M000210704

WINNING

Is an

ATTITUDE

WINNING

Is an

ATTITUDE

A Season in the Life of John Chaney
and the Temple Owls

STEVE WARTENBERG

St. Martin's Press New York

WINNING IS AN ATTITUDE. Copyright © 1991 by Steve Wartenberg. All rights reserved. Printed in the United States of America. No part of this book may be used or reproduced in any manner whatsoever without written permission except in the case of brief quotations embodied in critical articles or reviews. For information, address St. Martin's Press, 175 Fifth Avenue, New York, N.Y. 10010.

Design by Judith Stagnitto

Library of Congress Cataloging-in-Publication Data

Wartenberg, Steve.
    Winning is an attitude : a season in the life of John
Chaney and the Temple Owls / Steve Wartenberg.
       p.   cm.
    ISBN 0-312-05538-2
    1. Chaney, John. 2. Basketball—United States—
Coaches—Biography. 3. Temple Owls (Basketball team)—
History. I. Title.
GV884.C53W37   1991
796.323'092—dc20
[B]   90-48937
                                       CIP

First Edition: January 1991
10 9 8 7 6 5 4 3 2 1

For Mom and Dad. Thanks.

Contents

	Introduction	ix
1.	How You Start Is How You Finish	1
2.	You Can't Play Here If You're Going to Commit Turnovers	25
3.	I Get Emotional About Things That Are Unfair	61
4.	When You Fail in the Classroom, You Fail Out Here on the Basketball Court	90
5.	I Don't Think You Can Measure a Good Coach Based Just on Winning	124
6.	Being Told You're Wrong Is the Best Way to Correct a Problem	153
7.	The Battles Are Getting Tougher and Tougher for the Poor	176
8.	Heads You Win, Tails You Lose	210
9.	This Basketball Game Meant Nothing	246
10.	We Win Ugly Games	256
11.	College Is the Fountain of Life	279
	Postscript	285

Introduction

> *To be poor in our society is not to stand on equal ground.*
> *While the races may stand side by side, the rich stand*
> *on history's mountain and the poor stand in history's*
> *hollow. Until we overcome unequal history, we cannot*
> *overcome unequal opportunity.*
>
> —Lyndon Johnson

When John Chaney was named basketball coach of Temple University in 1982, he brought with him a slogan: "Winning Is an Attitude." This was something he had been telling his players at Cheyney State University (a small, predominantly black Division 2 school located outside Philadelphia) for ten years, and now that he was finally the coach of a Division 1 program at the ripe old age of fifty, he wasn't about to change. All the things that had made Chaney a success everywhere he had coached— first at Sayre Junior High School and Simon Gratz High School in Philadelphia, and then at Cheyney State—were the very same things that would make him a success at Temple.

In Chaney's second year, Temple went 26–5 and won the school's first NCAA tournament game since 1958. The next three seasons brought marks of 25–6, 25–6, and 32–4 and return trips to the "Big Show." In 1987–88 the Owls went 32–2 and were ranked number one in the nation for close to two months, finally losing to Duke in the Eastern regional final.

As Temple climbed up the rankings and Chaney gained recognition as one of the country's top coaches (after the 1987 season he was named national coach of the year by the United States Basketball Writers Association and after the 1988 season he was voted coach of the year by the USBWA, AP, UPI, and *The Sporting News*), his slogan captured the imagination of college basketball fans. It was repeated time after time in newspaper and magazine articles and on television by announcers quick to latch onto a catchy phrase. Today it appears on T-shirts, bumper stickers, posters and media guides put out by the Temple athletic office. It's even written across huge billboards in ten-foot letters that promote ticket sales for the upcoming season. Sometimes it seems you can't go anywhere in Philadelphia without seeing it. Another team at Temple wanted to adopt it, but Chaney said No way, that's my slogan. "I told them they could use 'winning is a learned behavior' instead," Chaney says and breaks out in a great burst of laughter.

But somewhere along the line, the true meaning of Chaney's slogan got lost in all the euphoria of winning and the resulting national acclaim. Contrary to popular belief, Winning Is an Attitude has nothing at all to do with the winning of basketball games. His slogan is about winning at the game of life, where the struggle to overcome and defy the odds is what's important.

"Winning Is an Attitude means that if something

around you is bad, is negative, is evil, then there must be something inside of you that says flip that record over because there is something better on the other side of the record," says Chaney, who loves to speak in metaphors. "When things are bad, real bad, you have to flip it over and make things better. This is the attitude I teach. I want to teach someone to say no to something that is negative and yes to something that is positive and right. If my players accept this, then they are winners before they ever step out onto the floor. They'll be winners in life."

He even has a specific way the slogan must be written. "Winning Is an" is written across the top line in small letters, and underneath in big, bold letters is the word "Attitude." "The key word is *attitude,* not *winning,"* Chaney says. "Attitude is everything."

Most of the kids Chaney coaches come from poor, inner-city neighborhoods, just like their coach. They do not stand on equal ground and Chaney believes it is his job to teach them their four years at Temple are their best and last chance to make something of their lives. "The only thing that can save a poor person's life is education," Chaney will tell his players and anyone else who will listen over and over and over. "It's the only thing that can save your life."

During the course of the 1989–90 season, Chaney will fuss and fight and pinch and poke and prod his players into learning this lesson and applying it to every phase of their lives. Like almost all the others who have played for Chaney, the members of his current team will fall in love with this man whose concern for them is so obvious. They will struggle at times, but, by season's end, will understand a little better how to be winners on and off the court.

I was fortunate to spend the 1989–90 season with Chaney and his team. I spent countless hours in his office or at his home discussing and arguing about the issues important to him and attended many of his famous (infamous?) 5:30 A.M. practices. At times they seemed more like philosophy classes than basketball practices, but that's what makes Chaney so unique and his story so important.

Chaney is a man who overcame the odds, who rose from the hollows of poverty, prejudice and lack of opportunity and today stands at the top of the mountain as a role model for his team, his university, and in some ways, an entire city. I saw and felt firsthand the passion, the anger, the frustration and all the love inside this man. By the end of the season, I learned where it came from and to look at Chaney, college basketball, the world around me, and even myself, a little bit differently.

"Stevie," Chaney told me several times, "I love to talk about life."

WINNING
Is an
ATTITUDE

I

How You Start Is How You Finish

9:14 A.M., Sunday, October 15, 1989. McGonigle Hall, Temple University. Philadelphia, Pennsylvania.

Today is the first day NCAA rules allow teams to practice. Some coaches started a little more than nine hours ago at the stroke of midnight ("Midnight Madness" they call it at the University of Kentucky), with an arena full of fans, cheerleaders, pep bands and television cameras. But that's not the Chaney way. "I'm not here for showmanship," he says. "I'm not involved in gimmicks. My goal is to put quality people on the floor." Today Chaney begins molding his team into quality people.

The only ones present this day are Chaney, his players, assistant coaches Jimmy Maloney, Dean Demopoulos, and Jay Norman, trainer Ryan Kling, student trainer Mike Flicker, and managers John DiSangro, Rob Jones, and Dan Marsh. This is the Temple basketball family.

Chaney begins speaking slowly and softly to his team,

1

which sits along one sideline of the court in front of the rolled-up bleachers:

> This is an extremely important day. The first day of anything is important. The first day you are born is a very important day. Anytime it's a first experience it's very important. Today is important because there are rules, and there are roles that we must involve ourselves in and understand. It's almost like formulating a contract. How you start is how you finish. If you start off being a family, that's the way you're going to end up.
>
> If you cannot live with the contract I'm going to spell out today, then we must know that. Because, as we go on tomorrow and the next day, as we move up the line and the ship is out to sea, you can't jump out of the ship. If you're going to throw the oars out of the ship, and if you're going to do something that is contrary to what we agree on today, then the ship is not going to go very far out to sea. We are not going to be successful as a team.

As Chaney continues, his deep, husky voice increases in intensity and volume until finally it seems to fill McGonigle Hall, bouncing and echoing off the 3,900 empty seats. This is the way it always happens. Chaney starts off so softly his players have to lean forward to hear, but little by little, all the passion and intensity that once made Chaney the toughest sonofabitch on the playgrounds of South Philadelphia comes pouring out as he tries desperately to make his players understand the importance of what he is saying.

Many people are surprised when they meet Chaney to find that he's only an inch over six feet tall. He seems so much bigger on television. "I may not be tall, but I'm a big person," he says with a chuckle. On mornings like this, when Chaney gets going, he is a giant, dominating everything around him.

Once, 150 pounds were stretched thinly over Chaney's frame. Today, he tips the scales at 200 pounds. By the end of the season it will be more. All the extra weight seems to have settled around Chaney's stomach and chest, which, coupled with his still rail-thin ankles and legs, gives Chaney a bit of a pear shape. He is wearing a green Adidas tennis shirt, cherry-red Temple sweatpants and white Adidas basketball shoes. As always, one of the legs of his sweatpants is hiked halfway up his ankle. Although his players tease him about this, Chaney never seems to notice, or maybe he just doesn't care. He paces back and forth as he addresses his team, periodically switching the basketball he's holding from under one arm to the other.

Every year Chaney begins the season with "The Speech." Former players, Chaney jokes, could come in here and recite it. "Shit, they heard it four straight years. They probably know it better than me."

There are different rules that exist when you try to live together as a family. You can do certain things as an individual and get away with it because you only have responsibility for yourself. But when you're on a team, when you're in a family, you have to always think about if what you're doing is going to create a problem for somebody else. This might be the only time in your life that you will be part of something so strong. A part of something so meaningful. You can't be successful, no matter how talented you think you are, if you decide to go in another direction than the one we agree on today.

This basketball bounces a certain way every time it hits the floor. It's not like a football. A

football bounces a different way every time. Your behavior must be like bouncing a basketball. I have to be able to predict success based on your behavior and your behavior must be the same every time I call on you. Every time I put my finger on the cash register and push down on the five, a five must come up.

If you don't go to class, if you don't function in the classroom, we can't function as a team. They are one in the same. They're no different. They're equal. If you're having a problem with one of your classes, raise your hand and say, "Coach, I have a problem." We'll get somebody to help you. Not somebody to do your work, but someone to help you engage your mind. I don't care how good a player you are, if you're not balanced I have to cut you off. This comes right from the bible. The bible says if my right arm is diseased, I have to cut it off. I HAVE TO CUT YOU OFF. It's that simple.

What I'm selling, you must buy. You have to buy it. If you don't buy it, we can't live together. The contract says you go to class, function in class, and then you can play basketball. One hand washes the other. It's very difficult to talk to somebody about life on this basketball court when he's not functioning in the classroom. Because then you're dealing with someone who doesn't think well, who doesn't respond.

I want to put good human beings out on the floor. People who are playing sports for the right reasons. Sports is a vehicle. It's a car that takes you from one point to another. You use sports to get your degree. That's the main reason you're here. Try to remember that the cost of education today is eighteen, nineteen thousand dollars a year. Your mother can't afford to pay eighteen

4

thousand a year, Ernest, can she? And now here you are about ready to graduate. Came out of a little pothole from around the corner in North Philadelphia, Ernest. The biggest surprise ever, Ernest. He's going to go home with that piece of paper. You're going to be able to get a nice job. Ernest is a good person.

Ernest Pollard meets Chaney's definition of a winner. He grew up a few blocks from Temple on the drug- and crime-infested streets of North Philadelphia—an area that resembles a war zone more than a neighborhood. A star at Roman Catholic High School (class of 1986), Pollard, a six-foot-six-inch forward, was recruited seriously by about a dozen colleges. He came to Temple for one simple reason: Chaney. "I could relate to Coach right from the start," says Pollard, who talks quietly. Pollard is a man of few words, even among his teammates. But when he talks, they listen. "Coach was poor growing up and knows what it's like growing up in North Philadelphia. When he came to my house, all he talked about was academics and life. He related basketball to life, just like he does in practice."

The fall of 1986 was the first year the NCAA's controversial Proposition 48 went into effect. Because Pollard, a solid B and C student at Roman, didn't score 700 on his SATs, he and fellow Prop 48 victim Duane Causwell had to sit out the year for the Owls. Now, four years later, Pollard has not developed into a star on the court. He'll spend the coming season on the bench cheering on his teammates. But Pollard has accomplished something even greater. He is on target to graduate in August.

"Ernest is the light at the end of the tunnel and not just another train," Chaney says. "He is someone who disproves the theory behind Prop 48 completely. He is not a star. He is not going to the NBA. He is someone from a poor, disadvantaged background who took advantage of his opportunity and worked his tail off to graduate. He proved that given the chance he could do college work and be a good student. Ernest is a role model, not just for the other guys on the team but for his entire community. Ernest isn't a brain. Ernest isn't a genius. But he works. He never misses class. He comes to every study hall. If the class requires twenty hours of work, he works twenty-five hours." In recognition of his attitude more than his playing ability, Chaney will later name Pollard co-captain along with Macon.

As Pollard listens to Chaney single him out during this morning's lecture, his blank expression never changes. But inside he is bursting with pride. "When he uses me as an example, talks about me to other people, it makes me feel real good. When I first came here, I wasn't really thinking about graduating and getting a job. I was thinking about basketball. But things changed. And I set new goals for myself and now I feel really good that I'm going to get them. And Coach is the one who set it all up for me and helped me. Now, when I see Coach working with the younger guys it makes me feel real good. I can see how he's trying to develop them as human beings and players."

After Chaney finishes with Pollard, two of his former players—Kevin Clifton (1986) and Derrick Brantley (1988)—walk into the gym. It's a coincidence, but the timing couldn't be better.

Look over there! Here come two of my graduates. Come over here. How nice to see you boys.

As they walk onto the court, Chaney grabs each in a big hug and plants a kiss on their cheeks. The two men look a little embarrassed at this display of affection, but it's easy to see they enjoy Chaney's attention. Neither can contain their sheepish grins. All former players—from Temple and Cheyney—remain part of the family and Chaney keeps close tabs on them. Often he'll end phone conversations by saying, "You know I still love you."

How much money you making now, Derrick? Fifty thousand? Sixty thousand? Here's a boy that went out and got himself a good job at IBM. Derrick is making good money. More money than me. Isn't that great? Can you get a job for Ernest? I don't want him working in a boxcar. I want him wearing a shirt and tie like you. And Kevin—he's going to law school. Gonna make a great lawyer one day. He'll get your asses out of jail one day.

After a little more teasing and another round of hugs, Clifton and Brantley head to the side of the court. After everyone stops laughing, Chaney gets back to business.

One of the things we can't involve ourselves with is someone with a weak mind that can be swayed in a negative direction. I don't care how poor you are, you cannot be the kind of person that will lean toward another value system. Just because you see someone walk around in expensive clothes and have gold chains around their neck and money in their pocket doesn't mean you can be swayed and forced to move in a direction that will mean a loss of our structure as a family. If you're going to let yourself down, you're going to let all of us down.

You have to put things in the right priority. You have a lot of long days ahead of you. Practice, classes, study hall. So something has to go. What goes? It could be your friends. It could be your girlfriend. If she can't type. If she can't type, you

7

shouldn't be going with her. Pick out the smart girls. Give them a test. Take them over to the computer center, put them on the computer and see how smart they are. Don't worry about pretty women. Just find one that's a good person, that's efficient. Then you go with her.

Ninety percent of you are going to have to find a nine-to-five job when you leave here. Kevin and Derrick heard me say that four years in a row. They are two of the finest graduates I have ever had in my life.

Chaney has been talking for thirty minutes, yet he has barely mentioned basketball. "You see, with Coach it's life first and then basketball and not the other way around," explains Mark Macon, Temple's sensational junior guard. Macon was Chaney's first blue-chip recruit, a high school All-American so talented he could have gone anywhere. Like Pollard, he chose Temple because of Chaney. "From the beginning I knew this was a man I could learn from. Coach brings it straight to you and that's why I love him. Right now he's almost everything for me: a father figure and a mother figure. I'm a long way from home [Saginaw, Michigan], and I know I can go to him and talk about anything."

At this morning's lecture, Macon sits up front, just a few feet from Chaney. He never takes his eyes off his coach and seems to soak up every word and gesture. Chaney says he can often feel Macon listening to him and can see the love in his eyes. What it takes some players several months, and in some cases, years to understand, Macon learned the first day he met Chaney.

Almost all of Chaney's players tell stories similar to Macon's and say they feel the same way about their coach. "Coach just has a way of communicating that feels so genuine," says Nate Blackwell, who was Chaney's first recruit at Temple and developed into an outstanding point guard. "Coach is like a father figure. He grabs you and tries to feel your strength and give you some of his. He makes you feel that he's really interested in you off the court. I could score twenty-eight points and after the game he'd be mad at me. He'd say one of my teachers called and said I was late for class. It really makes you feel good that the person you're working so hard for really cares about you." Blackwell knocked around the NBA and CBA for two years after he left Temple, but now he's back, working in the Office of Community Relations and taking courses. He's scheduled to graduate in August 1990 and knows what awaits him if he doesn't. "Coach said he'd kill me and then never talk to me again."

Donald Hodge, Chaney's second high school All-American and a seven-foot sophomore center on his current squad, has a similar story. "I knew he was someone I could trust, someone who would help me," says Hodge, who grew up with his grandmother in the Washington, D.C., area. "My parents separated when I was nine. Coach is like the parent I never had."

Chaney is a parental figure to many of his players and shows his concern through his constant teaching, lecturing, and hollering. Chaney never lets up on his players. "It's a form of testing out one's character," says Chaney, who believes that if his players can listen and learn from his constant criticism, instead of making excuses and disappearing, then nothing they will ever face—on the basketball court or in life—will be able to beat them.

Loving and caring for his players is not something a coach can turn on and off like a faucet. It's either there or it isn't and the players will be the first to know. Naturally Chaney has a metaphor—this one involves clothing—to help him explain his point. "You can't get it done by just saying 'I love you' over and over to your players. The only way you can do it is to be genuinely concerned about them and make it part of your everyday life-style. If you're not that type of person—and many coaches aren't—then don't wear that kind of suit. Find one that fits you or your players will see through it and it will work against you."

Unfortunately, most people don't get to see this side of Chaney. They don't get to see the patient and caring teacher who is a combination mother hen, Attila the Hun, best friend, bully, psychiatrist, and favorite uncle, who always has a cookie or piece of candy and a funny story to tell. They don't get to see the obvious love between teacher and pupil, coach and player. They don't see how this rubs off on the players and how they too form an unbreakable bond with one another that will last long after they have left Temple. Instead, on national television, they see the intimidating, snarling, screaming, sometimes out-of-control coach of the Temple Owls. To millions in Philadelphia and around the country who are ready to pass instant judgment, Chaney is like Indiana coach Bob Knight, a bully who screams at referees and his own players. And make no mistake, a screaming Chaney, arms waving and deep, catlike eyes glowing, is an intimidating presence to say the least. He could give Knight or John Thompson a run for their money in an intimidation contest. In the past, Chaney has even gone up into the stands after fans who threw things at him and his team or shouted racial slurs. He's even gone after opposing coaches.

At practice, I will often see this side of Chaney as he gradually works himself up into a state of extreme agitation as he discusses some sort of transgression from the previous practice or game. At first, I was a little intimidated, afraid to go up and talk to him after practice. Quickly I saw the other side of Chaney. In the midst of a tirade, a player sneezes and Chaney stops his lecture.

"God bless you," he says quietly, pauses another second and then starts yelling again as if he had never stopped. Or suddenly, he'll turn his anger into humor and tell a story so funny that all the players are doubled over in laughter. As soon as practice ends, the passion and anger disappear and Chaney wraps his arms around his players, pokes and pinches and squeezes them and lets them know he still loves them no matter what he has just said on the court.

"That was the most amazing thing for me," says Black-well. "He could come down on you so hard in practice, then you step off the floor and he's totally different. He never related his anger on the floor to how he felt about you personally."

After practice, a steady stream of present and former players parade through Chaney's office for no particular reason. They just want to be near Chaney, to trade insults or listen to him talk and feel the warmth of his love. Macon is perhaps the most frequent visitor, and sometimes, when he's killing time between classes, he'll fall asleep on the couch while Chaney talks on the phone or to someone else in the office. "A lot of coaches can't deal with this," Chaney explains. "They don't let people past their secretaries without appointments and they always keep their doors closed. My door is open all the time. This office might be the only place they have where they can come and feel wanted and comfortable."

This is Chaney's suit, and even if he wanted to, he can't take it off. He is a loving, generous man and his players pick up on this instantly.

"I have to believe that most people who only know me from the television think I'm mean and nasty," Chaney says with a grin, part of him proud of his con job. "I know, because I've gotten that kind of statement from people. But my friends, the people that know me, they know the

real me. They know that I really am mean and rotten."
Again Chaney breaks up in his extremely loud, high-pitched cackle.

"It's one of the greatest laughs I have ever heard," says Guy Rodgers, former Temple and NBA great who goes all the way back to the school yards of Philly with Chaney. "Even if you miss the joke and don't know what he's laughing about, you hear that laugh of his and can't help laughing yourself."

Character is very important for us. Make sure I understand what you are and who you are. I want gentlemen. I don't want guys who are heathens. You can't teach someone who is dumb. You just can't. Stupidity is something that is very difficult to deal with because it is forever. Stupid is forever.

I'm repeating a lot of this because I want repetition in what we do. Repetition means the possibility of you understanding it and remembering it.

You're at a stage now where the decisions you make, you are responsible for. Mom and Pop are not with you here. You've got to make the right decisions. It's very simple. If I'm walking down the street and there's a dark alley and I see twenty-five or thirty guys walking out of that alley with baseball bats, I know they aren't going to a baseball game. I run like hell. I get out of there. I don't go up and say, "Hey fellas, what's up? How you doing?" You have to make a good decision. You have to clearly read what's right and wrong.

I have to sit here and hope you're going to make the right decisions. The people who are very successful are the people who think well and

make the right decisions. IN LIFE. When you're on the basketball court and looking at the opposition, you have to take into consideration what is there. Do I step off it? Do I shoot? Do I pass? That kind of reading is very important and that is the same kind of reading you must have throughout life.

If I'm giving you hell on the basketball court because you're not functioning and you're not doing what you're supposed to be doing—after we have taught you and taught you and worked with you—you must realize it's not you I'm yelling at, it's your behavior. When your mother or father get after you for something you have done wrong and they put punishment on your ass, it's not because they don't love you. It's your behavior, it's the things you are doing wrong that they are yelling at. And you have to be able to separate the two.

Last year as a freshman, Mik Kilgore listened and watched as Chaney got all over senior shooting guard Mike Vreeswyk every day in practice. Nothing Vreeswyk did was good enough for Chaney. Somehow, despite all these shortcomings, Vreeswyk started on the number one team, was captain the next year and left Temple as the school's fifth all-time leading scorer.

Vreeswyk is back at Temple, working for the university and taking graduate courses with an eye toward getting into coaching. He is a frequent visitor to Chaney's office and later in the season will lament that if he had only red-shirted his freshman year he could still be playing and listening to Chaney get all over him on a regular basis. "I miss it," he says wistfully.

Kilgore, a six-foot-eight-inch center and forward in high school, was given the difficult task of learning to play the point guard and shooting guard positions at Temple. He escaped criticism last year, despite the multitude of mistakes he made game after game while learning his new positions. That's the Chaney philosophy: First-year players get a grace period until they have had a chance to learn the system. After that, they're fair game. This year, with Vreeswyk gone, Kilgore will become one of Chaney's favorite whipping boys. Kilgore, who grew up in West Philadelphia, is tough and stubborn and has a mean streak that comes out during the heat of battle. He also has a tendency to rebel when Chaney gets on him in practice. Chaney recognizes this and will tell Kilgore over and over he must change his attitude if he wants to be successful.

"Let's see if you can get it together and accept responsibility for your actions or just walk around blaming someone else for your problems," Chaney will tell him later in the season. "See how far your snap-back attitude gets you in life. What has been your detriment, Kilgore, is your head. You have as much talent as anyone here. There's no guy in the country six-eight who can handle the ball like you. But it just hasn't come. And it's because of your attitude."

It's hard to determine if Kilgore will ever fully understand Chaney when he says, "You have to understand it's not you I'm yelling at, it's your behavior." This is a difficult concept to accept, especially when you're on the receiving end of a Chaney outburst. Kilgore will take the abuse, just like Vreeswyk. "I think it might have bothered me if I didn't have Mike Vreeswyk here last year," Kilgore says. "I have never seen anyone get it worse than he did last year. And he took it and never said a word or even looked upset. He just tried to do what Coach said. And that's what I do."

Later in the season, after a particularly bad game the night before and a good tongue lashing in practice, Kilgore says to Chaney as they walk off the court, "I may not make good decisions on the court, Coach, but I'm a warrior."

14

"Shut up," Chaney says and slaps Kilgore on the arm. The two leave the court laughing.

Chaney doesn't try to analyze each player and determine how best to treat him. "I treat everyone the same. And they must understand when I'm fussing at them, snapping at them, cussing them, riding them, it's not them that I dislike, it's their behavior. I have to clearly distinguish for them the difference between loving them as a person and disliking their behavior. Once you get over that hurdle, your players will understand you. Sometimes it doesn't work. I've lost kids that never did understand. When we find a youngster like that, who is sensitive, he is very difficult to coach. He will not buy what you are selling and will be more concerned about himself than the team. That's the kind of person who looks in the mirror and only sees what is good. He'll never be able to see the bad things and develop the character he needs to overcome them."

I don't want a team that escapes from reality and escapes from the truth. I don't want people who are always escaping, who always have a story and are always conniving. An ostrich tries to escape from the truth. Isn't an ostrich the thing that puts its head in the sand? But guess what's sticking out when it does that? It's ass, that's what. I don't want a team like that. Because when you have a team like that and trouble comes, that team will not face the trouble. They become immersed in failure. They learn how to fail. They get good at being bad. Nobody wants to take the last shot in a game. No one wants to try. Because there's a comfort zone in failure. It's great. You don't have to try. I don't want a team that can't negotiate life, that won't take a chance at life. I don't want a team that avoids responsibility. I don't want a team built on fear.

If you can't learn a good lesson here, you can't learn a good lesson. You just can't learn period. And the lesson you learn here on the court is the same lesson you learn in the classroom. It's no different. Testimony of how it works is Ernest. Ernest is not a brain, he just tries. I have never in the four years he has been here got a report on him for missing classes. Never in four years. You know why? He tries. He just tries. Ernest, you're going to be important one day. You better graduate, Ernest. That degree, I want to see it. You don't have another way to go. You're not going to be an NBA player. You're not going to be the greatest player in the world, but you're going to be the greatest person with a degree, Ernest. And you're one of those Prop 48 kids they talk about. You are great testimony to how wrong that rule is. If you let us down, I'm going to tear you up Ernest. And then your mother is going to tear you up. How many credits you need to graduate Ernest?

"Twenty," Pollard says softly.

Twenty some credits. Is that all?

"Plus my senior field work."

Let's have a hand for Ernest. [Everyone claps.] I'm proud of you, Ernest.

With this, Chaney ends his first lecture of the season. The team runs through a few quick drills and then everyone—players, coaches, managers and trainers—forms a tight circle in the center of the court. Causwell, the team's starting center, shouts "TEAM!" and everyone else fol-

16

lows with "TOGETHER!" This is done three times at the end of every practice. The players then race over to a corner of the gym where donuts and fruit—a daily ritual—await them.

The 1989–90 season has begun and Chaney is pumped. "If you can't get excited at the start of a new season, it's time to get out of this business."

Things will change in the coming months. Problems on and off the court will add up to make this a very trying season. Chaney likes to call himself a modern-day Don Quixote, and the windmills he fights are overwhelming: poverty and prejudice, crime and drugs, difficult family situations, educational systems that don't educate, the hypocrisy and outright lying and cheating he sees going on around him in college athletics, the media, and most of all, the lack of opportunity for poor people. Chaney never backs down from these seemingly insurmountable obstacles and fights the only way he knows how: "Like I'm in a street fight."

"That's one of the things about John that causes him to be misunderstood and, in many cases, disliked," says Rodgers. "Here's a strong black man who's willing to take a stand, even if he's the only one willing to fight. A lot of people may not like him for this, but if they listened to him, they would have to respect him."

It may seem strange for a college basketball coach to take on such big issues, but to Chaney, basketball is just a metaphor for life. "Sports problems are no less solvable than society's problems," he says. "When we solve society's problems, we'll solve all the problems we have in athletics."

In the coming months, the windmills seem to pop up faster than Chaney can chop them down. In January, after a particularly tough week, Chaney will say, "I've reached the stage now where I'm thinking seriously about getting on my horse and riding off into the sunset. There are just too many windmills. I've been involved with youngsters for over thirty years as a teacher and coach and the problems are just getting worse. People do not have a clear understanding of what the real problems are: the problems of poverty and the problems of people who will never, ever get a chance in life. We have to start opening our minds and our hearts to these people before it's too late."

While Chaney coined the phrase Winning Is an Attitude in the early 1970s, its inspiration came from his mother, Earley. She was born Earley Williams on January 21, 1911, in Jacksonville, Florida, and lived a life similar to most Southern blacks of that era. "We didn't have nothing," says Earley. "We were dirt poor."

A month ago, Chaney went through the difficult task of putting Earley into a nursing home. Diabetes had rendered her blind and weak, and arthritis caused her constant pain and was so bad in her hip that she could barely walk. Although she hasn't been able to attend a Temple game in several years, Earley says she still "watches" them on the thirty-year-old radio she kept by her bed at home and brought with her to the nursing home. "I have a great imagination since I lost my eyesight," she says. "I follow them from one end of the floor to the other and sometimes I can see John jump up and holler. I tell him to stop all that fussing, you'll get a heart attack."

Chaney visits his mother two or three times a week and always brings a special treat, usually some sort of pork specialty that she loves so dearly, but isn't supposed to eat. An excellent cook, Chaney usually prepares the dishes himself. "Every time I go to see her, she always has a smile on her face, no matter how much pain she's in,"

Chaney says. "She's always concerned about others. asks how so-and-so is and worries about them and w ries about the team and that I'm being too hard on th boys. She's always been like this. You could feel a se of pride, a sense of caring and sharing for others, although she never said [Winning Is an Attitude], could see it in her deeds and words."

Until her later years, when her son was able to take of her, Earley lived a tough life marked by poverty. dropped out of school after the eighth grade to st working. She performed menial labor, cleaning other p ple's houses for a couple of dollars a week plus busfa When she was about twenty (she's not sure of the ex date), Earley married a man named Carter. A short ti later, on January 21, 1932—twenty-one years to the d after her own birth—Earley bore a son, John. A f months later, Earley's husband took off, and she ne saw him again. Earley and her older sister, Jessie, were l to fend for themselves and raise young John. While Earl supported the family, as live-in help for a wealthy wh family in the affluent Riverside section of Jacksonvil Jessie raised her nephew. Chaney grew up calling his au "Momma" and his mother, who was often away f weeks at a time, by her first name. Earley says she didr mind. "Everyone knew I was his mother."

Despite her absence, Earley had a strong impact on h son's life. In his lectures to his team, Chaney will repeat edly use her as an example of someone who overcome the odds with brains and attitude. Chaney still uses on of her lessons to test people. When he was about twelv an old woman who lived a house or two away aske Chaney to go to the store and get her a few items. Whe he returned with the groceries, she gave him a nickel a a reward. When he showed his reward to Earley, she go very angry and made him give it back. She told him tha you don't accept money for doing favors for people, espe-

cially elderly people who can't do for themselves. Chaney likes to quiz people, asking if they would accept money for doing a favor for a neighbor. If they say yes, they would take the money, Chaney tells the lesson he learned from his mother. If they say no, he congratulates them on being a "good person."

"She also taught me that you should be a person of your word," Chaney says. "From watching her, I could see she was someone who would stand up for a cause. She had a sense of honesty and of what was right and wrong to the point that it could be her failing." Although he is describing his mother, Chaney could be describing himself.

The two also share a love for a good argument. "We're both stubborn and argumentative," Chaney says proudly. "I'll take the con if you take the pro or the other way around, just to be devilish. My mom's like that too. We have a lot of fun arguing, but I always win. I make her laugh and that's it."

After Chaney was born, the family moved often. First to a tiny shack on Pearl Street in the Black Bottom section of Jacksonville, the poorest black section in the city. Next to a second-floor apartment in a small, three-story house on Madison Street, a dirt road one step up from Black Bottom. By this time Chaney was old enough to start school and he remembers walking to school every day, hiking through the woods and across a creek to the David Street Elementary School. A year or two later the family moved again, to Julia Street, and Chaney switched to Cookman Elementary, the same school Earley attended as a child. "Julia Street was perhaps the best street for blacks," Chaney remembers. "First of all, it was a tar street instead of a dirt road. Every Christmas they would block it off and have big celebrations. Everyone would rollerskate up and down the street and we could sit on the porch and watch."

About this time, Earley met Sylvester Chaney at a dance and a short time later they were married. Chaney isn't sure if he was ever legally adopted by Sylvester Chaney, but he assumed the name. In fact, Chaney didn't know until several years later that Sylvester wasn't his real father or that his younger brother and sister—Richard and Shelly, who have both passed away—were really his stepbrother and stepsister. "My mother never told me anything about my real father," Chaney says. When he was in sixth or seventh grade, Chaney went to a local department store and was given a brand-new bike by a woman working there. When he brought it home and showed it to Earley, she got furious and took it back. "We were too poor to have bikes, so it wasn't fair for me to have one if my brother and sister couldn't," Chaney says. "I cried and cried when she took it back."

A few years later, Jessie told her nephew that the woman in the store was his real father's sister and that Sylvester Chaney was his stepfather. "I think they didn't tell us so we would all get along better," Chaney says.

Despite the marriage and two incomes, the Chaneys were still very poor, a fact of life for blacks in Jacksonville and throughout the South at that time. "During that era, poor people didn't think about being poor and the hardships they had because it was commonplace, the norm, to scrape and scrap to get by," Chaney says. "You couldn't compare yourself to white folks, that was like comparing apples to oranges. There were only two things a black person could do in those days: perhaps go into entertainment as a tap dancer or something like that or work your tail off as a common laborer. There was no such thing as aspiring to go to college to become a doctor or a lawyer. And your family perpetuated this because they didn't have any other point of reference."

Earley continued to work as a live-in maid for the grand sum of three dollars a week and was away more than she was home. During the week, Sylvester washed cars at a Ford dealership in Riverside and on weeknights and weekends was a janitor and handyman at the Good Shepherd Church, also in Riverside. He always brought home the leftovers from the various church functions, so on weekends the family ate well. "We never had what one would describe as a close father and son relationship," Chaney says. "He was always working and the only time I ever saw him was for a minute or two on his way to work and in the evening when he came home all tired from work. He didn't talk much. He wasn't a caressing man who would put his arms around you and tell you he loved you."

Chaney is the complete opposite of his stepfather, who died in 1984. He is warm and affectionate and constantly puts his arms around his family, friends and players and tells them he loves them. This side of him must have come from Earley and her sister. Jessie, a major influence on the three Chaney children during their early years, was a lively, fun-loving woman who thought up games and helped the children with their schoolwork. Jessie spent hours with John, who always struggled in math, helping him learn his multiplication tables. As Chaney recalls, much of what he was taught in school was done through memorization and repetition. "As I see it, that's the best form of teaching," Chaney says. "I use those same methods as a teacher and coach."

Chaney was always a skinny little kid, an easy target for the bullies who wanted his lunch or just someone to beat up on. Although he didn't like to fight, primarily because he wasn't very good at it, Chaney was too stubborn simply to hand over his lunch. So he would run. "My attitude was I would never give in to the bullies," says Chaney. "They might run me home or beat up on me, but they never got my lunch."

The kids in the neighborhood managed to have plenty

of fun despite their poverty. With little money or equipment, they had to use imagination and resourcefulness. After watching the adventures of Red Rider and his sidekick Little Beaver at the local movie house Saturday matinee, they made bows and arrows from tree branches and twine. From the reeds they gathered at the river, they made pop guns, ingeniously shaving down broom handles until they formed a tight fit inside the reeds. Then they devised a trigger mechanism and spent hours shooting wild berries at one another. Slingshots made from old bedsprings were another weapon in their growing arsenal. They made scooters from old crates by attaching their rollerskates to the bottoms. "We were always wearing out just one shoe from pushing it," Chaney says. They would take old tires up to the top of a hill, lie down in the center of the tire and roll to the bottom, making themselves into "human wheels."

Perhaps the most creative invention was home movies. Chaney and his friends would gather old cigar boxes and cut small holes in the middle. Then they cut out strips of comics from the Sunday paper and rolled them around sticks. By spinning the sticks inside the cigar box, they could create movies and run them back and forth for their "show."

More than anything, Chaney loved sports and he was always one of the best athletes in the neighborhood. He wasn't big, but Chaney was quick, a student of every sport he played, and used his brains to gain the edge he needed. Baseball was Chaney's favorite. "I could always hit pretty good and catch the ball, but my problem was always grounders." Football was also popular. The one football in the neighborhood was in terrible condition and had to be stuffed full of newspaper. "When it rained and the newspaper got wet, that football was really heavy," Chaney says, adding that football was never one of his favorite sports. "I didn't like getting hit." One sport he didn't play was basketball. There weren't any courts in the neighborhood.

When Chaney was in seventh grade, Sylvester took a job in Philadelphia at the naval shipyards. Earley moved with him, while the three children remained in Jacksonville with Jessie. A year later, Sylvester sent for the children and Jessie. Once he got to Philadelphia, Chaney discovered something that would change his life forever: basketball.

2

You Can't Play Here If You're Going to Commit Turnovers

October 16

No night Owls, Chaney's players are early to bed and early to rise. The normal routine calls for 5:30 A.M. practices Monday to Friday (9:00 A.M. weekends and during school holidays), and sleepy-eyed players start wandering in a few minutes before the appointed time for treatment or taping or just to loosen up and shoot a few baskets. Today is the first early morning practice of the season and everyone makes it in on time, except Chaney. But this is by design.

Outside McGonigle Hall, it's still pitch black and cold. In the winter months, the five-minute walk from the dorms to the gym becomes a battle against the elements. Broad Street, which cuts through the center of Temple's campus and is one of the city's busiest, is virtually empty. The only signs of life are an occasional car and the lunch wagons, whose owners are just starting to arrive and claim the best positions for the morning rush, set to start in a couple of hours. If I'm lucky, one will be open for a much-needed cup of coffee. The lights from McGonigle Hall penetrate the darkness; the familiar and constant sound of squeaking basketball shoes can be heard from outside the building.

Pre-dawn practices have been a Chaney ritual since he was at Cheyney State. The idea is to get practice out of the way early, so the rest of the day is free for classes, tutoring and study hall. It also ensures that players go to bed early and avoid all the temptations that seem to come out after dark. Discipline is another goal. "I remember watching my mother and father leave every morning for work, even if they were tired or sick," Chaney says. "You hope ultimately you're teaching a youngster discipline, responsibility and character and nurturing his overall development into a man."

Chaney normally lets his assistants run the show and work on fundamentals for the first half hour of practice. Maloney works at one end of the court with the guards, and Demopoulos and Norman at the other end with the big men. Today Chaney strolls in a little after six, watches quietly for a few minutes, and then calls the players over to one end of the court for the morning's lecture.

Passing the basketball is the most important item of all. Being able to pass—whether it's hockey, soccer, football—is the most important skill of all. It's important because there is nothing you can do at any level without being able to pass the ball.

Dribbling is an individual skill, shooting is an individual skill. Passing is the only skill that can be individual and add to the team concept. All the Xs and Os in the world can't go anywhere without passing the basketball. I want to talk for a few minutes on passing. I want to talk for a few

minutes on protecting the ball. And I want to talk for a few minutes on proper spacing for passing.

Yesterday Chaney talked about how he expected his players to live and learn together. Today is the day he starts talking about basketball.

"I don't coach basketball; I coach elements," Chaney explains. By this, he means that every player on the floor has a specific role that is spelled out by the coaching staff. When each player understands and accepts his role and performs it properly, the Owls infuriate, frustrate and usually beat the opposition.

The 1987–88 Temple team came the closest to fulfilling Chaney's ideal of balanced elements working in harmony. This was far from the most talented team in the country, but each player understood his role, reined in the considerable ego that came with being the star of their various high school teams, and never (well, almost never) tried to do anything he wasn't capable of doing. Even more important, the players genuinely liked one another and achieved the mystical and much misunderstood "chemistry" that so many teams search for in vain. This was a team of overachievers who shocked the basketball world. "Temple who?" many asked as the Owls rose through the polls and were finally crowned number one by the AP and UPI on February 8, 1988—becoming the first team in the fabled history of the Philadelphia Big Five (LaSalle, Penn, St. Joseph's, Temple and Villanova) to be ranked number one during the regular season. But still there were skeptics, who argued that Temple's 18–1 record was built on beating a bunch of nobodies.

On February 21, 1988, the top-ranked Owls traveled to North Carolina and, before a national television audience, put this nonsense to rest, smashing the fifth-ranked Tar Heels 83–66 in a game that showed exactly what Chaney meant when he said he coached elements. Temple forced and frustrated North Carolina into twenty-nine turnovers and put the game out of reach with a 19–0 run early in the second half.

As Chaney and Tar Heels coach Dean Smith, cigarette in hand, walked past each other in the interview room, Chaney said to the only active coach with an arena named after him, "I keep telling you—give up those cigarettes."

"I think I might take up drinking," Smith answered.

The most important element on any Chaney team is always the point guard. The point guard is the orchestra leader, the coach on the floor, the postman who must always deliver, rain or shine, and a dozen other metaphors that spring from Chaney's fertile mind to denote leadership and responsibility. Chaney's point guards must have a feel for the ebb and flow and tempo of the game and involve all their teammates in the offense, often to the detriment of their own game. A former point guard, Chaney is always toughest on the players manning this position.

At Temple, Chaney has been blessed with a succession of fine point guards: Terence Stansbury, Nate Blackwell, and Howie Evans. Interestingly, none of these three players came to Temple as a point guard but were converted by Chaney, who saw leadership skills and intelligence in each.

Chaney's greatest point guard was Blackwell. During his three seasons at the helm, Temple was 82–16 and went to the NCAA tournament each year. But even he had trouble adapting to Chaney's system. "When I first got here I was very temperamental, hotheaded, high on myself and always had an excuse when I did something wrong" explains the six-foot-four-inch Blackwell, whom Chaney recruited out of South Philadelphia High School. "I was ready when Coach came at me and I went back at him. The other guys on the team took me aside and told me not to talk back, to just listen even if I didn't agree. It took a while, but by my sophomore year [when he took over from Stansbury (who was a first-round draft pick of the Indiana Pacers) as the starting point guard] I really started studying Coach and I'd actually say to myself during a game, 'What would Coach want me to do now?' " Eventually, Blackwell knew what Chaney was thinking without his having to say a word. A glance during a game was all it took. "We just had that about us," Blackwell says.

With Blackwell gone, the responsibilities of point guard for the 1987–88 team were handed over to Evans, a six-foot-one-inch senior who had been a starting shooting guard the past two years, although he and Blackwell played so well together they often switched roles during the course of a game. Like Blackwell, Evans had a stubborn streak, or as Chaney says, "Howie was a ram, always butting his head into walls." For one magical season, Evans played the point as well or better than anyone at Temple since Guy Rodgers back in 1958. Evans handled the ball against pressure almost flawlessly, fed his open teammates and set the Temple single-season assist record with 294 (8.7 a game). When the defense sagged off him, Evans (who scored 11.1 a game) nailed the open shot.

Along with Evans, three experienced players—junior shooting guard Vreeswyk, senior power forward Tim Perry and senior center Ramon Rivas—provided balance, another important element in the Chaney system. Each had limitations, yet they all grew and developed under Chaney into outstanding college players.

Vreeswyk, who at six feet seven inches played shooting guard in Chaney's three-guard offensive set and small forward on defense, came to Temple as a limited player. Although he was an outstanding shooter and scored 2,019 points at Morrisville (Pennsylvania) High School, Vreeswyk was not very quick, couldn't handle the ball a lick and couldn't create his own shot. "Mike was the turnover king in practice his first year," Blackwell says. But Vreeswyk was a tireless worker who listened to Chaney. He improved his ball-handling and learned how to use the offense and his teammate's picks and screens to get open jump shots. He averaged 16.7 points a game, hitting nearly 40 percent of his 226 three-point attempts. On defense, Vreeswyk again overcame his lack of talent with determination and intelligence and was very effective in Temple's assorted zones.

In Perry's first year, he was a "statistical nightmare" according to Chaney. "He averaged perhaps one rebound and one point a game," Chaney says. Actually it was 3.9 rebounds and 2.3 points. His point is that Perry was raw and unrefined. Three years later, Perry was a monster, a defensive intimidator who blocked 3.6 shots a game, altered another half dozen and pulled down 8.0 rebounds. Perry developed two or three strong moves to the basket and scored 14.5 points on .585 percent shooting. In May 1988, the Phoenix Suns selected Perry as a lottery pick.

Rivas, a six-foot-ten-inch, 260-pound block of granite from Puerto Rico, was another statistical nightmare. He was as slow as he was big, a "postage stamp" player Chaney says in honor of his inability to jump. But Rivas was rough and tough under the boards and used every one of his pounds to his advantage to set teeth-rattling picks, box out for rebounds and eat up a lot of space in the center of Temple's defense. Although statistics can't measure his contributions to the team, Rivas averaged 6.9 points and 7.1 rebounds. He was so good at doing the little things that go unnoticed on the basketball court that the Boston Celtics signed him as a free agent, and he spent the 1988–89 season sitting on their bench. This year Rivas is playing in Spain.

The X factor in the equation was Macon, one of the more highly recruited high school seniors in the nation the year before. Macon was voted Michigan's Mr. Basketball after his last season at Buena Vista High School and was not only selected for the McDonald's All-American game, but went home with the trophy as the game's most valuable player. The signing of Macon marked Chaney and Temple's first foray into the big-time recruiting wars.

From the moment he stepped onto the court (he scored 22 in his first game as the Owls beat UCLA at Pauley Pavillion), Macon was the team's best player, the one they turned to when they needed a big basket. A wondrous athlete—quick, strong, and intelligent—Macon is one of the gifted few who has the ability to beat his man off the dribble and take the ball to the basket, jumping over or around any and all players who try to stop him. Macon seemed unfazed as the Owls climbed to the top of the national rankings and more and more attention and praise was directed his way. On the court, his blank expression remained firmly in place no matter the score or situation. Nothing, it seemed, could rattle this child prodigy who played with the maturity of a senior. More a scorer than a shooter, Macon averaged 20.6 points on .422 percent shooting and pulled down 5.7 rebounds. He was voted freshman of the year by the UPI and the United States Basketball Writers Association. He even made the cover of *Sports Illustrated* and became Dick Vitale's favorite "diaper dandy." Vitale went so far as to call Macon the second coming of Oscar Robertson.

"I think what put it all together for us was to get a player like Mark," Chaney says. "He's perhaps the most well balanced athlete I have known."

The sum of these five players was greater than their individual parts. Together they were a well-oiled machine that blazed its way to a 32–2 season and provided a standard against which all future Chaney teams will be judged.

The 1989–90 team is generally considered to have even

more talent, although the Owls are still a far cry away from the talent of such perennial powers as Syracuse, Duke, North Carolina and the University of Nevada-Las Vegas. Over the next few weeks, Chaney's goal is to explain his philosophy, establish everyone's role and begin to develop the elements that lead to chemistry. "The first week is all fundamentals," Chaney explains. "It's long, it's tedious, it's mind-boggling. But I have to have a lot of patience and the players have to have a lot of patience. They have to have a great attention span because sometimes I lecture for forty-five minutes or an hour before we start playing." Starting today, and for the next five mornings, Chaney will address a different aspect of basketball: passing, dribbling, shooting, rebounding, and defense. Together, these five skills form the foundation of Temple basketball.

Everything Chaney teaches his players comes from within, from his experiences, his intelligence, the countless hours he spends watching tapes and games on television and his innate sense of what constitutes good basketball. "And he's never wrong," says assistant coach Jimmy Maloney, who's been around basketball almost as long as Chaney and in fact, has been in Division 1 basketball even longer. "Coaches tend to go to the same clinics and read the same books and watch the same tapes. They're all pretty much the same. But Coach came up with his own philosophy, his own style of play. It's different, it's well thought out and it works."

Chaney believes completely in what he teaches and has remained true to his philosophy over the years. Look at a tape of his 1978 Cheyney State squad—which won the Division 2 national championship—and you'll see the same offensive patterns and zones on defense. Only the names and numbers have changed. Why should he change? Going into the current season, Chaney's winning percentage (.785 after a 397–109 record in ten years at

Cheney State and seven at Temple) is the second highest among active coaches, behind only Jerry Tarkanian's .823 percent (530–114). Chaney must be doing something right. But there are always those who will criticize. Some say Chaney is behind the times, that his teams don't run or take full advantage of their athletic talents.

During the 1989–90 season, he gets a letter from someone who accuses him of coaching like a "white coach," like Knight or St. Johns' Lou Carnesecca. In this case, white basketball is defined as slow, disciplined, half-court basketball. As a point of fact, this is exactly the way Chaney coaches and he admires and respects Knight, Carnesecca, Villanova's Rollie Massamino, and above all, Princeton's Pete Carril. Even though all these coaches are white, they don't coach white basketball. They coach smart basketball. "Intelligent basketball has no color," Chaney says. Other coaches he respects are Clarence "Big House" Gaines from Winston-Salem and Vivian Stringer, who was the women's coach while he was at Cheyney and is now the coach at the University of Iowa.

The letter goes on to say, "You take black players and make them play white." This is a criticism Chaney hears often from the local media, from callers on radio talk shows and even from some Temple fans who aren't happy with a win and would like to see their team run up and down the court, fly through the air for monster dunks and score 100 points a game.

Chaney usually laughs at this stupidity, this overwhelming desire in others to see his team perform all kinds of "monkeyshines." This usually leads into Chaney's story about the organ grinder and his monkey. While the organ grinder plays, the monkey performs all kinds of fancy dances and flips and pirouettes as he goes from person to person with his little tin cup. "The people all love it until they're down the block and realize the monkey just stole their wallet," Chaney says. Exactly what this has to do with monkeyshines on the court isn't clear, but Chaney's point is that nobody is going to tell him how to coach his team.

"I know better than anybody else how well my team can play," Chaney says, adding that reporters and fans don't see his players every day in practice, don't spend hours watching tapes and analyzing their skills or lack of skills. "And I don't let anybody force me into playing any kind of offense or any kind of defense that they would like to see me play. I don't have a Heinz 57 team [a team that can do a variety of things well], not at all. I know these players, and I know how much depth we have. I can't afford to go out and give [the fans and the media] pleasure and let them say, 'He's a great coach—he plays fifty-seven defenses and fifty-seven offenses.' I just won't do it. We don't have the talent of a Syracuse, a Nevada-Las Vegas, a Georgia Tech. We've got two blue chippers on our ball club (Macon and Hodge). If I had ten or fifteen All-Americans like these other schools then you would see us doing a lot of things because, then, when you take an apple out of the game, you replace it with another apple. But when I take an apple off the court, I put in a lemon many times."

More than anything else, a Chaney-coached team is noted for hanging on to the basketball. A possession is an opportunity and a turnover is a wasted opportunity. Nothing in life is worse than wasting an opportunity and nothing on the basketball court is worse than a turnover. As far back as the early 1960s, when he was coaching at Gratz, Chaney kept track of turnovers during games and practices. At Temple, manager Rob Jones keeps a turnover chart during practice that lists each player and such negative statistics as turnovers, fouls, three-second violations, and allowed breakaways. On the positive side, Jones also records turnovers caused, steals, rebounds, shots made, and charges taken. At the end of practice he reads out each player's score.

"It's a unique philosophy," Maloney says of Chaney's fanatical hatred of turnovers. He admits he was a little skeptical at first, until he started seeing the results on the court. "Now, I think the strength of our program is that the players have accepted his philosophy. A lot of coaches say the same thing, but in reality they don't embrace it like John does. They'll say you have to take some chances and it's okay if you turn it over a few times. But John's philosophy is anything that will cause a turnover, he won't let his players do. Some say that could lead to players being afraid to do anything, but when you watch us play, you see aggressive, smart basketball and we don't turn it over."

Passing the basketball is a team skill. So being able to pass the basketball means there are a lot of things involved. You have to know what kind of personnel you are playing with. If I have a guy with bad hands, I don't care what he can do with that basketball. I don't care whether he can shoot it or not: sooner or later I'm going to throw it to him and he's going to drop it or miss it or do something that's going to cause us to lose the game. Who's fault is that? It's just as much my fault as it is his if I'm the guy making the delivery of the ball.

Perry was notorious for dropping passes in the open court. He could run like a deer and beat his man down-court, but every time someone threw him the long pass, he fumbled it out of bounds or was called for traveling. "Timmy would always say to me 'I was open, why didn't you pass it to me?' " Blackwell says. The two were roommates and remain close friends. "We'd argue back and forth, but I knew if I threw it to him and he lost it, Coach would holler at me. Coach was very frank, he'd tell Timmy he didn't ever want me to throw that long pass to him."

In basketball, you try to avoid as many mistakes as you can when you have possession. A great team—every time they come down the floor something good happens. They get a shot at the basket. That's good. If you come down the floor and don't get a shot at that basket, something bad has happened on the way to the bank. You were robbed, or you lost the money. Something bad happened on the way to the bank. So any way you look at it, passing is the key. Passing means there are always opportunities. It doesn't matter if the shot goes in—that's extra. What matters is you made the right decision, made the right pass. You can shoot a hundred percent. But if you came down the floor five times and shoot it two times and lose it three times, even though you're shooting one hundred percent, you're losing.

You cannot play basketball here if you're going to commit turnovers. You just can't.

Come over here, Victor.

Victor Carstarphen, a point guard and a transfer from the University of Cincinnati, who must sit out the season, comes out on the court and stands at the top of the key at the three-point line. Chaney takes a position ten feet to Carstarphen's left, also at the edge of the three-point line.

When you make a pass, spacing is very important. The person you are passing to must have proper

36

**spacing or you can't make the pass. Mark, come
out here.**

Macon comes out and assumes a defensive stance in
front of Chaney. When Chaney tells Carstarphen to pass
the ball to him, Macon steps in for the easy steal.

**This is a bad passing situation. There's no way I'm
going to make this pass, whether it's an
underneath pass, a chest pass, a bounce pass, a
two-handed pass. Something has to happen in
order for Victor to make this pass. Passing
requires distance, passing requires a proper angle,
passing requires proper spacing, passing requires a
clear view. These things build up confidence that
our pass will be successful. What we have is an
angle we want to work off of and we want to
work off of the box so we create a lot of space.**

Chaney then goes through the basic pattern for the
guards. The point guard holds the ball at the top of the
key while the shooting guards run through the box, free-
ing themselves through the courtesy of their teammate's
picks and screens. Once through the box, they pop out on
the other side. If everything works out right, the defensive man should be two or three steps behind. The shooting guard receives the pass, turns and fires up an open
jump shot. If he's not open, the point guard holds onto the
ball while the shooting guards go back through the stack
and try to pop open on the other side.

**It's just that simple. That's as simple as I can put
it. The box is your home base. Every player must
learn how to use it so I [the point guard] have
complete confidence when I make that pass. If he
goes back in that box and he can't beat his man**

**with that angle back to here, he should not be
playing this game. He should not be playing this
game. I want to have this kind of a view [a clear
view with nobody between the passer and the
receiver] when I'm making a pass. Who must
create it? The person who is going to receive it.**

For the next hour, Chaney lectures on passing. He will
talk about making passes to the wings, passes into the big
men, passes back from the big men to the guards, bounce
passes, chest passes and in-bound passes. Only at the end
of practice, for the last hour, will the players actually get
to scrimmage. The projected starting five—Kilgore at the
point, Macon and sophomore Mark Strickland at shooting
guard, and Causwell and Hodge inside—wear white,
while the second team flip their reversible practice shirts
to the cherry-red side. Even now, during the team's first
scrimmage, Chaney doesn't just let the two sides go up
and down the court. On almost every possession he stops
play and finds something to correct.

This is the way practice runs for the next five months.
The assistants work on fundamentals the first half hour,
then Chaney takes over, calling the players to one end of
the court to begin his lecture. Sometimes he talks about
life, sometimes basketball. Most of the time he finds a
way to combine the two.

October 17

Today's lecture is on dribbling, but you'd never know it
from listening to Chaney.

**While some of you have been here for two, three
or four years, some of you are hearing these things**

38

for the first time. When something is new, you
need time to absorb it. And you can't waste time
when you're trying to absorb everything we are
teaching and trying to prepare you for a game.
You only have one time to prepare and that is
now.

All of this has nothing to do with dribbling—he'll get
to that in due time—but it illustrates the Chaney teaching
method. His patience knows no boundaries, and he is
relentless in his pursuit of perfection. Many times, after
we've just spent the better part of an hour discussing
some topic or another near and dear to Chaney (Prop 48,
the media or education, for example), he'll pause and ask,
"Did I beat you yet, did I wear you down?" When I nod
my head yes, he'll break up laughing. "You're no match
for me, Stevie."

His players are no match for him either. Even when
they try to tune Chaney out, he'll stay on them and stay
on them until he wears them down and changes a negative attitude into a winning attitude.

You have one time to sharpen up your mind and
that's now. It's too late for me to say I'm going to
sharpen up my mind. I'm fifty-seven years old. If
you don't sharpen up your minds at a young age,
you'll never be sharp at all. If you don't spend
quality time doing what you're supposed to be
doing now, you can't look forward to doing what
you think you should be doing later on. Quality
time. That means you spend your time wisely.
You've got to try to absorb all the knowledge that
you can from working with us. You have to buy
what we're selling. You have to look at the
practice films and see if you're doing what we ask
you to do. And then after you learn what we tell

39

**you, you must begin to react instinctively. We
can't keep pinching and pinching and pinching
and pinching you without you sooner or later
saying "ouch." You have to have a feeling about
what you are doing.**

Repetition ("As I see it, that's the best form of teaching") is only one of the many tools Chaney has in his toolbox. "I try to use every teaching method you can think of, just like someone teaching English or math would do in the classroom," says Chaney, who has honed his teaching skills for the past thirty years in the classroom and on the basketball court. "The idea is to make it digestible for them. I use examples from my life; I use metaphors; I use humor; I demonstrate things; I use audiovisual aids. You name it, I'll do it to help them learn."

For this, Chaney has become recognized as not just a great coach, but a great teacher. During Chaney's first few seasons at Temple, Peter Liacouris, also in his first years as the university's president, was a frequent visitor to the 5:30 A.M. practice sessions. Eight years later he still attends from time to time. "I've been to as many as one hundred of his practices over the years," says Liacouris, who considers Chaney one of the top teachers at Temple. "I look at them as classes in life and he gives me insight into things. An outstanding coach is just like an outstanding teacher. He can understand and integrate theory and practice. In John's case he integrates basketball fundamentals and life fundamentals and teaches his players how to use them. In some ways I've been influenced by John. He sets clear goals. He may be reaching for the stars, but he has the discipline and perseverance to work toward them and never be discouraged."

What makes Chaney angry and will start him on an hour-long tirade is teachers who don't teach, teachers who think that just because someone doesn't attain a certain score on a standardized test like the SAT he can't be taught and doesn't belong in college. According to Chaney, a teacher's job is to teach those who don't already know and stimulate interest where there is no interest. "Anyone can teach someone who scores a sixteen hundred on their SATs," Chaney says. "Einstein didn't need a teacher; he was already a genius."

Chaney has seen a different attitude come into vogue at high schools and colleges, and even at Temple, which is still considered a school for the "common man." Chaney says many people, including professors at Temple, don't think athletes should be in college. "Teachers have taken on a new attitude," Chaney says. "A teacher says I can only teach the educated. But is a teacher indeed an educator if he can only teach the already educated? When a teacher raises his hand with pride and says that he flunked seven students, is he indeed an educator? When a youngster doesn't learn and fails, a teacher should say 'I'm at fault.' A teacher should never stop trying to teach." Because of this attitude, Chaney will tell his players never, ever to identify themselves as basketball players to their professors.

Education is an issue that has consumed Chaney for years and will continue to stir his passions in the coming season. "I know more about education than you can even think of," he shouts at Demopoulos in the midst of an argument on the subject. In the years he spent as a teacher in Philadelphia public schools (from 1955 to 1972), Chaney encountered hundreds of kids who weren't interested in learning, but he never stopped trying to teach them. Many failed, but even if he could ignite a spark in only a few, he felt as if he were a real teacher. "If you can get one kid into college, even for a year or two, you can change the aspiration level of everyone else in their family," Chaney says. "You can change the cycle for an entire family and perhaps make their life better."

Chaney has been making statements like this for thirty years, but it's only been in the last three or four years that he has had a national audience. In 1971, when the Philadelphia City Council threatened to drop varsity sports due to a budget crunch, Chaney, a coach at Gratz at the time, spoke out. "I'm extremely worried about the inner-city kid who has no hope," Chaney said in an article in the *Philadelphia Daily News*, ticking off the names of several basketball players he knew of personally who used sports to get them into college and change their lives. "I'm an example," the article continued. "I wouldn't have made it through high school if I wouldn't have played basketball." In an article in the *Philadelphia Inquirer*, Chaney stated, "The extracurricular activities serve as a force for motivation. But this has to be incorporated into the overall program. The system loses if it doesn't look at the student as an overall human being. [A city council member] said he was amazed that some kids just come to school so they could play ball. Well, it happens to be true. . . . Kids need every avenue of motivation whether it's basketball, art clubs, dramatic clubs or a home economics club. See, the whole thing is a cycle. Some kids are motivated simply by their classes. Others aren't. They only get a little motivation from class. But then other activities stimulate them. They stick it out and in the process they still learn and possibly go on to better things."

Chaney learned quickly that education is the only thing that can save a poor person's life. Now he's afraid that everyone else has forgotten this important message. He'll read an article in the paper that says the drop-out rate for blacks and Hispanics in Philadelphia's high schools is climbing at an alarming rate. He just shakes his head sadly, his eyes misting over. "You know something sad," he says softly, "there are more black youths in prison than in college. That's a tragedy."

October 18

"Sight and flight." This phrase—a Chaney original—is how he teaches rebounding, the topic of today's lecture.

Any time we're playing on defense, whether it's zone or man-to-man or matchup or rover, it's very important for you to keep a good relationship between the man, the ball and the overall floor. With us using a sideline or secondary break, everybody must rebound. There is no such thing as two or three guys rebounding [and everyone else heading upcourt for the fastbreak]. Everyone on this ball club must learn to rebound regardless of what position you play.

Sight, flight and quickness are the keys. By that I mean you must watch and keep in touch with the ball regardless of where it is on the floor or who is shooting it. You must have sight of the flight of the basketball. You must keep your feet situated so you can reach the basketball.

First Chaney starts with the guards, showing them how to position themselves for a rebound when the man they are playing takes an outside shot. He has back-up point guard Michael Harden play offense, Chaney guards him. As Harden shoots, Chaney turns and watches the ball go toward the basket, at the same time moving away from Harden until he is a few feet in front of the foul line, in position to grab a long rebound.

**We don't use the old-fashioned method of turning
and putting your body on the man.**

He has Harden shoot again and demonstrates the old-
fashioned method, turning quickly as Harden shoots and
jamming his butt and back up against Harden. This is how
many coaches teach their guards to block out, but not
Chaney.

**You can get a foul this way. Plus, there is no way
this man should ever be able to beat you to the
ball if you do it like I showed you. He's up in the
air shooting and you're already turned and moving
toward the spot where the ball should be going.
No matter how quick he is, it's virtually
impossible for him to beat you to the ball.**

Next Chaney turns his attention to the inside players,
starting with the defender playing the weak side—the
side opposite where the shot is coming from. Then he
works through each position on the floor, showing what
the player should be doing in every conceivable situation
that can occur during a game. Chaney talks about "sight
and flight" for more than an hour before the team finally
scrimmages.

October 19

It seems that some players have been making the daily
trek to practice in their good basketball shoes, tracking
mud and rain into the gym and at the same time dirtying
their expensive Adidas sneakers.

**Have another set of shoes you wear from your
room to the gym. The weather has changed and**

it's raining a lot and we don't want you getting your shoes wet and tracking water in here. And don't be walking around bareheaded and with open shirts and no jackets. You can't expose yourself. You can't afford to be sick. Flu season is coming up.

This is an example of how Chaney involves himself in every aspect of his player's lives, whether they want him there or not. Chaney likes to tell the story about the night he paid a surprise visit to the dorms during his first year at Temple. He knocked on the door of Jimmy McLoughlin, a star guard on the team, at approximately 10:30 P.M. There was no answer, so Chaney left a note that said: "Dear Jimmy, I was here at 2:30 in the morning, where were you?" The next morning at practice, McLoughlin pleaded with Chaney to believe him that he was in his room asleep at 2:30.

"I wanted to serve notice that they shouldn't be surprised to see me anywhere at anytime," Chaney says. "I checked up on them in the dorms, in the cafeteria, even followed them to classes. It's not enough to tell players how you feel about them, you have to show them every day that your interest in them goes beyond the basketball court." At first many of Chaney's players resented his intrusion into their personal lives. Little by little, one by one they came to realize that their new coach really did practice what he preached and did indeed care for them as people as well as players.

After he's finished telling his players how to dress, Chaney changes the topic to turnovers. Suddenly he remembers a particularly bad one Harden committed a year ago during practice. Chaney seems to have a photographic memory of every turnover commited by every one of his players over the last twenty years. On this particular play, the other team had just scored a basket.

45

While the nine other players headed to the other end of the court, Harden brought the ball upcourt all by himself. For no apparent reason, he dribbled the ball behind his back. It bounced off his backside and rolled out of bounds into the alcove behind the court. He went chasing after it, while the other nine players wondered what happened to him and the ball. "I turned around and said what the hell happened, where did he go?" Chaney said. "And then he walks into the office later like nothing happened. 'Hey Coach,' he says, 'how you doing?' "

Even when we have the basketball, we must be playing defense. It's like having money in your pocket. It's something of value, something you have to protect. I'm still concerned with the fact that we are losing the basketball too much. I don't want you to relax at any time on the court, especially when you have the ball. People who relax find themselves being surprised by the defense. Your man will make a stop-and-go move at you to disrupt your pattern of behavior and force you into a mistake. Come over here, Shoun.

Shoun Randolph, a backup guard/forward who played with Macon at Buena Vista, heads out onto the floor and assumes a defensive stance at the top of the key in front of Chaney.

It's extremely important that you learn to go from point A to point B without having to expose the basketball. I know that many of you guys learned how to use the crossover dribble in [summer] camps, but that's not what I want to see.

Chaney then demonstrates another way to switch the ball from one hand to the other without exposing the ball

to the defender. The method involves taking a step backward and shifting his hips so they remain between the
ball and the defensive player, as he switches the ball from
one hand to the other. It's not as flashy as the crossover
dribble or putting it between the legs or behind the back,
but it's more efficient.

You just step off and change over without
exposing the ball. If you keep exposing the ball
[with a crossover or between the legs dribble], you
are creating a problem not only for you but for
your teammates as well, because four other
players are depending on you to get the ball from
point A to point B.

Instilling this philosophy in players who grew up
watching run-and-gun basketball (and plenty of turnovers) on television is one of Chaney's harder sales jobs.
Convincing his first Temple team was the toughest sale of
all. "One of the things you have to understand," Chaney
explains, "is that the returning players, who were recruited by Don Casey [the coach before Chaney] and had
played for him the past few years, are going to automatically resent a new coach at first. And my approach to
coaching is different. The way I teach, the importance of
fundamentals and the length of time I take in establishing
a platform for teaching was different than anything they
were used to. Plus, I came in with the philosophy of never
beating yourself—no turnovers—as an overall philosophy for the team. It took a while for them to accept what
I was saying, especially since we weren't winning."

The entire 1982–83 season was a struggle. The Owls
were coming off a 19–8 record and a trip to the NITs,
where they lost to Georgia 73–60 in the opening round.
With several starters back, expectations for the 1982–83
season were high despite the team's move into the much

tougher Atlantic-10 Conference. Things started going wrong immediately. During preseason practice, starting guard Ed Coe went down with a knee injury that would sideline him for the season. Five games into the season, star center Granger Hall went down with a knee injury that required major reconstructive surgery many feared would end his career. A third starter, forward Charlie Rayne, limped though the season on yet another injured knee. The bulk of the scoring was left in the hands of guards Terence Stansbury and McLoughlin. Chaney started calling his Owls the two-guy team.

Chaney won his first game at Temple, a 68–67 nail-biter at George Washington on a free throw by Stansbury with four seconds remaining. Next came a 73–62 win over Rhode Island in the opening game of the Stanford Tournament, followed by a tough 77–70 loss to Stanford in the finals. The game featured a brief confrontation and shoving match between Chaney and Stanford coach Tom Davis. With sixteen minutes left in the game, Temple's B. J. Jones was ejected for a flagrant foul. "Stanford had been hand-checking and belly-checking all night and when one of our players [Jones] retaliated on a rebound, he was tossed out of the game," Chaney said after the game. "Tom Davis stormed onto the court in the direction of my player. I stepped in to restrain him. I'm quite sure he wasn't going to really go after my player. He was excited and he was trying to intimidate the officials. They didn't need his help."

Maloney still teases Chaney about the incident. "Here I am trying to get one of my kids into Stanford and he goes and creates an international incident." (His son got in anyway.)

During the 1984–1985 season, Chaney got into a shoving match with George Washington coach Gerry Gimelstob as the two teams headed off the court at halftime, with the Owls ahead and on their way to a 93–77 win. Chaney was unhappy with what he considered the overall physical play of the Colonials' center and wanted to discuss this with the officials. When Gimelstob joined the argument, tempers flared, words were exchanged and suddenly Chaney's hands were around Gimelstob's neck. The toughest sonofabitch from the playgrounds had struck again. "That means you're a coast-to-coast assassin," Maloney will remind Chaney from time to time. "If we ever play overseas you can become an international killer."

The fourth game of the 1982–83 season brought a 76–68 loss at Missouri, followed by a 62–61 win over William and Mary in Chaney's first home game. This was the game Hall went down and with him went most of Temple's hopes for a winning season. On February 19, 1983, Big Five and Atlantic-10 rival St. Joseph's crushed the Owls 88–59 to drop their record to 8–14, including losses in eight of their last nine games. "It was a tough time," Chaney says. "There was a possibility we could completely disintegrate and fragment into pieces. We had so many injuries, most of the team was in the training room instead of practice."

Somehow, probably through the sheer force of his will, Chaney was able to keep his team together and they closed out the regular season with four straight wins. In the opening round of the Atlantic-10 Tournament, the Owls went up against St. Joe's. This proved to be the turning point of the season and the game in which the Owls finally bought what Chaney was selling. "At halftime we were up by about thirty points and as we ran off the floor into the locker room everyone was screaming and yelling," Chaney recalls. "But not because we were up by thirty, but because we had only one turnover the whole half. That's when I knew they had finally reached the stage where they believed in my philosophy, that they thought they could win if they didn't throw the ball away. That game convinced them."

The Owls went on to win 88–69 and next topped Rutgers, the league's regular season champion and a team that featured two future NBA players (Roy Hinson and Cliff Battle) by a score of 72–67. Late in the game, disaster struck. With Temple safely ahead, McLoughlin broke his hand. "We were up ten or twelve with a minute or two left and he dove trying for a steal," Chaney says. "That's the kind of player he was. He didn't care about the score or how much time was left, he always gave a hundred and fifty percent." McLoughlin was out of the tournament and the Owls were down to a one-guy team—Stansbury. Despite 31 points from a double-teamed Stansbury, West Virginia beat Temple 86–78 for the Atlantic-10 championship and the automatic bid to the NCAA tournament. "After that game, I said the lowly touted had become the highly touted," says Chaney, who shed a few tears of pride that night. "We ended up on a high note [14–15], in that we played for the conference championship and a trip to the NCAA tournament despite so many injuries. It was the most amazing kind of turnaround to see players who were not really of that caliber come in and do their job. Role players went out and did what had to be done. Against West Virginia, only Terence was equal to the talent they had." The Owls' performance in the tournament, plus the return of Hall the next year, set the wheels in motion for a 26–5 record the following season and a 65–63 win over St. John's in the opening round of the NCAA tournament.

Although Chaney's current team understands and accepts his system, they will struggle all season to develop the proper elements and chemistry and to hold on to the basketball the way Chaney would like them to. Part of the problem is that since Evans graduated after the 1988 season, Chaney has yet to find a point guard who can do the job on a consistent basis. Last season, Kilgore and Harden, and even Macon, took turns at the point. The offense never got untracked, and without the inside-out balance Chaney wanted, opposing teams doubled Macon game after game. The Owls struggled to an 18–12 record and were beaten by Richmond 70–56 in the opening round of the NIT Tournament.

This season, Kilgore will start the season at point guard, as Chaney tries to go with a huge lineup of Kilgore (6' 8") at the point, Macon (6' 5") and sophomore Mark Strickland (6' 9") at shooting guard, and Hodge (7' 0") and Causwell (7' 0") inside. This just might be the tallest starting lineup in the country and is bigger than most NBA teams. Harden will be the first man off the bench, followed by Randolph and Chris Lovelace, a six-foot-ten-inch sophomore who is on the comeback trail from major reconstructive knee surgery.

With all this height comes a lack of ball-handling skill. A point guard who could assume responsibility for the ball and provide the type of leadership that Blackwell and Evans once provided would solve many of the problems of Chaney's young and inexperienced team. But five days into the 1989–90 season, Chaney is not confident this will happen and is worried that many of the same problems that plagued his team in 1988–89 will rear their ugly heads in the months and games to come.

October 20

As usual, the three assistant coaches work with the team for the first half hour of practice until Chaney arrives. At one end of the court, Maloney has the guards run through the offensive patterns. Unlike Chaney, Maloney rarely

51

shouts. He is as low-key as Chaney is hyper, with a sly and sometimes biting sense of humor. At the other end of the court, Demopoulos works with Causwell and Hodge. They take turns posting up the other, while Demopoulos assumes the role of point guard and feeds the offensive player the ball from the three-point line. Demopoulos is almost as intense as Chaney, often screaming and cursing to get his point across. Over on the side, Norman works with Lovelace and Jan Post, a freshman center from the Netherlands who lacks many of the fundamental skills of basketball, but is more than willing to learn.

When Chaney came to Temple, one of his first tasks was to decide whether or not to retain Maloney and Norman as assistants. It wasn't a tough decision. Chaney had known both men for several years, respected their basketball knowledge and considered them good friends. He and Norman, who was a grade behind Chaney, grew up playing with and against each other in the school yards, various summer leagues and the Eastern Pro League.

A star at Mastbaum High School, Norman remembers the first time he played against Chaney's Benjamin Franklin High School team, early in the 1949–50 season. Norman was a sophomore and Chaney a junior. Mastbaum was a predominantly white school at the time, and Norman was the only black player on the team. "Franklin was a very intimidating school," says Norman, a six-foot-two-inch center who made up for his lack of size with aggression and determination. At the time, Franklin was an all-boys, mainly black school, which received incorrigibles from around the city. "They had a reputation for fighting," Norman says. "If there were five hundred people in the gym, four hundred ninety-five of them were black. It was hard to pick out a white face. For most teams, the game was over before it started. But I was too dumb to be scared. I didn't care about any of that stuff, I just wanted to play." Franklin won that game and the rematch the next year at Mastbaum. Although the two didn't become friends until a few years later, Chaney made a lasting impression on Norman. Chaney was one of the first in a long line of great Philadelphia point guards. He was so tough, legend has it, that anyone foolish enough to try to take the ball off him would wind up with a broken leg. Like all legends, this one is exaggerated, but based on a true story. In the semifinal game of the Public League play-offs in 1951, Chaney's senior year, an opposing player was foolish enough to try and steal the ball from Chaney. He wound up with a sprained ankle.

"During that era, there was no such thing as the term point guard," Norman says. "John was just the player who ran the offense and scored. If you were looking for an all-around guard, he would be the first guy you would pick. He ran the offense and made sure everyone was where he was supposed to be. He was a great person to play with."

Norman went to Temple on a football scholarship in 1952, but he wound up a basketball star. After two years in the military he returned for the 1955–56 season. This was the golden era of Temple basketball, as the Owls, under Harry Litwack, advanced to the Final Four in 1956 and 1958. Norman was the starting center on both Final Four teams and is a member of both the Temple and Big Five Halls of Fame. In 1968, Norman, who was a teacher in the Philadelphia public schools until he retired in the summer of 1989, was named a part-time assistant by Litwack and remained through the Casey years (1973–82).

Over the years, Chaney and Norman developed a deep and lasting friendship. Each uses the words "like a brother" to describe their relationship. "It's not like we set out to be best friends," Norman says. "It just happened, and we've stood the test of time, so to speak. Now, the great thing is to be in a situation here [at Temple] where I can do something to help a friend."

Maloney, one of the all-time leading scorers at Niagra University, and later head coach there for two years, joined Casey's staff in 1973 after several years as an assistant to Lefty Driesell at the University of Maryland. Maloney was born and grew up in North Philadelphia, not too far from Temple. He discovered basketball on the neighborhood playgrounds and was a star at Roman Catholic High School.

Maloney left Maryland to join Casey at Temple because he wanted to spend more time with his family, which includes his wife Barbara Ann and five children—four boys and a girl. At Maryland, Maloney was the top recruiter for the powerful Terrapins teams of the late 1960s and early 1970s and was on the road more than he was at home. As an assistant at Temple, which did not have as high-powered a program as Maryland and didn't yet recruit on a national level, Maloney could spend more time at home. One of the first things he did when he took the job at Temple was buy a big old house in a nice neighborhood in Haddonfield (New Jersey) and put up a basketball court in the backyard.

Maloney is a simple, straightforward man. His whole life revolves around basketball and his family, although not necessarily in that order. During the coming season, he will talk constantly about his youngest son, Matt, a star guard at Haddonfield High and one of the most sought-after seniors in South Jersey. The big topic of conversation is where Matt will decide to go to school (he eventually chooses Vanderbilt) and how he is adapting to the switch from shooting guard to point guard.

Maloney is one of the most respected assistant coaches in the country. Dick Vitale calls him one of the top five, and Chaney says there is no question he is the best. After Casey left Temple for a job as an assistant in the NBA,

Maloney applied for the job of head coach and was one of the finalists. Over the years, Maloney has been offered several jobs, as assistant coach for high-profile college teams and NBA teams. But he has remained at Temple, in part because of his loyalty and respect for Chaney and because he didn't want to keep relocating his family. Now that Matt, the youngest, is ready to graduate from high school, Maloney is starting to think more seriously about becoming a head coach again. "I have the credentials and the contacts," Maloney says matter-of-factly.

Maloney, fifty-two, was not a school yard contemporary of Chaney and Norman, but he has played against both. While Chaney was at Cheyney State, and during his first few years at Temple, before his back and legs gave out, he, Maloney, Norman and several others would meet at McGonigle once or twice a week to play pickup games. Afterward they would go out for a beer or two and brag about how great they used to be.

"He cheated," Maloney says, making sure Chaney hears his accusation. Maloney can do one thing on the basketball court: shoot. Even now, no one on the team can beat him in a three-point shooting contest. His whole game was getting free for a quick jumper and he likes to brag that he never passed once he got the ball. "My only pass was to the basket," he says. "It was always open. My passes were ten feet up and with an arc." Chaney quickly learned that all Maloney liked to do was shoot and he stuck to him like glue in their pickup games. "Didn't you ever learn anything about weak-side help?" Maloney lectures Chaney. "Don't you know you're supposed to step off me and help your teammates when they get beat?"

Chaney will have none of this. "I stuck on him and just did this all day," Chaney says, moving his arm up and down in a hatchet motion. They both laugh.

Chaney felt confident that his first important decision at Temple—retaining Maloney and Norman—was a good one. The only problem was that Norman, who was a full-time teacher and part-time coach, was not always able to travel with the team, nor could he spend as much time on the road recruiting as the job required. "We did fairly well for a year, but then it got to be too much," says Chaney, who was trying to build Temple into a national power, and the best way to do this was recruiting, recruiting, and more recruiting. This left him with two options: He could let Norman go and replace him with a full-time assistant, or, add a full-time assistant and retain Norman.

Chaney is a firm believer in small coaching staffs, with three being the number he feels most comfortable with. "I hate it when you look out there and see five or six guys in suits all gathered around strategizing and trying to make a mystery out of a simple game," Chaney says. "I hate it when you see more coaches out there than players."

Chaney didn't want to lose Norman and the contributions he made to the team, so he kept him on as a part-time assistant and added a full-time assistant for the 1984–85 season. This is when Demopoulos, twenty-eight years old at the time and a complete unknown with virtually no coaching experience, entered the picture. He had been a teacher and high school junior varsity coach for a few years in the late 1970s and played pro ball in Greece in 1980. After Demopoulos got back from Greece, he was a part-time graduate student at Temple and worked for Liacouris, who at the time was the Dean of Temple's Law School and in the midst of an unsuccessful bid for the Democratic nomination for governor. "Deep down, I knew I wanted to get back into basketball," Demopoulos says.

Before the 1982 season began, Demopoulos summoned up his courage and walked into the Temple basketball office deep in the bowels of McGonigle Hall. Chaney wasn't there, so Demopoulos introduced himself to Maloney and said he was interested in working for the program. "I guess I was one of maybe a thousand people who did that," Demopoulos says. "Coach Maloney was very cordial, but basically what he did was blow me off and tell me they didn't have any openings. I went back the next day because I wanted to get to Coach, but Coach Maloney was the only one there. I think he started to get a little annoyed."

On the third try, Chaney was in and Demopoulos finally got a chance to talk with him. He said he would do anything Chaney wanted, and do it for no salary, just to be a part of the program and learn how to coach. Chaney politely told him that he didn't believe in volunteer coaches, that he only felt comfortable when he was paying someone and had some sort of control over him. Next, Demopoulos asked if he could just come to practice and sit up in the stands. Chaney said yes, never dreaming that Demopoulos would attend all but one or two practice sessions that season. Every morning at 5:30, Demopoulos was in the stands, sipping coffee, taking notes and inhaling everything Chaney said and did. After practice, Demopoulos would corner Chaney in the office and pester him with questions about why he did this or that. "He bribed me with coffee and donuts," Chaney jokes.

At the start of the next season (1983–84), Demopoulos was back in the stands. As the season progressed and he began to realize Demopoulos wasn't going to go away, Chaney invited him to come down onto the court to help out. Demopoulos threw balls into the big men during drills and spent time after practice in the office helping with the mail. He even tutored a few of the players. "At this point, I had fallen in love with the guy," Demopoulos says. "Here he was, the best in the business, spending all this time with me and never getting upset or impatient when I kept bothering him. Other coaches, guys who didn't have an ounce of what he had, wouldn't even give

57

me the time of day or an interview for a terrible job in a terrible program."

Still, Demopoulos never expected to get a job at Temple. He knew Chaney only wanted two assistants and thought Maloney and Norman would be at Temple for a long time. What he hoped to gain was knowledge and a recommendation or two from Chaney. Twice, Demopoulos almost got jobs, first at West Catholic High School [in Philadelphia] as the freshman coach and then at Lehigh University as an assistant. Both fell through at the last minute and Demopoulos was beginning to feel desperate. He hit bottom when he couldn't even get an interview for the job as an assistant at Drexel University, a job that paid only $5,000 a year.

During this same period, Chaney was coming to the realization that he had to add someone to his staff. "The key ingredients you look for in an assistant are loyalty and recruiting contacts," Chaney says. "You don't need a great Xs and Os man; that's my job. You need someone who is loyal to your philosophy and someone who can recruit. You can't win at this level if you don't have players."

Although he had a file full of letters from highly qualified college assistant coaches, Chaney kept leaning toward Demopoulos. He had all the right ingredients: His loyalty was unquestionable, and what he lacked in recruiting contacts he could make up for in enthusiasm and hard work. "Dean just seemed like someone I could not deny the opportunity," says Chaney, adding with a smile that Demopoulos "just wore me down. I couldn't believe anyone in their right mind would have done what he did over those two years." Chaney was willing to overlook Demopoulos's lack of experience because he felt he had a lot of potential. "The things I look for you can't measure on any kind of test," Chaney says, equating Demopoulos's situation to a youngster who is denied the opportunity to play because he didn't score a 700 on his SATs. "There is no SAT test for coaches. You can't sit them down in a room and give them a test. There is no way to know for sure until you give someone a chance. Dean was someone I knew had potential and would listen and work hard and learn. Now, he has proven he can do the job and he'll make a very fine head coach."

When Chaney offered him the job, Demopoulos was stunned. "I thought maybe he was going to offer me a part-time spot, but when he offered a full-time position I almost went into shock. I couldn't believe it. Here I was upset I didn't get the job as freshman coach at West Catholic and I end up a full-time assistant at Temple." Even now, five years later, Demopoulos gets choked up when he tells this story and can't hold back the tears. "This is embarrassing," he says as he regains his composure.

Chaney has become more than just a boss and a mentor for Demopoulos. His father died when he was five and he never had a strong male influence in his life until Chaney. "It might sound strange to say someone is like a father figure to you when you're thirty-five, married and a father yourself," says Demopoulos, who has a three-month-old daughter. "But he is. He's taught me things that no one else ever has."

At times it seems that Chaney and Demopoulos are more like husband and wife than father and son. They argue over almost everything—especially Demopoulos's driving. Even when Chaney agrees with Demopoulos he fights him ("I take the con if you take the pro or the other way around, just to be devilish"). This is all part of Demopoulos's ongoing education. "I just want to slow him down sometimes," says Chaney, who says that Demopoulos is indeed like a son to him. "Dean has a tendency to go right from A to Z. So even if I agree with him, I disagree just to slow him down and get him to look at all the letters between A and Z."

If there is such a thing as chemistry among a coaching staff, these four men have it. They work hard and have fun, setting the tone for the players. Maloney, Norman, and Demopoulos all buy what Chaney is selling, not just because he's their boss, but because they embrace his philosophy wholeheartedly and agree that he is one of the top coaches in college basketball. "He's not just the best coach, he's the best person," Maloney says.

In another week, there will be a change in the chemistry. Norman, ready for a new adventure after more than twenty years as an assistant, accepts a job in the sports marketing department at Temple, where his biggest duty will be as color commentator for Temple basketball. "I'm excited about it, but I know I'll miss being with the team," he says. "One thing I won't miss is getting up at four in the morning." Despite these words, Norman will frequently attend early-morning practices in the coming season. Unable to just watch, he'll revert to form and do a little coaching. "It's hard to get out of your system."

3

I Get Emotional About Things That Are Unfair

October 23

This evening the team gathers in McGonigle Hall for the annual media day, the first chance for newspaper, radio and television reporters to meet Chaney and his players. It's a relaxed, informal affair for the most part; the start of the season is still a long way off and this is your basic "get to know us" event. The players enter in ties and jackets and have head shots taken for the media guide and program, then change into their uniforms for the official team portrait.

The reporters watch and wait, growing more and more impatient by the minute as the photo session drags on. Finally, it's over and the coaches and players are available to the press. Half the reporters and television crews gather around Chaney and the other half circle Macon. One or two of the more enterprising reporters corral Causwell or Kilgore for a couple of minutes.

First-year players—sophomores Hodge, Strickland and

Lovelace, who all had to sit out last season due to Prop 48, and freshman guard Johnnie Conic—are all off-limits to the press. At last year's media day, Chaney only allowed two players—seniors Vreeswyk and reserve Jerome Dowdell—to talk to the press and said he hadn't decided yet if he would change this policy once the season started. This created quite a stir, but Chaney didn't care. He did what he thought was best for the team.

The year before, after Temple became number one, the demands from the press got to be too much, Chaney explained, especially for Macon. Although he was a freshman, Macon was getting the bulk of the publicity, with reporters calling him in the dorm day and night and actually following him around campus trying to get an interview. "Fifteen guys would run in and put a microphone in front of Mark after a game and ignore everyone else—the guys who had made this program and gotten us to this point. As soon as they were finished with Mark, they would run out. How long could I, as a coach, allow this to go on before it would start to disrupt my team?" Finally, Chaney decided Macon was off-limits to the press, and Macon, who only wanted to fit in and be one of the guys, said he was relieved to be out of the harsh glare of the spotlight. A few days later, Perry told Chaney he was starting to become distracted by the press and asked if he too could be placed off-limits. "I didn't care what the press thought or wrote about me for that," Chaney says. "I can't allow them to control my team and create problems."

Last season, Chaney eventually decided to allow all his players to talk to the press, with only Harden off-limits. This was Chaney's way of fighting against what he believes is an unfair characterization of Prop 48 players as dumb. He knew that instead of asking Harden questions about basketball, all the reporters would be interested in was talking to him about Prop 48 and the year he had to sit out. "These kids are stigmatized and traumatized by being labeled Prop 48s," Chaney says. "The 'color casters' are on the TV going, 'There's Prop 48 taking the ball out of bounds. There's Prop 48 at the free-throw line.' He's the only kid in a class [at Temple] where everyone knows his board scores. The kid goes to his tenth class reunion and a person is going to walk up to him and go 'Oh, I remember you. You were Prop 48.' "

Chaney saves articles in which a reporter interviews a Prop 48 kid and asks him if he benefited from his year out of basketball, leading the kid to say it was indeed good and helped him concentrate on his studies. "What else do you think the kid is going to say?" Chaney says. "But the truth is different. What is honest, what is fair, is to ask that kid the same question later on, after he becomes eligible and finds out what he was missing. Or ask him after he graduates. Only then can he answer the question intelligently. But these guys already have an answer formulated in their heads before they ask the question. They come in with their own agenda, their own morality and ask their slick little lawyer questions to get the kid to say what they want."

This evening, Chaney is subdued as six or seven reporters and two television crews gather around him near midcourt. When one of the reporters makes an attempt at a joke, Chaney doesn't even smile. "Come on, John, lighten up, that was a joke," he says, but Chaney stares blankly ahead, waiting for the next question. He answers all queries matter-of-factly, minus the usual Chaney wit and exuberance. He says he's not happy with the guard play so far, saying he's still searching for a point guard and some leadership. "Leadership comes from the guy who handles the ball. Mike Vreeswyk had an easy job [last year]. All he had to do was shoot it. What we're looking for now is someone to make the delivery. When we have that problem solved, everyone fits into the equation pretty good."

The topic swings over to Temple's big men, with someone saying this seems to be an area of strength with Causwell, Hodge and Strickland forming one of the biggest frontcourts in the country. Chaney disagrees, saying that in college basketball—because of zone defenses—it is sometimes hard to take advantage of big people. He stresses that unless the guards come around and start hitting consistently from the outside, other teams will double Macon and pack their zones tight around Causwell and Hodge and keep them from operating down low. "Right now I only have one player [Macon] who has identified himself as a good perimeter shooter. The others [Kilgore, Strickland, and Harden] haven't identified themselves yet. Good teams have balance."

Someone brings up Macon, asking if he'll be back to the All-American form he showed two seasons ago as a freshman. This immediately sets off Chaney, who gets angry when people try to tell him Macon is coming off a bad season. Although his scoring average dropped from 20.6 to 18.3 and his shooting percentage dipped from .454 to .407, Chaney says Macon actually had a better year in 1988–89. He had to do more things for the team—like play point guard at times—and carry a bigger load with Evans, Perry and Rivas gone. "From the very first game, coaches were running doubles on him or triangles and twos. We needed someone to take the pressure off of Mark by shooting the ball well, but Mike Vreeswyk had a terrible year [he averaged 17.8 a game, but shot only .414 percent]. Mik [Kilgore] didn't shoot the ball well from the outside [.394 percent overall and .313 from three-point range], and we need him to this year or else Mark will be looking at another year of double coverage and triangles and twos."

On he goes for another few minutes until the questions end. The two groups of reporters switch, leaving Chaney and Macon to answer the same questions again.

* * *

In the past, Chaney has received generally favorable press locally and on a national level. As the Owls climbed up the polls during the 1986–87 and 1987–88 seasons, newspapers around the country wrote about Chaney, his life, his philosophy and his team of overachievers. Various headlines from around the country proclaimed: "Owls' Success Reflects Coach" (*New York Post*), "Suited to Coach" (*Los Angeles Times*), "John Chaney Has Lifted Temple to a Higher Ground" (*St. Petersburg Times*), "Chaney: This Owl Is Finally Flying High" (*Las Vegas Review-Journal*), and, "Owls Learning to Give Nothing Away" (*New York Times*).

In many ways, all this acclaim rubbed Chaney the wrong way. The things he said that were suddenly being hailed as genius were the things he had been saying for thirty years. The only difference now was that he was the coach of the number-one team in the country. Too many coaches who do not have great winning percentages or nationally ranked teams, Chaney insists, still have a tremendously positive impact on their players and deserve recognition. But public perception, spurred on by the media, believes that the winning of basketball games somehow makes one coach smarter, perhaps even a better person, than another with a lesser record. "The winning or losing of basketball games should not be the thing that gives me access to having an influence on someone's life or to be viewed as a good coach or a good person," Chaney says. "The thing that should give me access is the fact that my major concern is to try and develop good character in the people I have under my wing. I value this more than winning, because winning, without question, speaks for itself. But it should not be the only measurement by which a coach is judged. What is truly important is the growth of another human being and knowing you had something to do with it."

Chaney often gets angry at what he reads in the newspapers and watches on television. The worst offenders, he says, are the color commentators who rave and fawn over coaches of the elite teams, the teams that are ranked in the Top Ten year after year. It's not that they're better coaches, Chaney says, it's that they have better players. "You know who said it better than anyone?" Chaney asks. "John Wooden. He was perhaps the greatest coach, but he'll be the first to tell you he won because he had great players. So what right does a sportscaster have to start off saying the equation is equal—that both teams have equal talent—when they don't? And then they develop a thesis and a theory and end up giving the wrong prognosis. All they're doing is promoting that program and that coach, perpetuating their success. I get emotional about things that are unfair. But when things are unfair you have to *say* they are unfair and not become a part of it. I don't credit my success to anyone except those who have made it possible: the players."

For these reasons, Chaney is wary of the press. "You can't beat a reporter at his own game. His interest lies in his story, especially here (in Philadelphia) where there is a lot of competition among reporters and the television people. A reporter has a competitive spirit too, where he's competing against other reporters to get the best story and best angle he can. If there's no story there, he'll create one. They have one of the most powerful weapons in their hands."

Although he won't admit it, sometimes Chaney takes his criticism of the press too far. There have been times in the past, and during the 1989–90 season to come, that he will become too defensive about what is written and said about him, his players and college basketball in general. He will look for and find something negative when there is nothing negative. But this comes from his overall frustration at the wrongs he sees committed in society, not just in basketball, and at the hypocrisy that tries to rationalize unethical behavior. Chaney always takes what he calls the "high moral ground," and unrealistically expects everyone else to as well. He believes the media has an obligation to look at issues such as Prop 48 and dig deeper than just trying to find out which players qualify and which must sit out. Reporters must look at the overall picture: the plight of the poor, the lack of opportunity and education in the inner cities, and the damage drugs are doing to the nation's youth. The fact that many basketball players are scoring less than 700 on a standardized test is a symptom of what is wrong in this country, not what is wrong with college basketball.

Despite his feelings for the press as a whole, Chaney has a good relationship with the beat reporters who cover Temple on a regular basis. They respect him and like him, knowing he will always return their calls, answer their questions and say what is on his mind. Even more important, Chaney doesn't hold grudges. In fact, once a reporter gets hold of Chaney, he often has a hard time getting away. For Chaney, there is no such thing as a quick answer to a question, especially those involving issues outside basketball. He will spend as much time as it takes to explain his point of view, overwhelming his audience with the sheer power of his presence and the passion of his beliefs. Every interview is an opportunity to preach what he believes and Chaney is tireless, wearing down reporters as he does his players. Just as he believes that giving one kid a chance at college can raise the aspiration level of that kid's entire family, he believes that influencing what one reporter thinks and writes can also have a rippling effect.

October 24

Now that his players have been exposed to the press for the first time this season, Chaney wants to make sure they understand his views on the media.

> **Newspaper people are always being strategists. They talk to the public every day and say why didn't he try this or that? What the hell do they know? Newspaper people don't know anything about basketball. There is always someone out there who says you should be doing something else. Here we win thirty games [thirty-two, actually, in 1987–88] and some asshole says, "But Mark Macon doesn't have a smile on his face when he plays." Well, he's going to work out there. [The newspaper] shouldn't be your motivation. It doesn't matter what people write or say about you. What's important is that you play for the right reasons and listen to what we say.**

Macon understands: "I don't read the newspapers." This proves to be a good idea in the months to come.

During his freshman season, Macon was the toast of the town. An article in the *Philadelphia Inquirer* stated: "The Most Remarkable Owl Ever," and went on to call Macon, who at that point had played a grand total of fourteen college games, the greatest player in Temple history. A January 25, 1988, article in *Sports Illustrated* titled "Freshman at Work" called him "a freshman of such tender brilliance and luminous skill that to expect anything less of him than sudden stardom would, in this city of stars, have been folly indeed." Macon shrugged off all this acclaim and continued to play with a singleness of purpose that never wavered. Part of his mystique became his fixed blank expression. It fascinated and infuriated fans who wanted to know what was going on inside this freshman prodigy.

In the Eastern Regional final against Duke that year, Macon had his worst game of the year, shooting 6 for 29 for 13 points and Temple, which as a team shot 18 for 63, went down 63–53. After the game, Macon's mask came down for a brief moment. As he sat quietly in front of his locker, a few tears rolled down his cheeks. While many thought he was upset about the game he had just played, Macon says that's not true. "I cried because they [Perry, Rivas, and Evans] were leaving and I knew we'd never play together again," Macon says. "I already missed them. We were so close that whole year. We did everything together."

In 1988–89, as the team struggled, the press started asking what was the matter with Macon. Some suggested that he was never that great, just the beneficiary of talented players around him. Others blamed Chaney's system, saying Macon would be better off on a run-and-gun team. "What do they know that you don't?" Chaney would ask the press after games when they suggested Macon had a bad night. By this, Chaney meant that if opposing coaches put two men on Macon and devised all sorts of trick defenses to stop him, then they must think he's still something special. In the coming season, opposing coaches will continue to have their defenses pay special attention to Macon and his shooting percentage will drop for the second straight year, even though his points per game will top even his freshman year and his all-around game will continue to grow. The *Inquirer* will ask: "Whatever Happened to Mark Macon?" and the *Providence Sunday Journal* will proclaim: "Macon No Longer Bringing Home the Bacon."

All this would be enough to shake the confidence of even the most self-assured player. But not Macon. His faith in himself never waivers and he continues to play with the same grim determination and blank expression. If his shooting is off ("I'm a scorer not a shooter," he says), he works even harder on defense or rebounding, somehow finding a way to help his team win. For those who understand the game, it's easy to see that Macon is a brilliant player and one of the top three or four shooting guards in the country. "The best guard in America," Chaney states and refuses to even consider arguments to the contrary.

"I planned out my life a long time ago," says Macon, who sometimes acts and sounds like he's forty rather than twenty. "I want to play basketball, graduate and be a husband and father." A career in the NBA is part of the plan and Macon is looking forward to the day when he can take care of his mother. "I want to tell her, 'You've been working and struggling and worrying long enough. Now it's time for you to relax and get your vacation in life and have no more worries.' "

Macon will not let anything stand in the way of these goals and has a single-mindedness about him that borders on fanaticism. Macon allows himself to go out and party only two nights a year. The rest of the time he can be found in his room studying or listening to music. In high school a broken relationship with a girl got him off the track briefly. "I lost my focus," Macon says. "I cried and cried and walked around all heartsick and made a fool of myself. I promised myself I'd never let a girl do that to me again." This doesn't prevent him from dating. In fact, he has had a steady girlfriend for the past two years at Temple. "I love her a lot, but I can't let her come between me and my goals. I can't totally commit to her until I reach my goals. She could get tired of me and drop me, but I won't lose my focus."

To help him keep his focus, Macon thinks up inspirational messages, which he writes down and tapes up on the wall of his dorm room: THE THREE S'S OF LIFE—SUFFERING + SACRIFICE = SUCCESS; OBSTACLES ARE WHAT YOU SEE ONCE YOU TAKE YOUR EYES OFF YOUR GOAL; IN A TRUE WINNER'S BRAIN THERE MUST LIVE A MAN WHO IS HUMBLE AND HUMANE. Every day Macon touches each saying before he leaves his room.

Macon is a bit wary of the press, who in turn have become even more determined to discover what makes him tick. But Macon refuses to pour out his heart. He answers any and all questions thoughtfully and at length, but never reveals as much as the questioner would like. "I'm hesitant to open up," he says. "Coach says you have to be careful who you trust, who you're friends with." Some mistake Macon's caution for aloofness, or even worse, a big head. But with his teammates he's just one of the guys, playful and friendly. Every once in a while he'll even break into a dance step in the locker room or dorm. During the 1989–90 season he'll even try a few jokes with the press. About half get a laugh, which isn't too bad a shooting percentage.

October 26

In practice, you develop muscle memory from repetition. Just like you do in the classroom. So when you call on it in a game it's there. Sooner or later you will react without thinking about it because you have done it so many times in practice. But you have to develop this in practice through repetition.

Chaney developed his basketball muscle memory when he got to South Philadelphia the summer before he started eighth grade. The Chaneys lived on the 1700 block of Ellsworth Street, a poor, working class neighborhood that included Italian, Jewish and black families. The homes in South Philadelphia are all row houses: blocks and blocks of small two- or three-story homes. They all have front porches—or stoops as they are often called—where everyone sits to pass away the time on warm summer evenings.

Ellsworth Street was alive in the late 1940s, Chaney explains as we took a tour of the neighborhood. Today it's a quiet, deteriorating street, with many of the stores closed and a few houses boarded up. "The trolley cars used to run right down Ellsworth," Chaney says as we pull up in front of his old house, which he says looks exactly the same as it did forty years ago. "We lived right there, the house with the garage," he says pointing toward 1707, the smallest house on the block. The Chaneys never owned a car, but Sylvester kept his tools in the garage and on weekends—summer and winter—he'd make extra money washing and waxing cars. "Then we moved across the street to 1706," Chaney says, pointing toward a slightly bigger house. "It was a big step up for us."

Everything the Chaneys needed was within a few blocks of their house. On the corner of 17th and Ellsworth the Good Shepherd Mission Church of God still stands. Halfway down the block is the Globe Theater, where Chaney spent many a Saturday afternoon watching the nickel double features. It's been shut down for years. "We didn't call it the Globe; we called it the dump," Chaney says. "I loved the cowboy pictures, especially the Durango Kid. I used to dream about being a cowboy. But the only horses I ever saw were the old, broken down ones pulling the garbage trucks."

Down the street from the Globe is a warehouse that used to be an ice factory. Another block up is Washington Street, which used to be lined with slaughterhouses and

72

warehouses. "You could smell the sheep factory [slaughterhouse], especially in the summer," Chaney remembers.

The center of Chaney's world was the school yard behind Barrett Junior High at 16th and Wharton. "Everyone came to Barrett," Chaney says as we pull up to the chainlink fence that surrounds the small school yard behind the big, red-brick school. Three courts occupy half the yard and the other half is open space. "This place was always packed. There were little kids playing tag and older guys in the corners playing cards. There were always basketball games going on and behind them there were always two softball games going on, one in each corner. You can see there's not too much room, so you always had to keep one eye out so you wouldn't get hit in the head by a softball."

Chaney fell in love with basketball immediately, even though it was a year or two before he was good enough to make it into one of the playground games. At first, all he could do was watch. "We'd have to pick out all the odd hours [to play] when the big guys or the tough guys weren't playing," Chaney says. Unable to afford a basketball, Chaney and his friends would play with a tennis ball, dribbling and shooting until the ball cracked. Then they would cut it in half and play halfball (a form of stickball) in the street. In the winter they'd even shovel off the courts and play until the bigger kids chased them off. "Sometimes one of the gym teachers would give us an old volleyball or a busted basketball we could stuff with newspaper to use until the older guys came and took it away from us."

As Chaney got better and better, basketball became an obsession. "Basketball provides you with instant gratification," Chaney explains. "There was satisfaction in knowing that I could be good at something. The other kids and people in the neighborhood started to look at me as a good athlete. I began to feel as though I was a very important person and people on the street I didn't know would recognize me. Basketball became everything for me."

Chaney played all day long and often well into the night, frequently missing dinner. When he got home Sylvester would give him a whipping, but Chaney didn't care. A few minutes of pain was worth it to play basketball. On weekends, Sylvester wanted his stepson to do carpentry work with him, but Chaney would get up before him and sneak out of the house. Chaney would play by himself when there was nobody else at Barrett, working on his shooting and dribbling, never satisfied and always striving for perfection. "Somewhere inside me there was an inner drive that said I wanted more out of life. I can't explain where it came from, but it was there and basketball became the way. There were a lot of bad influences in the neighborhood, but I avoided them. You could influence me to go anywhere to play in a basketball game—through a den of evil people or jump on the back of a trolley or slip underneath the turnstile to get on the subway—but I would never steal or rob or hit people over the head. Basketball, although I didn't know it, was my way to a better life."

Sam Browne, a gym teacher and the basketball coach at Franklin, discovered Chaney in a gym class during his sophomore year and persuaded him to come out for the team. Sylvester was reluctant to allow Chaney to play. He thought sports were a foolish waste of time. "He thought all you should do was go to school, come home and do your chores, go out and work and make money and come home and sit in your room," Chaney says. Browne met with Sylvester and convinced him to let Chaney play. Once on the team, Chaney quickly became a starter and star and one of the leading scorers in the city.

Chaney developed a close relationship with Browne— whom he calls "my white father"—that continues today.

"He was a person who really cared so much about us," Chaney says. "He would come and visit us in our houses or invite us over to his house for dinner."

"I'm so proud of John," says Browne, who retired several years ago. "People say he's a lot like I was as a coach and that makes me feel good. I remember I told all the fellas the same thing my high school football coach told me: 'When you go out for a sport, you have to give everything you've got and if you don't, you're not going to get a uniform from me.' "

Browne didn't have to worry about Chaney, who was as tough and tenacious as any player who ever laced up a pair of sneakers. Chaney was also an angry player and he sometimes let his emotions get the best of him. "I was a bad person in the early portion of my career," he says. "I remember once a foul was called on me and I spit and growled at the referee and a technical was called on me. Later I apologized and tried to show I was a good person. At the end of the year the referee came up to me and said he could see a change in my behavior. That still stands out in my mind today, knowing that kids sometimes make mistakes or have bad attitudes, but you can't give up on them. There has to be some sort of redemptive value."

Chaney teamed with six-foot-five-inch Bob Gainey (they were known as Chaney and Gainey) to form one of the top scoring tandems in the city his senior year and lead Franklin into the play-offs. In the Public League semifinals, Chaney led Franklin to a win over Southern at the famous Palestra on the campus of the University of Pennsylvania. In those days, teams had an option to shoot foul shots or take the ball out of bounds. With Franklin up by close to 20 in the second half, Browne decided to put the game on ice and instructed Chaney to freeze the ball. "I could dribble the ball all night long and nobody could ever take it off me," Chaney says. "So they kept fouling me and we kept taking it out of bounds. They must have fouled me twenty straight times. I scored twenty-six points, which was a Palestra record at the time, but I could have had forty if I got to shoot all those foul shots."

In the finals, Franklin went up against West Philadelphia, which put a box-and-one on Chaney. "It was the first time I had ever seen a box-and-one," says Chaney, who still managed to score 15 points. "It was very disruptive." It worked well enough for West Philly to come away with a 41–37 win and the Public League championship. "That was perhaps the most crushing blow for us," Chaney says. "It was neighborhood versus neighborhood for bragging rights to the city."

The blow was tempered a little when Chaney was named the Public League's most valuable player after the season. LaSalle High School's Tom Gola was the Catholic League's MVP. Gola went on to a brilliant career at La-Salle University, four times earning All-American honors and leading the Explorers to the 1954 NCAA championship. "That was my crowning moment," Chaney says of the banquet where he received his award. "Yet it was also my most embarrassing moment."

Chaney had to wear a suit to the banquet at the elegant Warwick Hotel. "We were very poor and I only had one suit, a brown houndstooth suit. My father said I couldn't wear it, that this was a formal affair and I had to wear a more formal suit. So he made me wear his suit, a dark blue zoot suit with pinstripes that hadn't been in style for years. I was real skinny and the big shoulders on the suit hung way down and the pants were too long and I looked ridiculous. I was so embarrassed that when I got there I didn't mingle or talk to anyone. I just hid in the corners and I ran into the bathroom when they took the pictures. They had to come and get me out."

Chaney's forte was dribbling and scoring (he was one of the first high school players in the city to come up with a jump shot) and he would control the ball for a minute or two at a time, until he could create his own shot or dish it off to an open teammate. He could be fancy when he had to, going behind his back or between his legs to keep the ball away from the defensive player.

"I have to laugh at John now because he did everything he would yell at one of his players for now," says Victor Harris, a playground contemporary of Chaney. Harris first played against Chaney in 1948 at the Christian Street YMCA. "I'll never forget seeing John play for the first time. I was guarding him and he got a rebound. I thought I had him covered, but he faked me out and dribbled down the floor for a lay-up. The next time he got it, I told one of my teammates to get him; I didn't want to be embarrassed again."

Harris's playing days came to an end in the summer of 1950, when he contracted polio just before he was to enter Temple on an academic scholarship. He was paralyzed and his doctors didn't expect him to live. Harris pulled through and eventually graduated from Temple with a degree in accounting but has been plagued by medical problems ever since and has been confined to a wheelchair for the past twenty years.

By the summer of 1952, Harris could hobble around on crutches. He wanted to get back into basketball and organized the Haddington team and entered them in the Narberth Summer League, the premier league in the city. In 1953, Chaney, at Bethune-Cookman College by this time, joined the team, which also included such great players as Hal Lear, Sonny Lloyd, Cloyd Gross, Jackie Moore, Tee Parham and a shy, seven-footer still in junior high school named Wilt Chamberlain. "This team was a joy to coach," Harris says. "I just sent them out there and watched them play." Harris's Haddington teams may have been the greatest ever assembled in Philadelphia. They almost never lost and beat a league all-star team that included future NBA stars Gola, Ernie Beck and Paul Arizin.

Chaney was the star of the team and the league's most valuable player. Chamberlain was a shy kid thrown in with high school and college players who was already starting to change the game. There was no such thing as offensive or defensive goal tending in those days, so Chamberlain was free to stand under the basket and swat away opposing players' shots or stand under his own basket and guide or tap his own players' shots into the hoop. "One time we were playing an all-star game, Philly versus New York," Chaney says. "I took a shot from the corner and Wilt just grabbed it as it was about to go in and he put it in. I called a time-out. I was the star of the team. I walked up to Wilt and I said 'I don't care what you do, but don't you dare touch my shot.' He just kind of looked at me and didn't say a word. But he didn't touch another one of my shots."

Harris and Chaney have remained friends over the years. "I'll tell you how close we are," Harris says. "I have two blood brothers, but I'm closer to John. I've had a lot of problems over the years and every time something happens, John is one of the first people I call. And he's always there for me. Whenever I try to thank him, he just brushes it off. John is just a giver, a very, very special person."

November 6

Chaney is determined to cut down on all outside distractions this season. "Time is my most important commodity," Chaney says. "I'm not interested in speaking engagements, clinics, doing radio programs or commer-

cials or anything that will take me away from my team."
By eliminating all of the above, Chaney also eliminates
the opportunity to make a lot of extra money. But he
doesn't care.

Today, after practice, Chaney makes one of the few
exceptions to this rule. As a favor to a professor at Temple, he will talk to her class about Proposition 48 and
Proposition 42. "Talking to students or disadvantaged
youngsters is something I'll still do." Chaney lectures the
class as if they were members of his team:

**In my opinion, this is an issue that goes far
beyond athletics. Everyone [he motions toward the
eighteen or twenty students in the class] has to be
concerned with education in this day and time.**

By now, the history of these two pieces of NCAA legislation is well known. In short, Proposition 48—which was
approved at the NCAA convention in 1983 and went into
effect for freshmen entering college in the fall of 1986—
was the method the NCAA, panic stricken at the time by
the low graduation rate of football and basketball players
and the growing public outcry over this very real problem, used to ensure "academic integrity." The new rule
mandated that incoming athletes had to have both a 2.0
grade average and score at least 700 on their SATs in order
to play as freshmen. Anyone who achieved one, but not
both requirements, would have to sit out his freshman
year and would then have three, not four, years of eligibility remaining. A student who did not meet either requirement could not be offered a scholarship at all.

Prop 42 was passed at the 1989 NCAA convention and
took Prop 48 a step further. It stated that, starting in the
fall of 1991, anyone who did not meet the 2.0 and 700
requirements could not receive a scholarship and would

have to pay their own way to school for a year. If they maintained a 2.0 average that year, they could then be eligible for a scholarship.

At first glance, these requirements don't seem that prohibitive. A "C" average in high school and a 700 out of 1,600 on the SATs don't seem unreasonable requirements for potential college students. The NCAA thought their new rule would force high school athletes hoping to receive scholarships to study harder and ensure that those who did receive scholarships would be better equipped to handle college work, thereby increasing the percentage who graduated. However, this was an oversimplified solution to a problem that is complex and involves every aspect of the American educational system, as well as sociological, economic and environmental factors.

As soon as Prop 48 was passed, Chaney was one of the first to grasp its implications: The NCAA—an organization founded and designed to govern intercollegiate athletics—was suddenly in the admissions business, telling universities across the country who they could and couldn't admit. Plus, Chaney also predicted this new rule would disproportionately affect poor people and blacks.

This is exactly what happened. In 1986 and 1987, of the 150 Division 1 basketball players who did not meet the requirements of Prop 48, 138 were black. This shouldn't come as any great shock. The U.S. Department of Education has identified school systems in major urban centers—who serve a high percentage of black and Hispanic students—as offering the poorest education in the country. This finding is backed up by results of the SATs, which are generally regarded, even by the Educational Testing Service—the organization that administers the test—as being culturally biased against blacks. Year in and year out, blacks score 150 to 200 points lower than whites, with Hispanics slightly ahead of blacks, but still well below whites. In 1985 for example, blacks averaged

722, Hispanics 777, and whites 940. Other studies have shown a link between high family income levels and high test scores. "Prop 48 was like punishing a youngster because he hadn't had the opportunity for a quality education," Chaney says. "That's like punishing him twice."

From the moment Prop 48 passed, Chaney led the fight against it. While others criticized the new rule, saying it was unfair and would discriminate against kids from poorer backgrounds, Chaney took it a step further. He said Prop 48 was out-and-out racism. Along with Georgetown's John Thompson, Chaney became a national spokesperson against Prop 48.

During the 1988–89 season, when Prop 42 was passed, Chaney received and answered literally dozens of phone calls a day from reporters. This sometimes took four or five hours. The electronic media was just as demanding. Someone seemed to stick a television camera in his face every time he turned around. Chaney was on "Good Morning America" to plead his case against Prop 42. On "Nightline," he got into a heated argument with former tennis star Arthur Ashe, whose argument was that if poor black kids would spend more time studying and less time playing sports, they wouldn't have any problem getting into college. This line of reasoning infuriated Chaney. He says Ashe was someone who was "sponsored" by wealthy people throughout the early years of his career and doesn't know what it is like to grow up poor. Chaney penned articles against Prop 42 for several publications, including the January 23, 1989, issue of *Sports Illustrated,* where he wrote: "Proposition 42 will do one thing: punish blacks. This is racism. I believe that, as colleges have increasingly relied on black athletes, the public response has been: 'Let's do something about these black athletes. There are too many.' Could it be that the NCAA voted for the measure to make it impossible for some black athletes to get into college?

81

"Under Prop 42, numerous athletes—most of them black—will have to pay their own way to school, and many of them won't have the money. The result is that they won't be able to attend college. This is absurd.

"Athletes don't need punishment, they need inspiration. If you put another hurdle in front of them, the likelihood that they will succeed at both academics and athletics becomes slimmer. What we should be saying to our black athletes is that we will give them an opportunity by providing them scholarships, but they have to go to class and produce like everybody else.

"What's America afraid of? Education isn't a privilege for the privileged, it's a necessity for all—athlete and nonathlete alike. But educators have a negative perception of athletes. They see all the money that a few athletes end up making, and they're envious. It's easy to educate the bright kids, but even a deficient student should have the opportunity to get an education. I say don't discard a youngster because he doesn't have good grades or test scores. Educate him. . . .

"Get rid of Proposition 48 and Proposition 42 because they are antipoor and antiblack. Get the NCAA out of the academic arena, which should be the domain of the universities. And let's give economically disadvantaged athletes a chance."

It's difficult to dispute Chaney's claim that Prop 48 and Prop 42 are racist when you look at the facts. A headline in the NCAA's own newsletter read: "Poll shows most ineligible grid freshmen are Blacks." The article stated that "an Associated Press poll of all 192 NCAA member institutions playing football in Divisions I-A and I-AA indicates that 86.5 percent of 213 football players who are ineligible this season [because of Prop 48] and identifiable by race are black."

What is even more telling is the fact that the Ad Hoc committee of the NCAA that proposed Prop 48 to the

1983 convention—an Ad Hoc committee that did not include a single black member—had in their hands statistics that indicated this was exactly what would happen once Prop 48 went into effect. They knew that according to the College Testing Board, the average yearly SAT scores for whites between 1976 and 1982 ranged from 924 to 944, and that for blacks, during this same period, the scores varied from 686 to 707. Estimates made before the rule was adopted predicted that 50 to 60 percent of the black scholarship athletes currently in college would have been Prop 48 nonqualifiers. The question, then, is knowing this information beforehand, how could the Ad Hoc committee recommend a proposition that would disproportionately affect blacks?

"To me, what they did looked premeditated," says Chaney, his voice rising and his anger starting to spill out. "If they knew going in who this rule would affect, then the only conclusion I can draw is that this was their intention. I can't read minds; I can only look at the facts." To Chaney, the facts screamed racism.

These are some of the points Chaney wants to get across to the students he is lecturing today. To him, one of the sadder aspects of Prop 48 and Prop 42 is that as Temple travels to different schools around the country to play, students will yell "Prop 48, Prop 48" at players like Causwell and Hodge when they step to the free-throw line. Some of these schools even have Prop 48 players on their teams. Chaney sees the younger generation buying into the age-old stereotypes about athletes and blacks and perpetuating the same prejudices he has seen all his life.

My suggestion is we don't need a guillotine at this level, at the higher education level. We don't need to destroy a vision, someone's dream. Very few blacks can afford to go to school anyway. We're already costing them out. Temple has more black

students—not that we have a super number—than all the schools in Philadelphia combined, including a black school like Cheyney State. That's because we have a diverse approach to education. We afford more opportunity to more people in this university than perhaps any university. With that in mind, legislation [such as Prop 48 and Prop 42] would alter our founding policy. This university was founded for the common man.

There are all kinds of colleges. You have elite colleges like the Ivy League, which have higher standards. Or you have colleges that are for a wider range of people. So why should we dream up some legislation that's going to legislate people out of higher education at a time when we have a high dropout rate among blacks in higher education; when we have an even higher dropout rate among blacks in high school? Why should we dream up some legislation to keep out the people who need education the most? There are more blacks in the jails than in higher education. This is tragic. It seems as though there is something more important and that is a concern for people who come from very, very tough backgrounds.

And now they've come up with a piece of legislation—Prop 42—that stretches its arms a little farther. At least Prop 48 said we're going to give you a little bit of a chance. At least we'll let you come to school and give you a chance to shoot yourself in the foot. But Prop 42 says if you do not pass the test you cannot get a scholarship at all. So here goes all the hope and the aspiration of a youngster who feels the only way he can get out of that poverty cycle; the only way he can break free, is through perhaps the only vehicle he has: athletics. We're talking about destroying hope and when you destroy hope you destroy the human being.

What is the answer? It's very simple. We're focusing in on the problem at the wrong end. The problem is not the fact that a youngster couldn't pass a test to get into higher education. The problem is that he wasn't educated at an early age. If you couldn't read or write in twelfth grade, that means you couldn't read or write in third grade. Anytime a person is poor, the chances of him getting a good education are very unlikely. It seems to me a kind of perpetuation and the same thing's going to happen to his family.

My first year at Cheyney State, the first youngster I recruited I found playing right here in Pearson Hall [a gym at Temple]. McKinley Walker was his name. Came from right around here, a very poor neighborhood. Lived with his mother and brothers and sisters. I'll always remember going home with him—in the winter—and all they had for a front door was aluminum foil over a screen door. This was all they had to fight off the elements. I walked in and said, "Mrs. Walker, I'd like to see if I could take McKinley to college." She said she don't know about college, but I convinced her. I knew how tough it would be for McKinley. I couldn't give him a scholarship. He had to apply for all kinds of grants and aid and borrow money.

I always remember what Dr. Marcus Foster—who was the principal at Gratz High School when I was a teacher there—told me. He said if you could go into any poor family and it seemed as though generation after generation of that family were poor, if you could go into that family and take one kid out of there and get that kid through college, you would raise the aspiration level of everybody in that family. You want to break the cycle? That's how you do it. That's what we did with McKinley. Here was a kid who was poor. He had a bullet in his back. One day when he was in high school, he was walking to school and got shot. He had to go to the hospital once a month to get the bullet checked. They couldn't operate to get it out because it was too close to his spine, but they checked to see if it moved. I didn't know it at the time, but he had zero vision in one eye. We finally noticed it when we passed him the ball—he had to turn his head to see it and catch it. One time he got hit in the face and we finally found out.

In his fourth year, when it was time for him to graduate, he came to me after a couple weeks of practice and said he didn't think he would be able to play. I said what the hell are you talking about? He was my starting center. He said, "Coach, you know how much you talk about graduating and getting that degree. I need to work on my studies and have to drop basketball so I'll graduate."

I went home and tears came to my eyes.

The ultimate statement I want to make to you is if you diagnose the problem wrong—if you use the wrong instruments [the SAT]—you'll end up with the wrong prognosis. Sooner or later we have to reach some common denominator, some common ground, and state what the problem really is. The problem is the fact that we have a lower standard of education in the poverty belt. You have colloquialism where a youngster only learns what is two feet from the right of him and two feet from the left of him and does not get an opportunity to get introduced to anything else.

How can you use an instrument such as the SAT, which does not measure the character of someone? It doesn't measure what's in here [he points to his heart and head].

Chaney has a surprising ally in his contention that using 700 on the SATs as a cutoff point to deny youngsters is unfair: Gregory Anrig, president of Educational Testing Service, the organization that administers the SAT. In a January 19, 1983, letter to Walter Byers, then executive director of the NCAA, Anrig wrote: "I have serious concerns, however, about the particular effects of using the SAT in the manner decided [by Prop 48]. Based on the enclosed 1981 figures, for instance, the fixed requirement of a combined SAT score of at least 700 would have eliminated almost 51% of the Black males and 60% of the Black females. . . . I certainly support the strengthening of standards through requiring specific academic courses and a minimum grade point average for the courses. It is possible that SAT performance can be used fairly as part of these basic standards in some way. The particular use of a fixed cutoff score as contained in [Prop 48], however, may undermine the overall effectiveness of this worthy effort to raise standards for athletes."

Anrig went on to offer his and his organization's assistance to study the implications of Prop 48 and "possibly consider modifications to better achieve the objectives of this goal." Byers didn't take him up on his offer. On January 18, 1989, a few weeks after the NCAA approved Prop 42, Anrig tried again, sending a letter to Richard Schultz, who had replaced Byers as executive director of the NCAA. Anrig wrote: "I want to express concern again at this time about the [SAT] test use provisions of the recently enacted [Prop] 42. With this rule, as with its predecessor, admission test scores are used in a manner inconsistent with the way they [are] properly used in combination with other student information in reaching admission decisions at colleges and universities."

After Chaney concludes his lecture to the class, he asks if there are any questions. A student asks how can you explain to someone with good grades and a good score on the SATs why he or she can't get into a particular college, while an athlete with poorer grades and a lower score on the SATs is there on a full scholarship?

That's a big argument a lot of students have. The answer is, unfortunately, there is no market for you. There is a market for sports. But you have to take this equation and use it for everything else in life. People say why does that guy make two million dollars playing baseball? Well, hell, if people stop going to the ball park, he wouldn't be making two million. Why not tell all schools to drop all athletics [and athletic scholarships]? I have no problem with that at all. But until that happens, we're dealing with a situation that says there is a market for athletics and athletes. What do you have to sell [he asks the student who asked the question]? You could have 1,200 on the SAT and the school says we don't want you, we can get somebody else with an even higher score.

Another student says it's all well and good to let kids from disadvantaged backgrounds into college, even if their scores and grades are low, but what happens to them if they don't graduate?

That is another big discussion and a very valid point. I don't think you can legislate success or guarantee success. You can if you are a Princeton,

where you get the very best students. But my point is, you still have to give those youngsters from disadvantaged backgrounds a chance, even if you can't guarantee their success. That's why we have a fair amount of youngsters in this school from disadvantaged backgrounds. Our approach is different. We have seven hundred Hispanics over here in a bilingual program that takes six years to graduate from. That is addressing the needs of this community and I applaud that. I don't know how many of those youngsters will graduate, but at least they have a chance to succeed.

What would happen if disadvantaged youngsters aren't given a chance at all? Where are all the black youngsters today? One, they're in jail; two, out in the streets homeless; three, out looking for a job; or four, involved with drugs. So even if [only a small percentage graduate from college] isn't it worth it? Even if someone doesn't graduate, maybe that little bit of education, that little taste, will enhance his life. I don't know. I don't have any way to measure that. But I do know you guarantee the other things if you don't give him a chance. That's a hundred percent. I certainly know the most important thing is never destroy opportunity for a youngster. Never.

4

When You Fail in the Classroom, You Fail Out Here on the Basketball Court

November 8

Tonight the season starts, sort of. The Owls host Soder-talje, a Swedish professional team touring the states. Chaney treats this as if it were any other home game, which means he's holed up in his house incommunicado all day. He won't answer the phone, and since he hates them, Chaney doesn't have an answering machine. If his phone rings, he'll call his secretary, Miss Davis, at the office to see if it was her. Maloney, Demopoulos and DiSangro (the team's business manager) know this is the only way to reach Chaney. He'll watch tapes, make something for lunch, or just sit quietly and think about the game. If he gets restless or wants to get his mind off the game for an hour or two, Chaney will go shopping at Bloomingdales or Saks ("I like to see where the rich people shop") and look at ties, or head over to a farmers' market to squeeze the tomatoes and smell the melons.

Chaney times his drive so he arrives at McGonigle about forty-five minutes before the start of the game. The assistant coaches and players are there well before him. As he enters, Chaney tries to avoid fans and friends. His mind is on the game and he doesn't want to be distracted by well-wishers. Chaney heads for his office, where he sits quietly, sipping a cup of coffee. "I begin to think about the game again," he says. "I play the game in my mind and formulate the kind of approach I want to make to the team, what things I want to emphasize. I want to come up with a theme, so that the players can identify with it." With about fifteen minutes on the clock until the start of the game, DiSangro will summon the players into the locker room and Chaney will talk to them briefly for about five minutes. He'll remind them to look inside first to establish the big men ("That's important because the big people don't handle the ball and need to get involved early") and control the tempo, then he goes over the different defensive and offensive sets they will use. Then Chaney asks for a moment of silence, after which everyone gathers around Causwell, who leads them in a "team together." The players head back onto the floor for the final few minutes of warmups, while the coaches remain in the locker room discussing the game. Finally, just as the clock ticks to zero and the horn sounds, Chaney, Maloney and Demopoulos walk out onto the court.

As they are introduced, Temple's starters—Causwell, Hodge, Strickland, Kilgore, and Macon—amble onto the court, seemingly emotionless. The most they'll do is nod toward one another or lightly slap each other's hands. There are no high fives or waves to the crowd. Macon is always the last to be introduced. He heads onto the court, his fist in the air. The reserves follow him until everyone is together. Even this is done calmly. Macon's expression is as it always is during a game: emotionless. His fist is raised not as an act of defiance or a way to get the crowd going, but just as something for his teammates to attach themselves to as they gather together and draw strength from one another.

"I've never liked high-fiving and all that other stuff," Chaney says, explaining his team's demeanor on the court. "Football teams have to do it, I guess, to get all pumped up, but in basketball, if you're in a tough road game, you can't rely on emotion to get it done for you for forty minutes. That surge only stays with you a short period and can give you a false sense of security. I don't want my players to only play good at home because someone is cheering for them and not against them. To me, that's a coward. That's why you don't see our kids hand-slapping and running up and down doing all kinds of monkeyshines. I don't allow it. I don't like to see them look for encouragement from the stands. You're not playing for them. You're playing for me and your teammates."

Tonight the crowd is friendly, but the opposition a little tougher than expected, especially Bill Magarity, a six-foot-five-inch forward and former high school star in the Philadelphia Catholic League. In the first half he hits five of eight shots (four for seven from three-point range) for fourteen points and Temple, led by Causwell's eight points, leads just 34–33. In the second half Sodertalje's outside shooting finally cools down, and Temple pulls away to win 76–69.

The key to the win is the play of the guards. Macon plays like Macon, which means he does a lot of everything. He scores a team-high twenty-one on nine of twenty shooting, leads the Owls with ten rebounds, and adds an amazing nine steals and four assists. Kilgore adds seventeen points and commits only one turnover. With Strickland struggling (two of seven from the floor and only two rebounds in seventeen minutes), Chaney replaces him with Harden, who assumes the point, with Kilgore taking Strickland's spot at three. The offense seems to move better with Harden at the point. In twenty-one minutes, he connects on three of six shots for nine points, hands out four assists, and most important, doesn't commit a turnover.

November 11

Chaney has received reports that a couple of players have missed a class or two in the past two weeks. He wants this nonsense stopped immediately.

When you fail in the classroom, you fail out here on the basketball court. They work hand in hand. You can't be successful out here if you're failing in life. You just don't die one place and live another. If you die you're dead and you can't function anywhere.

Since Chaney has been at Temple, he has had a total of twenty-two players complete their eligibility for Temple (plus two transfers). Of this total, fifteen have graduated and three are currently in school and working toward a degree. Four have left school without a degree and are not presently in school. Of the four who left without degrees and are not in school, three—Stansbury, Rivas, and Perry—are playing professional basketball in either the NBA or in Europe.

Despite the high percentage of his players who have graduated, Chaney insists coaches don't have graduation rates. "Universities have graduation rates, not coaches," he says. Chaney won't buy into the theory that coaches use players, funnelling them through the system until their eligibility and usefulness are used up, not caring whether or not they learned anything or graduated. "An even swap ain't no robbery" is Chaney's way of saying a scholarship is one last chance for a disadvantaged kid to get an education. "It's his fault if he shoots himself in the foot."

"But Coach," I ask, "isn't a coach using a player if he doesn't help that kid graduate?"

"How the hell am I using you?" Chaney says. His voice is rising and is closing in on shouting. This happens often during our discussions. It takes a while to realize that he's not yelling at me, and that he's not mad at me. Chaney is just so passionate and believes so strongly in what he's saying that he can't help getting angry at all the wrongs he sees in the world ("I get emotional about things that are unfair"). Far from being mad, he enjoys a good argument and the chance to vent his frustrations.

"If a coach gives a youngster an opportunity to get an education," he continues, "how the hell is he using him? Let's say the kid is ignorant, stupid even, doesn't even know his ABCs. I'm still giving him another chance to learn. It's like Ernest [Pollard] says, you have to use the university. I've heard athletes who became sour after they have been given a chance and fail. And when someone says to them, 'Hey, that university used you,' he says, 'Yeah, you're right, they used me.' It was his responsibility to take advantage of the opportunity."

I press on, unwilling to let the coaching profession off the hook so easily. "But suppose a coach really doesn't care about a kid's education and doesn't push him to attend class and study and graduate. Then is he using the kid?"

"All a coach can do is open the door and let you in," Chaney answers. "I can open the door and let you sit down at my dinner table. I set the table for you. I set out a knife and fork. I set out the food. There it is, there's your meal. Now, if you walk out of that house hungry, whose fault is that?"

I'm caught up in his metaphor and think I can use it to disprove his point. "You may give a kid a knife and fork, but what if he's never used them before? What if he doesn't know how to eat? Isn't it your responsibility to teach him. If you don't, isn't that using a kid?"

"I might personally feel that way, but I'm talking about coaches in general. When a youngster I bring here to Temple doesn't make it, I, John Chaney, take it personally. But the coaching profession as a whole should not feel responsible or guilty of using a youngster when he fails."

In a way, the whole discussion is a moot point with Chaney. While he sticks to his guns and says a coach's only responsibility is to set the table and it's up to the players to partake, in reality he shoves the food down their throats whether they're hungry or not. He just doesn't want anyone to tell him this is his responsibility as a coach. He believes it's his responsibility as a person. That's the suit Chaney wears, but he's not about to force everyone else to wear it if it doesn't fit them.

You missed a class. [He points to a player.] You're losing by default, and that is pure ignorance. You don't have a choice. People who have choices are people who have alternatives. A poor man doesn't have choices or alternatives. You're the kind of person who goes along and you do fair and you think you have money in the bank. So then you screw up and go in another direction and you convince yourself you're doing good. It's not going to come out clean in the wash; it's going to come out dirty. What equals success? Your behavior.

The four years Chaney spent at Bethune-Cookman College (a small black school in Daytona Beach, Florida) changed his life in ways he never dreamed possible. He left Philadelphia in the fall of 1951 a skinny and scared eighteen-year-old boy and four years later he came back a man. At Bethune-Cookman, Chaney's world expanded from the blocks surrounding his South Philadelphia home and the school yards of Philly to include new ideas and philosophies and the realization that he was more than just an athlete. "A great deal of what I am comes from those four years," Chaney says.

"John just blossomed like a flower," says Dr. Hubert Hemsley, Chaney's roommate, best friend and teammate.

Chaney almost didn't go to college. After being named the Public League's top player, he should have been heavily recruited by the local schools. But this was 1951 and blacks didn't get scholarships. The idea of paying his own way wasn't even an option. "The concept of college was very difficult for many black families to understand," Chaney explains. "It represented a new kind of commitment that cost a lot of money and did not necessarily guarantee that the youngster was going to turn out special. In my family, the mind-set was after high school you got a job."

This is exactly what Chaney did, unloading boxcars at Sears for sixty dollars a week. "As I saw it, this would have been my job for the rest of my life," Chaney says.

One of his former teammates at Franklin, who was playing at Bethune-Cookman, recommended Chaney to the team's coach—Rudolph "Bunky" Matthews—who called and offered him a tryout, not a scholarship. This meant Chaney had to buy his own train ticket to Daytona Beach and if he made the team he would get a scholarship. If he didn't, he'd be on the next train home. Chaney decided to take the chance, confident that his basketball skills would take him to the next level. He had a hard time convincing Earley and Sylvester that this was a good idea. Sylvester wanted him to get a job. Earley was opposed for a different reason. "He didn't have the things that the other boys in college had, like clothes and money and good shoes," she says. "I told him I didn't think he should go. But he told me a story about some man who didn't have any money and went on to be successful and I didn't say any more."

So Chaney put his few possessions into a paper bag and boarded a train for Florida. "It was more a case of me running away from something—a way of life I didn't like—than running toward something I did like," Chaney says.

Bunky Matthews was a big man in both size and voice. He was also the football coach and an English teacher and a great orator. He would often captivate groups of students with his recitations of Shakespeare or poetry. "He'd sit under a tree reciting and twenty or thirty students would be gathered around him," Chaney says. "Much of what I learned in terms of public speaking came from him." According to Chaney, Matthews wasn't a great coach but was a great leader and motivator.

"When I first arrived I don't think he was too happy to see me," Chaney says. "I was very skinny and scrawny and didn't look like someone who was a basketball player. They didn't have a gym, so we had to walk three or four miles to the Cypress Street Rec Center (the team played its home games at the Daytona Beach YMCA). He threw the ball out and watched us play. I played very well. I shot well, ran the team, did everything. From that day on I was like his son."

Chaney quickly became the team's star and leading scorer and a crowd favorite wherever Bethune-Cookman played. Chaney was on the Southern Intercollegiate Athletic Conference (SIAC) all-league team in 1953–55, the NAIA All-American team in 1953–55, was named to the

NAIA national championship tournament team from 1953–55, and was most valuable player in the tournament in 1953, even though his team didn't win. He scored more than 2,000 points in his career and was voted into the school's sports hall of fame. "A lot of people thought I was the best black player in the country," says Chaney, who grows less and less modest about his playing days as the years go by. "But they didn't have the type of national coverage we have today, and we didn't really know about the other guys from around the country."

The SIAC included schools from black colleges throughout the South, including Morris Brown and Savannah State in Georgia, Tuskegee in Alabama, South Carolina A&M, St. Augustine's in North Carolina, and Florida A&M. This meant trips through the segregated South.

"This was my first introduction to American style apartheid," Hemsley says. On the train ride down to Florida, Chaney and Hemsley got a taste of what was to come. They rode on "Jim Crow" cars, meaning they had to switch in Washington, D.C., from the desegregated cars of the North into the segregated cars of the South. Lynchings were not uncommon and Hemsley remembers reading about one in nearby Augustine during his first few months at school. In Daytona Beach, blacks had to carry identification cards in the white sections after dark. "When we traveled we had to be very careful," Chaney says. Matthews drove one station wagon and Jack McClaren, the team's center and the current athletic director at the school, drove the other. There were very few restaurants that would serve the team and they often brought enough sandwiches with them to last the entire trip. They'd drive slowly through the small towns of Georgia and Alabama, afraid to draw the wrath of the redneck cops. No matter how slowly they drove, they always managed to get stopped and taken to the local courthouse and fined. "The police always seemed to be about six–five and weigh two hundred fifty pounds," Hemsley says. "And no matter how much they hassled us, we always had to be polite or we'd really be in trouble. Plus, they resented us because we were black and in college."

Years later, Chaney is free to travel wherever he wants to in the United States. Wherever he goes he is recognized and greeted warmly, by whites and blacks. This doesn't mean racism has vanished or that Chaney will ever forget what it was like for a black to travel in the South in the 1950s. "You have to have a strong sense of history to understand the present," Chaney says. "You can't divorce yourself from the past or forget that racism is our holocaust."

More than just exposing Chaney to racism, his four years at Bethune-Cookman showed him the best way to overcome it: education. "The lack of education is what keeps you at the lowest rung of the ladder," he says. Chaney didn't go to college to learn, he went to play basketball. "I wasn't a student; I wasn't a brain. I couldn't have passed any SAT test. They had to trick me into learning, into passing, so I could still play."

But a funny thing happened on the way to the court: Chaney began to enjoy learning. Bethune-Cookman was a wonderful place for young black students to learn and grow. It was a small, pretty campus where the professors took an interest in their students and instilled in their students a sense of pride in themselves and the belief that they could become anything they wanted. "They nurtured us," Hemsley says. "The people there showed affection for us and made us feel that we were more than just jocks and were expected to learn." The matriarch and guiding spirit of the school was Mary McCloud Bethune, who died in 1955. She founded the school in 1904 as the Daytona Normal and Industrial School for Negro Girls, was a leader in the civil rights movement and served as President Roosevelt's adviser on minority affairs. "She predicted that one day the barriers would come down and that we had to be prepared to take our place," says Hemsley, who, through his deeds, showed Chaney what a poor person from a deprived background was capable of accomplishing when he put his mind to it.

Hemsley grew up in West Philadelphia and wasn't a particularly good student in high school. But on the entrance exam at Bethune-Cookman, he scored the highest grade of any incoming freshman and so encouraged, challenged himself to do well in school. He was a straight A student. Hemsley switched his major from phys ed to science and math and then to medicine. "At that time I had never even seen a black doctor," he says. But still he was determined to become one. He was accepted to Jefferson Medical School in Philadelphia—one of only two black students in the school—and worked two jobs to pay his way through school and support his wife and two kids. Today Hemsley lives in Los Angeles and is a prominent obstetrician/gynecologist.

"He was my inspiration," Chaney says. "He proved that given a chance he was capable of remarkable things. And he made me stay in the room and study. He told me, 'One of these days you'll be out of here and people will quickly forget you were once an All-American basketball player.'"

Later this season, Hemsley, in town for a medical convention, makes a surprise visit after an Owls win at McGonigle. The two hug and it's easy to see the affection they hold for each other. "I love John and have an all-abiding faith that it's mutual," Hemsley says. "I just have a warm glow inside from knowing someone like him." Although they haven't seen each other in months, it's as though they were never apart and they immediately start teasing each other. Hemsley mentions Chaney's ever-enlarging stomach. "I guess you can't fit into my suit any-more," he says and they both burst out laughing. In college, Chaney didn't have a suit, which was required at Sunday church services. Hemsley had two—a wool suit for the winter and a gabardine one for the summer. In the winter Chaney wore the thin gabardine and froze. In the summer he wore the woollen suit and sweated.

Next Chaney tells the story of how Hemsley tricked him into embarrassing himself in front of the entire school. At Sunday services, students often got up and recited poetry and Shakespeare. Hemsley had a photographic memory and would often rise from his seat and give impassioned recitations, with Chaney sitting next to him in a jealous snit. "Hemsley was the one who always brought up the curve for the rest of us," Chaney says, unable to keep from laughing as he tells this story. "Miss Berhl, our English teacher, would say, 'That Hemsley, he's my boy.' I begged and begged him to teach me a poem and finally he did." Only Hemsley taught him the poem—"Invictous," by William Ernest Henley—incorrectly.

"It matters not how straight the gate," Chaney begins, reciting the poem he still remembers—sort of—almost forty years later, "or charged with punishment the scrolls. God is the captain of your soul and I am the master of my fate. Or something like that. So I'm all proud and ready, and I stand up and recite it. The next day I come into class all happy and whistling and ready for Miss Berhl to reward me. But she says, 'Chaney, you're the stupidest person I ever met, you read the ending backwards.' I said 'but Hemsley taught it to me.'"

By his second year at Bethune-Cookman, Chaney found himself turning into a good student. "I couldn't have escaped it even if I wanted to," he says. "They pulled and pushed and pinched at me until I learned. There were no people cutting classes, there were no people who didn't want to be there. Everyone wanted to learn and after class we would find ourselves continuing the discussions."

Chaney still remembers a course called American Institutions where he learned about the law, political systems, religion, marriage and the family. In humanities he learned "about the world around you and the world above you" and was first introduced to Cervantes's classic, *Don Quixote.*

Hemsley joined the Kappa Alpha Psi fraternity and a year later Chaney pledged. "It was looked upon as the top frat on campus," Chaney says. "The people in it were recognized as the good students." To get in Chaney had to maintain good grades and also go through all the rituals of hazing. "We had to buy five pounds of beans and paint the fraternity initials on every one. Then they'd wake you in the middle of the night and make you walk to the beach and get a bucket of sand. The beach was five miles away." The fraternity also put on skits and built floats for the homecoming parade and was involved in projects in the community, including raising money for black scholarship funds.

At Bethune-Cookman, Chaney met his future wife, Jeanne. Until this time, Chaney had been too preoccupied with basketball to spend much time chasing after girls. In fact, until he met Jeanne, he had never even been out on a date. "The first time I saw her was in the lunch line in the cafeteria," Chaney says. He found out she worked in the registrar's office and began to think up excuses to stop by and say hello. He finally worked up the nerve to ask her out and Jeanne said yes. Chaney's only problem was he didn't have any money. "I had to convince her that if she lent me the money, I'd pay her back. I never did."

After this first date they began seeing each other regularly, studying and going to the library together or just walking around campus. Occasionally they'd go to a movie. The summer before their senior year, the two got married in Philadelphia. Once back at school, they moved in with Hemsley and his bride (Hemsley has since remarried) into a small apartment on campus. Both women became pregnant and there were some tough times. "Hemsley and I played basketball, worked a job waiting tables and studied," Chaney says.

"Then we'd come home and our wives would be waiting for us to make them dinner," Hemsley says. "Both of us were better cooks than our wives."

Despite the hardships of a new family and the demands of school, basketball and a job, this was a golden era for Chaney. "I shudder to think about what my life would have been like if I hadn't gone to college," Chaney says. "I have nightmares even thinking about it. I would have wound up on the streets like many of my friends. Sometimes I drive around and see them or people just like them on the streets, homeless and hopeless and I can't help but cry."

Not surprisingly, much of what Chaney teaches his players and many of his views on the world around him can be traced back to his four years at Bethune-Cookman. The amazing metamorphosis he underwent there is why he is so vehement in his objection to anything—such as Prop 48 or Prop 42—that would deny a kid from a poor background the opportunity to go to college and reach his full potential. If he could do it, Chaney figures, anyone can. All someone needs is an opportunity and a push in the right direction.

November 15

Today Chaney tells his players about the time his oven "captured" a ham hock. In addition to being extremely

103

funny, Chaney uses the story to drive home the theme for the day, which is that you must learn to control the little things on and off the court, and sooner or later the big things will fall into place.

In life, not just basketball, the key is to be able to control the little things. No human being is capable of overcoming all the big things in life, the things that aren't within your control. I'm a guy who gets angry at the things you can control and don't. A person is an idiot if he doesn't manage the things he can manage.

One time I bought this big ham hock. So I put it in the oven and cooked it up with all the seasonings I like. Then I couldn't get it out of the oven. I kept pulling, but the pan was stuck, wedged in. And I couldn't get the heat to shut off. I got a screwdriver and pulled that door off, but I still couldn't get that ham hock out. I called the gas company. They said it wasn't an emergency, they'd come in two days. I said, "I need you now." I couldn't tell the man I have a ham hock stuck in there, that's too embarrassing. I just said it was an emergency. I kept working at it and just destroyed that oven. Finally my wife came home and asked what the hell was I doing. I said the damn oven has captured my ham hock and won't let it go. She finally went upstairs and got HER tools. She's the mechanic. She took the back of that oven off and got that ham hock out. While she was doing this, I just went up and locked myself in the bedroom. Finally she came up and handed me a bill for a new stove.

I learned I couldn't manage the situation. I should have run for help from the start. So, the things you can manage, you have to control. The little things make you win games. That's why we work on them every day. Put them inside your pocket and that's your bank account that you can draw on whenever you need it.

"Is this a true story?" I ask Demopoulos.
"I never heard it before," he says.
Later in the office, Chaney confirms that this is indeed a true story. He does admit he might have exaggerated a little.

November 17

At the end of practice, Chaney looks at his players and makes an observation. "We sure have a lot of players whose names start with M or D," he says, looking at Mik, Michael, the two Marks, Duane, and Donald. "M, Ds. But that sure doesn't stand for doctor. That means MMMMMMMMMM Dumb."

November 20

Chaney is in a giving mood after the Owls 97–95 win over USA Verich Reps, an AAU team from Ohio that has no business coming within twenty points of Temple. To John DiSangro he gives his brand-new cashmere topcoat. To Demopoulos he gives his expensive Italian designer silk tie. "I don't want them anymore, they're bad luck," Chaney explains.

Chaney believes the clothes he wears can affect the outcome of a game. Once he finds a particular article of clothing is cursed, he gets rid of it as fast as he can rip it off. Demopoulos and DiSangro—who aren't as superstitious—each have half a dozen ties, a sweater or two, and other assorted articles courtesy of the Owls' poor play over the years. DiSangro even has a pair of $150 Italian leather shoes. Conversely, once an article of clothing proves itself a good-luck charm, Chaney will continue to wear it to games.

After tonight's game, Chaney is lucky to leave McGonigle wearing anything at all. The Owls do everything in their power to give the game to Verich Reps. With Temple up twenty points midway through the second half, Verich Reps begins pressing fullcourt. Several turnovers later (Temple commits seventeen in the game), the lead is down to twelve and Temple has yet to show it can get the ball upcourt against Verich Reps' mediocre press. "Right now we are just having trouble beating the press because we are not getting good guard play," Chaney says. "Sooner or later I'm going to have to abandon those big guys."

Chaney does in fact take Strickland out as the big lineup struggles to get the ball upcourt. Harden comes in and the ball-handling improves—but not by much.

To make matters worse, Kilgore pushes an opposing player under the basket after Verich Reps scores midway through the second half. The official toots a personal foul on Kilgore, who continues to argue until he is hit with a technical. Verich Reps makes four foul shots and gets possession of the ball. Naturally they make the most of their opportunity and Bill Toole hits a long three-pointer for a seven-point turnaround. On the Chaney scale, a technical foul is even worse than a turnover.

Verich Reps keeps pressing and hitting long bombs and the lead is down to 95–92 with a minute to go. After Macon is fouled and makes only the first free throw, Toole hits another three pointer and the lead is 96–95 with forty-five seconds remaining. Temple breaks the press and gets the ball into the frontcourt. The game clock and shot clock are almost exactly the same, which means all the Owls have to do is hold on to the ball, let the clock run and wait for Verich Reps to foul them. But Strickland (who's back in with Kilgore fouled out) gets impatient and rises up for a jumper from twelve feet with about twenty seconds to play. Chaney, Maloney and the entire bench rise almost as one shouting, "No, no!" The shot misses, Verich Reps gets the rebound and calls a time-out to set up their final play. After working the ball around they miss a long shot, but get not one or even two, but three offensive rebounds. Each putback somehow finds a way to roll off the rim and finally Strickland grabs the ball and is fouled with a second remaining. He makes the first, misses the second and Temple escapes with a 97–95 win.

Outside shooting is the key for Verich Reps, which hits fifteen of thirty-four three-point attempts. Toole connects on eight of eleven, including five in six in the second half during his team's comeback. Most of his shots were from three or four feet behind the three-point line. "I've never seen a team shoot the ball so well," Chaney says to the press after the game. "That one guy [Barry Mitchell, who connected on five three-pointers] was hitting them from the bleachers. One time he was so far over toward the sideline, I couldn't even see him. All I saw was a ball come out of the stands and go into the net."

"What happens if you play a team during the season that shoots that well?" a reporter asks Chaney.

"We lose. You can just write that down now and send it in. Whenever we play a team that shoots that good, you just write down that Temple just lost."

Giving away his clothes after a bad game is only one of Chaney's many superstitions. (It is, however, his most expensive one.) In a sense, they are more rituals than superstition, with a little bit of common sense added in for good measure. Proper respect for these rituals means good luck. Despite what referees and opposing coaches may think, Chaney has never put a curse on anyone. The closest things to voodoo in Chaney's repertoire are his "Reckless Eyeball" and "One-Eyed Jack" stares. But more about them later, when poor officiating necessitates their use.

Many of Chaney's superstitions revolve around clothing. As a player, Chaney always put his pants on last. "I would always have everything else on but my pants," he explains, "and I would walk around the locker room like that. Then I would always go to the bathroom right before the game started—whether I had to go or not—and then come back to my locker and put my pants on. Then I always had to be the last one out of the locker room."

In recent years, Chaney has begun wearing cardigans instead of jackets to games, but this has nothing to do with superstition. He sweats a lot, which can ruin his expensive jackets. Sweaters are a lot easier to clean and cheaper to replace. Chaney will wear only two sweaters this season—one black and one a very dark blue that looks black. The year Temple was number one, Chaney wore the same black cardigan during the Owls' eighteen-game winning streak. He retired it after the loss to Duke. Last season marked the end for his lucky T-shirt, a sleeveless number made of cotton and rayon. Chaney had worn it for years at Cheyney State and Temple. During tournaments, he would wash it out at night in his hotel room and hang it up on the shower rod to dry so it would be clean for the next night's game. Finally, it became so worn and frayed and ripped that he couldn't wear it anymore. "I had on this beautiful white silk shirt," Chaney says. "The only problem was it was sheer and everyone could see through it and see all the rips and tears and holes in my

T-shirt. I looked like a ragamuffin. I hated to do it, but I had to get rid of it.

"And after that we went on a rage of losses," Chaney says, believing the two events were connected. He and Demopoulos spent last season searching everywhere for an identical T-shirt, but to no avail. "They just don't make them like that anymore," Chaney laments.

To make up for the loss of his lucky shirt, Chaney makes sure to adhere to his other clothing rituals. His game-day tie must have splotches of red in it to approximate the cherry of the Owls' uniforms. Luckily Temple's colors are cherry and white instead of green and white: Chaney hates green and won't buy any article of clothing that has green in it. Chaney loves to shop, especially for ties. His taste is impeccable and he only buys the most expensive designer clothes, admitting this is a weakness. "But look," he explains, a little defensively, "I lead a simple life-style. I've been in the same house for thirty years, I don't go out much or go on vacations. This is my hobby."

Chaney has an extensive wardrobe of suits, ties and shoes, and almost all are from Italy. But he is most comfortable at work in sweats and basketball shoes and at home all he ever wears is a bathrobe. Even during games he doesn't wear his "A" clothes. "I don't want to show up the other coach," he says. But even the items from his "B" list often cost a couple hundred bucks a pop.

Chaney has influenced Demopoulos's taste in attire and he too spends much of his spare time shopping (Maloney is a K-Mart kind of guy). Ties are a particular weakness for both. It has gotten to the point where the owner of a very exclusive shop on Rodeo Drive sends a box full of the latest seventy-five-dollar Italian silk ties to Chaney a few times a year. Chaney and Demopoulos pick and choose what they want, often fighting over the same tie, and send the rest back. Chaney usually buys three or four, while Demopoulos can afford only one at a time. But in the end, Demopoulos—one of the best-dressed assistant coaches in America—usually winds up with more ties than Chaney. He knows his boss is a big-time soft touch. Demopoulos keeps admiring a particular tie until Chaney finally gives in and hands it over to him. Chaney doesn't mind; this just gives him an excuse to go shopping for more.

Other superstitions include a fear of black cats ("If I see one in front of my car as I'm about to leave, I don't go"), no open umbrellas in the house and no hats on the bed. A relative taught him to spin around three times whenever he stubbed his toe. This would keep him from stubbing the same toe again. Now, whenever a player gets hurt, he has the player stand in one spot and turn around three times. This won't prevent all injuries but will keep the player from suffering an injury to the same area again. When Chaney was recruiting Macon, who suffered a serious sprained ankle his junior season in high school, he had him turn around three times in his living room. "You ask Mark," Chaney says. "He's never had any trouble with that ankle since." He passes on this tidbit to Ryan Kling, the team's trainer, and the next day he dutifully has two or three players turn around three times in one spot to keep them from reinjuring assorted fingers, shoulders and ankles. "You never know," Kling says.

November 21

With the late game the night before, Chaney decides to have practice at 6:30 in the evening. His players think they're getting a break. They're not. All this does is give Chaney more time to think about the game. The more he thinks about the seventeen turnovers, the seventy-eight shots Verich Reps took, the four chances they had to score in the last few seconds, and Kilgore's personal foul, the angrier he gets.

You have to realize and take seriously my frustration. I have never, ever, as long as I have been in this business, had as many turnovers as we had last night [that's not true, but Chaney never lets facts get in the way of making a point]. And then, you let a team get three shots in the last second to almost beat us. You stood idly by, right here [Chaney stands under the basket where the criminal act took place the night before], watching the ball being bounced back and forth. When we need a rebound everybody has to go and get involved. You got to get the ball and rip it off the boards.

And your play was an act of stupidity worth eight points [he says to Kilgore]. Eight. All because of an attitude. And the day before I talked about attitude. Keep your mouth shut.

Chaney isn't finished with Kilgore yet. Kilgore is like Chaney was at a similar age: a street kid with a lot of inner anger. They're both tough and stubborn and won't back down from anybody. Chaney learned to rein in his anger and use his energy constructively, not destructively, on the court.

That is what he will struggle to teach Kilgore in the months to come. Kilgore understands, but says he can't help himself. "Coach teaches us to try to put our emotion and fire into our feet," Kilgore says. "But I still keep my emotion up here [he points to his head] and walk around the court when I should be running." Sometimes Kilgore plays defense with his hands balled into fists and takes jabs at the ball, instead of moving his feet to get into position to cut off the opposing player.

I can't believe it. Seventy-eight shots. Here's a gun. Shoot me. I'm going to give you six bullets and I'll have a gun with six bullets. Let's count ten paces.

Chaney has Kilgore come out on the court with him and the two line up back-to-back near the free-throw line for a mock duel. Kilgore isn't sure what to do or what Chaney is up to, but he has no other option than to play along.

Start counting to ten and then we turn around and shoot. But why would you wait until ten? Why wouldn't you be able to count off five and then turn around and shoot the bastard in the back? See, that's what you need to do. Cheat to win. One, two, three, four, five, six and then turn around and BAM! Seventy-eight shots. Why should you count to ten and make it fair for the other team? I expect you to ambush them. AMBUSH THEM! Ain't no way the other team should get seventy-eight shots. That's like shooting ourselves through the heart.

Chaney walks back toward Kilgore. The two are now standing at the foul line, while all the other players are under the basket.

Turn around.

Kilgore turns, his back to Chaney. Chaney reaches in his pocket and peels off a hundred from his wad of bills. He reaches into Kilgore's shorts and deposits the money.

I'm paying off a hundred for you from the other team. Right here. To your ass. Now get the hell out of here.

Kilgore joins his teammates, but not before Chaney grabs his money back. Everyone is cracking up, doubled over in laughter. Even Kilgore can't hold back and laughs as he looks helplessly toward his teammates.

After practice, Chaney shoots a few baskets while his players crowd around the water cart and grab at the donuts and fruit. A member of the women's team walks in and immediately goes over and teases him about his shooting ability. "Nobody needs you here," he responds. He loves to tease and flirt with the women around campus. "Why don't you do something useful? Go take a home economics course. Learn to cook." Chaney breaks into a cackle and the two start slapping at each other.

Both the *Inquirer* and the *Daily News* come out today with special college basketball sections that preview the coming season. The Owls are ranked twelfth by the *Daily News*, which notes: "The Owls' size and power inside, and Mark Macon's leadership should more than offset the inexperience of towering newcomers Donald Hodge, Mark Strickland and Chris Lovelace and the absence of a consistant jumpshooter. Shades of Final Eight in 1987–88?" The *Inquirer* rates Temple seventh, stating: "This is the year we find out whether to believe the hype about Mark Macon or begin to wonder whether he's overrated. Despite his resourcefulness, Macon has yet to show consistency with his jumper." This is exactly the kind of criticism of Macon that angers Chaney.

In the AP poll Temple is ranked fifteenth and the UPI has them seventeenth.

All in all, this is a pretty optimistic outlook for a team

that has only one proven scorer and star (Macon), a center who is still a work in progress (Causwell), a sophomore guard still trying to learn how to play point guard (Kilgore), three Prop 48 guys who have never played a game in college (Hodge, Strickland and Lovelace) and almost no depth. Much of this optimism and the high rankings is a testament to Chaney, who is recognized as a man who has done a lot with a little in the past. Now, everyone believes, he has a lot. Even though his team is young and inexperienced, the feeling is that Chaney will whip them into shape.

November 23

It's Thanksgiving Day, but the Owls still practice long and hard starting at 9:00 in the morning. Many teams are off during Thanksgiving, so the players can be with their families. But to Chaney, the team is his player's family ("The greatest assurance of success is that each and every one of you must agree that you are in a family setting") and it's important that they spend the holidays together. Some of the players can't afford to go home, or they come from broken homes where there isn't much to be thankful for. "In many cases they wouldn't have an opportunity to sit around a table in a family setting on Thanksgiving even if they were home," Chaney says. "This gives them a chance to be part of a family and gives them pause to think about what a family should be."

The team dinner is scheduled for midafternoon at the Hershey Hotel in center city—the team's home away from home. Whenever school is out and the dorms are closed, they stay here. A big buffet table is set up and loaded with enough food for an army, which means there will be just enough for the hungry team. Everyone is there—except Maloney, who's with his family—including the managers and trainers. Chaney sits at the head of a long table and says grace. He gives thanks and wishes everyone and their families the best. He adds that he hopes that this is just the first of many times when they will be together as a family and "break bread." Then Chaney gives thanks for the "little bit we have already accomplished in our lives" and asks the Lord to give everyone the strength they will need to continue to grow and succeed in life. "Then everyone eats as much as they can and takes the leftovers to their room," Chaney laughs.

From the Hershey, Chaney rushes over to the nursing home to pick up his mother and takes her to his house, where his second Thanksgiving dinner awaits.

Chaney keeps his two families separate. His wife, two sons and daughter sometimes attend home games, but when they do it's on their own and they never talk to Chaney before or afterward.

"I have a different view than a lot of other coaches who involve their wives in the basketball aspect of their lives and have them travel and be on committees and perform all kinds of functions," Chaney says. "The time I would have to spend with her on the road is time spent away from the team and preparing for the game. My peace of mind comes when I can get the hell away from my job. I don't need to come home and talk about basketball with my wife. I have to have a place to run to where there is no basketball."

Jeanne Chaney has her own career, apart from that of her husband. She recently retired after more than thirty years as a teacher in the Philadelphia public schools. Now she spends her time doing community service and rearranging her husband's spices in the kitchen. "How come every time I clear a little space and set up my special

115

spices, she moves them?" Chaney asks no one in particular, while he searches for the oregano to add to his simmering pot of chili. "Don't ever trust a woman; they always hide things on you," he says and breaks out in a cackle.

Chaney loves to fuss and fight with his wife, but Jeanne, who calls her husband "Chaney," knows how to handle him. "I just ignore him," she says.

"Oh no, you don't," Chaney says and tries to start a tussle. If Jeanne doesn't respond, he'll call Demopoulos, who's always ready for a good argument.

November 24

Today turns out to be a long day for Chaney. It starts with a fiery lecture, followed by a fire in Chaney's house and his third Thanksgiving dinner.

We're going to talk about special situations today. Not only must the coach be ready for them, the players must be ready for them as well. If a hospital didn't have special situations, there wouldn't be emergency rooms. But every hospital has an emergency section, a trauma section for life-threatening situations. A situation where time has been reduced and the length of time you have to do something for somebody has been reduced.

Special situations are those that come at the end of the game, when the outcome is on the line. But before Chaney gets down to specifics, he wants to make sure his players learn how to control their emotions when the game is on the line and the fans are going crazy.

If you go to any kind of contest overly emotional, it's almost like being drunk. It's like drinking a bottle of whiskey before the game. In any aspect of life, you just can't be emotionally drunk. Emotion only stays with you a short period. What you want is a sustained effort of performance. Not just on the basketball court, but throughout life.

I had a player at Cheyney that was always emotionally drunk. He was seven feet tall and wasn't a good player in the first place. I can remember a game I put him in, started him, and he played for twenty minutes and didn't play well at all. The fans didn't cheer him on, so he wasn't inspired. It got to a really crucial point. We had a run of six or seven, took the lead and I put him back in. We were shooting a foul shot. We missed, but he was there. The ball hits his hands, bounces off his head and goes in the basket. KABOOM! He thought that he had just done the greatest thing in the world. He went running down the floor jumping and fighting and scratching. People were yelling and screaming. Then he went down and stole the ball. Gave it up to the guard, ran down the floor, got it back and dunked it. I called time out and took him out of the game.

He could not understand why I took him out. He sat next to me and kept saying, "Coach, can I go in?" This went on the whole second half after he had committed what I called an atrocity. He was out there playing for the wrong reasons. He was playing for his girlfriend and his mom and pop and his friends in the stands. I wasn't putting him back in there for that. I wanted him to learn a lesson. If you listen for the rah-rahs and the hah-hahs, sooner or later you're gonna get the boo-boos.

Chaney wants his players, especially his point guard, to always be thinking about time, situation and score, and what they have to do to make the most of all three. So far, he's doing all the team's thinking, literally coaching the players up and down the floor on every possession.

"In practice my senior year, he didn't have to tell us anything," Blackwell recalls. "He would just coach the red team and set up the time, situation and score for us. He'd say, 'White team, you're down three points with thirty seconds to go and you have the ball. What you gonna do?' Or he'd say, 'You're down three and the other team has the ball.' Then we'd get together real quick and figure out what to do."

I had players say, when there was one second left, "Let Terence [Stansbury] do it." I said okay. And we won. We beat the same team we're playing Tuesday [Penn] with a ninety-foot pass and last-second shot by Terence. When we sat down on the bench at the end of our first game in the NCAAs, guess what fellas? Granger Hall said, "Hey, Coach, let Terence do it. He can do it." Three seconds left and he makes a twenty-five-footer. BOOM. That shot was heard around the world [and gave Temple a 65–63 win over St. John's]. All our diagrams and fancy plays meant nothing, because we had players on the floor who knew what to do. They were tuned in, not tuned out. Terence said, "I'm ready, I'll do it," and everyone else believed in him. You see, it wasn't the fact that the ball went into the basket. That's not the success, that's not the point. The point is he wanted it. He stepped up to a challenge. When the ante was raised, he raised himself. Now, if he was emotionally drunk, he would have missed.

Now that the lecture is over, Chaney begins working on special situations. The first is getting offensive rebounds on missed foul shots at the end of a game. He has the players get on the line and shows his players how to use a drop step to circle around the man with inside position and beat him to the ball. Then he shows the inside man how to prevent this from happening. "You must make contact with your man," he says, taking a position along the foul line and showing Causwell how to do it. "Use your body. Know where your man is."

Next they work on defensing inbound plays at the end of the game, when the Owls need a steal. "Double the man who gets the ball." This leads Chaney into a story about the whippings he got from his mother for staying out late playing basketball. "She would whip my ass until it started smoking," Chaney says. "I would try and fool her and put cardboard or something in my pants, but that only made her madder and she'd just whip me longer." Finally he delivers the moral. "You got to get your ass out there [on the man with the ball] or else you're gonna get an ass whipping. And not from me, from the other team."

Chaney sets up a special situation. He gives the red team the ball and tells the white team—Kilgore, Harden, Strickland, Hodge and Lovelace are in; Causwell and Macon sit on the sideline, resting minor injuries—that there are ten seconds left and they're down a point. "Time is now your enemy. In order to make it your friend you must stop the clock." The red team inbounds the ball and Strickland immediately fouls Randolph hard. "That's an intentional foul," Chaney screams, "an act of stupidity. That's what you call a Mik Kilgore. And he's like Sherlock Holmes, only he doesn't have a clue."

In the next situation Chaney sets up, the red team is up one with ten seconds to go and Conic is at the line shooting one-and-one. The freshman makes both shots and his

119

side is up three. Kilgore signals a time-out. "This is a test. I'm not telling you anything," Chaney says.

"Go ask Coach Maloney," Causwell shouts from over on the sideline and Chaney just laughs. The white team inbounds and gets the ball across midcourt and quickly calls another time-out.

"Five seconds left," shouts Rob Jones, who serves as the official timekeeper and calls out the seconds as they tick off.

"That's your last time-out," Chaney says.

"They're looking for Mike Vreeswyk," Causwell says and Chaney laughs again. He's enjoying the white team's confusion.

"The League of Nations can't meet forever," Chaney says, and the white team sets up to inbound the ball. They get it in to Kilgore, who misses a three. Hodge rebounds and tosses it out to Harden, who misses, while Jones counts down to zero. Chaney is pleased, even though he doesn't say anything. The red team got the ball to the right person—Kilgore—and when Hodge grabbed the rebound he correctly threw it back out for a three instead of going back up with the shot.

Next the white team has the ball. They're up one with three seconds to go. All they have to do is inbound and wait to get fouled. But the red team is making it tough for them to inbound the ball. Harden finally works himself free, but he loses his balance as he grabs the pass and steps out of bounds. It's the red team's ball. They get it to Randolph, who scores at the buzzer. The red team goes crazy.

After practice, Chaney goes home and prepares another turkey, this one with his special oyster dressing. Next to shopping, Chaney's favorite hobby is cooking and oyster dressing is one of his favorite dishes. He has been making it for years and has the recipe down to a science.

The first step is to put the neck and giblets from the turkey into a pot with some water ("You can put some parsley and mushrooms in for an extra taste") and simmer for an hour. This will be used later to baste the turkey while it's in the oven.

Next, put a little butter and olive oil in the bottom of a frying pan. Cut up some onions and celery and cook them for about ten minutes in the pan along with some sage ("a lot of sage"), salt and pepper. Garlic is optional ("I love garlic"). After they're done simmering, stir in some corn bread ("You can use the stuff you get at the store, but I like to make mine. Don't mash the corn bread up and make it all mushy 'cause when you stuff it in the turkey it gets mushy enough"). Then you take the raw oysters ("Make sure to get the fresh oysters, not the stewing ones that are real tough"), cut them up into nice-size chunks and add them to the mixture. Don't cook the oysters too long or they'll get tough. Stuff this mixture into the bird, stick it in the oven and leave it in seven or eight minutes per pound of turkey.

Once the turkey's in the oven, Chaney still has a few tricks left. He puts a couple of pieces of bacon on top of the turkey to add flavor, as well as a grease coating that keeps the meat moist and lays a piece of tinfoil on top ("to maintain the heat at a constant") and removes it a half hour before the turkey is done so the skin can brown. You have to baste the turkey every fifteen minutes with the broth. Afterward the drippings can be used for gravy— mushroom gravy if they're in the broth ("You can put a little cornstarch in it for thickening").

Once the turkey is in the oven, Chaney washes up and goes upstairs to watch a quadruple-header of college basketball on ESPN. "I'm feeling great," Chaney says.

"There's no one home—my wife's in Atlantic City—and I got the game on and the turkey in the oven. Then all of a sudden I hear *Boom!* I say 'what the hell is that?' and run downstairs. I look in the oven, but there's nothing wrong. I wonder if maybe the satellite dish fell off the roof. I go out back in my bathrobe to check, but it's all right. I figure someone must have thrown something at the house, so I go back upstairs. I'm watching the game and *Boom!*

"I run downstairs and open the basement door and all I see is black smoke. I say 'oh my God' and grab a scarf. I pour water on it and put it over my mouth and try to go down to the basement. I get halfway down and I'm gagging. I figure I better not do this. I try to cut the basement lights on, but they won't work. I figure the house is gonna burn down. I don't even know who to call, but I remember 911. I call and they come in two minutes. I am at the front door and all the neighbors are out watching the fire trucks. I'm in the doorway, and here comes a guy with a big hatchet. Another fireman comes up and says, 'Hey, Coach, how you doing?' I say, 'Coach my ass, put out the fire.' Another guy comes in with a big hose and another with a battering ram. They ask where the fire is. . . . They knock the [basement] door down and put out the fire."

It turns out that his wife had left some cleaning supplies on top of the washing machine, next to the heater. The *boom* Chaney heard was two of the cans exploding. "That's how lucky I was. If there was no *boom* I would never have known. The fire would have come right up the stairs. And I was lucky I could make the phone call. A few minutes later the telephone wires burned through."

After the fire company left and the neighbors went back to their houses, Chaney went inside to clean up, watch the basketball games and eat his turkey. "Then, when my wife came home, she had the nerve to be mad that I told the neighbors how the fire started. That's how a woman's mind works. She was more worried about what the neighbors thought than my black ass being burned up."

5

I Don't Think You Can Measure a Good Coach Based Just on Winning

November 28

Temple's regular season begins tonight, with the Owls playing Penn at the Palestra, a 9,000-seat bandbox of an arena that reeks of history. "Any Big Five game here is always a tough emotional struggle," says Chaney, who played here when he was in high school and has coached here on a semiregular basis since his days at Gratz.

Penn comes within a heartbeat of adding to the long list of memorable Big Five upsets, falling to the Owls 55–54 when a last second shot from just outside the foul line misses.

Despite the Owls' overwhelming height advantage (Penn's frontline is 6' 7", 6' 7", 6' 4"), the determined Quakers outrebounded Temple 34–32. "Teams like this give us problems and always have," Chaney says. "Small teams like this use their quickness to get to the boards."

Temple maintains a small lead throughout the game, but the Owls are never able to pull away. Every time they threaten, they seem to go through a three- or four-minute stretch without scoring, allowing Penn to claw its way back into the game.

With 4:48 remaining, Hodge hits a twelve-footer to give Temple a 53–50 lead, but Penn answers with a seventeen-footer at the 3:04 mark to chop the lead to 53–52. Causwell is then fouled, and the big center, in the midst of an off night (one for nine for five points), hits both for a 55–52 lead with 2:06 left. Again Penn answers, hitting another long jumper at 1:41, and the Quakers are down 55–54.

Temple works the clock and with a tick left on the 45-second clock, Causwell forces up and misses an eight-foot turnaround. Penn grabs the rebound, calls time-out, and first-year coach Fran Dunphy sets up the final play. During the time-out, Chaney changes his defense from a zone to a straight man-to-man. "I was trying to take them away from their pattern and force them into a mistake," Chaney says after the game. But Temple makes the mistake. After Penn works some time off the clock, Paul McMahon suddenly finds himself free as he drives to the basket. As he gets closer, Causwell recovers enough to worry McMahon and his shot bounces too hard off the glass. The two teams scramble for the rebound, with it finally going out of bounds to the Quakers with fifteen seconds to go.

Penn gets it inbounds to forward Vince Curran. Hodge jumps out to cover him, and with nowhere to go and no one to pass it to, Curran calls Penn's final time-out with eleven seconds remaining. The Quakers inbound and again Temple's swarming defense causes problems, with Harden deflecting the ball out of bounds with six seconds left. Again Penn inbounds to Curran and again he is immediately swallowed up by Hodge. With time running out, all Curran can do is turn and fire up a desperation shot that is well off the mark as the horn sounds.

Once again, Chaney is forced to take Strickland out (he played only twelve minutes) and go with Harden to "give us more speed and ball-handling." Penn uses a box-and-one on Macon for most of the game, with six-foot-six-inch guard Jerry Simon hounding him all over the court. "We recognized it and went to a set that could work against it," Macon said. "But then we got kind of lax and started standing around on offense." With everyone else standing around, this made things even tougher on Macon, who was forced to create and fight his way to the basket against two and sometimes three men. Still he manages to score twenty-one (eight for seventeen shooting), but no one else is able to get untracked. Hodge had eleven, Kilgore ten and Causwell, Strickland, and Harden combined for only thirteen.

Later, as Chaney leaves the Palestra and walks slowly to his car, acknowledging congratulations and stopping to talk and joke with friends and fans, he sums up the game: "We were lucky to get out of here alive."

November 29

During the team's afternoon study hall, Blackwell shows up and addresses the team. Although his playing days were over before any of the current team members arrived, he's still part of the family and close to several of the players. He comes to practice every now and then and frequently stops by Chaney's office during his lunch break. The two have a lot in common. Both grew up in South Philadelphia, less than ten blocks apart. "We learned to play on the same courts," says Blackwell. "Coach always talks about how they used to get the five best guys from the neighborhood together and go around the city and play the best five from other neighborhoods.

That's exactly what we did. We played on the same courts as Earl Monroe, Walt Hazzard, Guy Rodgers, Wilt Chamberlain and John Chaney; all the great players, the legends."

Blackwell was at the Palestra last night and didn't like what he saw. "I told them I wasn't angry that they didn't play well," Blackwell explains later, adding that he rarely talks to the team like this, but just felt it was something he had to do. "I was angry because I didn't see togetherness. I didn't see guys helping each other out there on the floor, talking to each other. I told them that in order to be a great team they would have to find that kind of togetherness that we used to have during my years here. Right now they're still searching for it and it shows."

The team listens intently as Blackwell talks. "We know he's speaking from Coach's mouth, the way Coach would say it," Kilgore says, "But it's like hearing it from one of your friends instead of Coach. He's been through everything we're going through and he's been to the NCAAs."

Blackwell didn't clear his talk to the team with Chaney. In fact, Chaney doesn't hear about it until the next day when some of his players tell him. "That made me feel very good about Nate," Chaney says. "He's a guy who is still very close to us and to the players. Any one of my former players can walk in and talk to them like that. They don't have to be a star like Nate was. We all love and respect each other, even if you're the last man on the bench."

December 1

The Owls are in Syracuse to play in the Carrier Classic. They face Arkansas State tonight in the first game, with

Syracuse taking on Virginia Commonwealth University in the nightcap. The winners meet tomorrow night for the championship.

After the team's short shoot-around in the morning, Chaney talks briefly about togetherness.

Everyone has their own way of looking at sports. Our way is we're a family. On the day of a game, we will work toward being one, in developing a oneness. That one bolt of lightning can do a lot of damage if we're all together. As long as you possess an inner strength, you can overcome mistakes.

That's it for the day. Chaney calls his players together for a "team together." Afterward they shoot a little longer, until the vans come to take them back to the hotel. Maloney notices a couple of players dribbling the ball hard, smacking it against the floor. "Hey, don't do that," he says. "You have to make the ball your friend. If you slam it down hard and get it pissed it won't go in." Maloney bounces the ball gently and fires up a shot from well past the three-point line. It hits nothing but net. "See what happens when you treat the ball right?" he asks.

At the tournament banquet the night before, Arkansas State coach Nelson Catalina quipped, "I grew up wanting to play in the NBA. Now I wonder what it would be like to coach in the NBA. I'll get my chance tomorrow. John's team is bigger than anyone in the NBA."

Welcome to the NBA, Coach. The Owls roll to a 65–41 win over the Indians, who have a bit of height of their own, including six-foot-nine-inch, 260-pound center Greg Williams and Al Banister, a seven-foot-five-inch, 290-pound backup center from England who is as big as a building and only a little more mobile. "That's the first time Duane ever had to look up to someone out there," Chaney says after the game.

The game is close for a half, with Temple taking a 27–21 lead. Then Macon takes over, hitting six of ten shots and nine of thirteen free throws for a total of twenty-eight points, including eight straight Temple points midway through the half to stake the Owls to a 50–30 lead. Causwell also plays a dominating game with seventeen points, ten rebounds and three blocks.

Syracuse, ranked number one in the nation, races to a 57–28 halftime lead and crushes VCU 100–73.

December 2

At this morning's shoot-around, Chaney is absolutely, positively convinced his team can beat Syracuse. The Orangemen boast an incredible array of talent, including Derrick Coleman, a six-foot-ten-inch All-American power forward; Stephen Thompson, a six-foot-four-inch leaper who was an honorable mention All-American last year; six-foot-nine-inch Billy Owens, a member of the freshman All-American team last season; and LeRon Ellis, a six-foot-ten-inch center and transfer from Kentucky, where he averaged sixteen points his last year. In all, Syracuse has six McDonald's All-Americans on their roster and as many as five future NBA first-round picks.

But still, Syracuse doesn't have the proper elements in place to be considered a great team by Chaney. Thompson, although a talented and explosive player, is not a true point guard and Owens is really a small forward playing shooting guard. The Orangemen will turn the ball over and don't shoot well from the outside. Plus, Coleman, their best inside player, likes to roam outside and launch jumpers instead of posting up down low where he belongs.

There are a few keys to this game. First, we have to get back on defense to stop their break. They love to run. Get back and force them into a halfcourt game. They have some very talented athletes, but they have the wrong guys shooting the wrong shots. There will be fifty NBA scouts here tonight [twenty actually], and they want to show them what they can do. So they may come out with their own agenda. They may not play within themselves.

The Carrier Dome is unlike any other college basketball arena in the country. It's really an indoor football stadium that can be set up for basketball. More than 30,000 fanatical, orange-clad fans routinely fill the arena. Tonight there are 30,049, and not too many are rooting for Temple. While the Owls are being introduced, the fans—who are very organized—scream "Who's He?" "Who Cares?" and "Big Deal!" to let the players know how welcome they are.

For fifteen minutes Temple seems determined to spoil the party. The Owls play exactly as Chaney prescribed this morning, controlling the tempo, the boards and the game. Causwell starts things off with a block of Coleman on the game's first possession and on the other end Strickland cans an open twelve-footer for a 2–0 Temple lead. With 11:51 remaining, Macon picks up his second foul with Temple ahead 16–12. Chaney normally takes a player out once he gets his second foul in the first half, but tonight he leaves Macon in, gambling he won't pick up a third. In the next few minutes the gamble pays off. Macon hits two jumpers and the Owls stretch their lead to 22–15.

130

But then Strickland, who up to this point has been playing his best basketball of the year with six points and two rebounds, gets whistled for his second foul and Chaney takes him out. With five minutes left in the half, Temple ups its lead to 28–19, and Chaney finally decides he's gambled long enough and takes Macon out. "I decided to leave him in and shifted around the defense to try and keep him out of trouble areas," Chaney says. "But my better judgment finally told me to get him out of there after he almost got called for reaching in. But that's characteristic of Mark. Whenever's he's in he fights like an assassin. So I had to take him out."

Without Macon, the Owls struggle and the Orangemen come alive, outscoring Temple 18–8 the rest of the way to take a 37–36 halftime lead.

Macon scores on a pull-up jumper to start the second half and Temple regains the lead 38–37. The game stays close, with Hodge hitting two free throws with 12:18 remaining to pull Temple to 47–44. At this point, Syracuse coach Jim Boeheim switches from man-to-man to a 2–3 zone and Temple doesn't score for the next five-and-a-half minutes. By this time Syracuse is in control 56–45.

"I was surprised they went to the two–three," Chaney says. "We feel there are very few teams that can play us zone. We ran screens and cuts for Mark, but we just failed to recognize the defense and negotiate it properly."

"We were only going to use it for one or two possessions," Boeheim says, "but when they didn't score, we left it on. They only scored four times in eighteen attempts once we went to the zone. The kids did a real good job recognizing where Macon was and not letting him shoot the ball in good position."

The Owls pull to within 62–54 with 2:19 remaining, but down the stretch Syracuse—not known as a good foul shooting team—hits seven of ten from the line to wrap up a 73–56 win.

131

"I think we played a real strong ball club and did quite well," Chaney says after the game. "It's real tough when you don't have the kind of bench strength we'd like to have. I think we brought out some character in them by making them prove they could shoot free throws and hit from the outside. They showed everyone they are for real and deserve to be number one."

December 5

We need ball control and recognition of what's on the floor, of what kind of defense the other team is operating and how to attack it. The guards are responsible for that job, and if you don't take it seriously and work at it and get better, we can't get better as a team.

Howie Evans is an example of a great point guard. He wasn't as good an athlete as you [he points toward Harden]. But you could never take the ball off him. That's because he played the way we taught him.

Chaney has his players work on beating the press today. Against Syracuse they had problems, especially late in the first half when the Orangemen made their comeback. If a player commits a turnover today, Chaney pulls him out of practice and has him run laps. Hodge is the first to start running, then Kilgore, Macon, Lovelace and Conic. "I'm gonna eliminate all your dumb asses, even if I have to put in Rob [Jones]," Chaney yells. "I knew I'd get you," he screams in delight when Harden finally screws up. Strickland makes a good play and looks over at Chaney for a sign of recognition. "Don't be looking at me when you do something good," Chaney hollers.

Two plays later Strickland throws the ball away and starts running without Chaney telling him to. "I knew I was going to get your ass again."

After practice, the coaches gather in Chaney's office. Maloney and Demopoulos discuss the Syracuse game while Chaney goes through his mail. "Hey look at this," he says holding up a letter. The envelope is addressed to Chaney, but the letter is made out to Georgetown's John Thompson.

The next letter is from a basketball player in Guyana. "He says he's one point nine five meters tall," Chaney says. "How tall is that?" Nobody can answer. "I'll have John [DiSangro] figure it out later," Chaney says.

DiSangro started out as a manager his freshman year at Temple, which was Chaney's second year as coach. Over the years his responsibilities grew, and two years ago, after he graduated, he took a job in the business office of the athletic department. He is now Chaney's right-hand man and takes care of everything that goes on in the basketball office. "John was one of the greatest things that ever happened to me," Chaney says. "All I know is that when something's supposed to be done, it's done and done right. John is a perfectionist. Everyone on this campus—including the president—wants him to come work for them, but I'm not letting him go."

A few minutes later a secretary from the athletic office comes in and tells Chaney her car was broken into and the window smashed. Chaney calls a friend of his at Wilkie Buick down the street from Temple and makes arrangements for her to bring her car in for repairs. Next he writes out a check to a student scholarship fund that Liacouris has set up in memory of his mother. "Don't let Peter know about this," he says as he gives it to Miss Davis. This week he's also written checks to St. Christopher's

Childrens Hospital and Cheyney State, but again he doesn't want anyone to know.

The next letter he opens is from the U.S. Olympic Festival saying that he has been named coach of the East team for the 1990 festival. "I told them I wouldn't do it," Chaney says. August is his only break of the year and the last thing he wants to do is coach basketball.

"This is your chance to give something back to your country," Maloney teases, but Chaney just laughs and shakes his head no.

After Chaney finishes with his mail, Maloney, who has learned to wait until he has his undivided attention, brings up a new offensive set he would like to see the team run. It would have Hodge up high, at the foul line. He diagrams it on the blackboard behind Chaney's desk and goes over the different patterns that could be run for this set.

"You see a problem with our offense against man-to-man," Chaney finally says, after he's absorbed what Maloney says. "But I don't."

"We don't swing it enough; this will give us more movement," Maloney responds.

"We're setting up a situation where [Hodge] can make more mistakes," Chaney says. "Against Syracuse he got the ball up there and turned it over too many times."

They go back and forth for a few more minutes. Finally Chaney vetoes the idea, although later in the year they will add something similar. Strickland walks into the office in a good mood after his improved play at Syracuse.

"Get a ball and practice your dribbling," Chaney tells him, a smile on his face. "Learn how to pass the ball."

"Coach, I know how to pass; I'm the only one who can get it inside."

They kid around another minute or two and then Strickland leaves. "Learn how to dribble," Chaney hollers after him.

A few minutes later, someone from the student newspaper comes in to interview Chaney. At least twice a week someone from the paper or a journalism student working on a class project or a student in education or health and physical education comes in to interview Chaney. He never says no and will spend as long as it takes.

More than an hour later, the interview is over. By now it's past 2:00 and time for Chaney to leave. He's headed over to Germantown Friends to watch Jonathan Haynes play. A few weeks ago, Haynes, a gifted six-foot-three-inch point guard who can also play shooting guard, signed a letter of intent to play for Temple. Haynes is one of the top fifty seniors in the country and Chaney's third national-level recruit. Haynes is lightning quick, can shoot, penetrate and pass and play tenacious defense. "He plays like I did," Chaney says. "Although I didn't do all those spin moves in the lane he does." Chaney hates spin moves in the lane.

Haynes is also a confident young man, another trait he has in common with Chaney. Later this season he'll go over the 2,000 mark in career scoring. "Think you can get two thousand at Temple?" I ask him jokingly and Haynes holds up three fingers, indicating he'll score 3,000. When I tell Chaney, he laughs. "Maybe he will."

Today Germantown Friends is hosting Episcopal Academy, which will end the season as the top-rated team in the city. The game is scheduled to start at 3:30 and Chaney arrives a few minutes before the appointed time. He sits at the top of the bleachers in the small gym, but the word quickly gets around that he's here. A minute later, Haynes's father comes over, they embrace and joke around for a few minutes, and Chaney goes over to sit with the Haynes family. Pretty soon students come over for autographs.

"How come you fell apart against Syracuse in the second half?" a brave kid asks. Chaney just laughs as he signs his name on a slip of paper. A girl comes over and asks for an autograph. "That's gonna cost you," Chaney teases. "You got any Goobers?" All she has is a chocolate bar, but Chaney takes a piece anyway and signs the autograph in return. Later he'll get more candy, but no Goobers, his favorite.

Game time comes and goes. The second official has yet to show so the players continue to warm up. Chaney, who's been up since 5:00 this morning, is starting to fade. His back is aching and he tries to rest it by sitting in the top row of bleachers and leaning back against the concrete wall. Finally, the game starts at 4:10, and Episcopal opens in a box-and-one on Haynes. Germantown Friends' other star, center Malik Nagel, is out with a broken hand, and Haynes is on his own. With two and sometimes three men on him, Haynes struggles and gets more and more frustrated as the game progresses and his team falls further and further behind. But still there are flashes of brilliance: a head fake and pull-up jumper with a smooth, quick release that hits nothing but net; quick hands that slap away the ball on defense; the ability to dribble in traffic and beat the press almost single-handedly; and quick passes to wide-open teammates under the basket. Chaney also sees something he doesn't like: a spin move in traffic. "He's going to have to stop those spins. That's like trying to be good at being bad." Haynes scores twenty-four, but his team loses 74–51.

After the game, Haynes and his coach, Alfred Johnson, gather around Chaney. On a piece of paper, Chaney diagrams an inbounds play designed to get the ball to Haynes and also a couple of offensive sets to get him free when the other team is playing a box-and-one on him. "This is what Mark [Macon] is up against every night," Chaney says and Haynes hangs on every word. "You have to be patient. Give Mark a call tonight and talk to him about it. He'll help you."

By now the junior varsity game has started and Chaney, tired and his back aching, desperately wants to leave. But the son of a very good friend, who's in the stands and has been chatting with Chaney the past hour, is playing for Episcopal's junior varsity, and Chaney says he can't leave just yet. "That would be rude," Chaney explains. "He's a good friend and it would be an insult if I left."

His friend's son makes three or four good plays in a row early in the game. "Did you see that, John?" the father asks proudly.

"I saw it and it's making me sick," Chaney says with a smile. "If he makes one more play like that, I'll never hear the end of it."

Finally at halftime, Chaney decides he can leave. It's after 7:00 and he's been on the go for more than thirteen hours and still has several game tapes to watch. He heads home, but not before stopping at Sonny's, a rib joint near his house, for a take-out order of extra hot ones.

"You be careful with these, they'll burn your mouth," Chaney warns after treating me to a rack. He's right and I call him later to tell him my mouth is still on fire. For the next few minutes all I hear on the other end of the phone is Chaney's booming, cackling laugh.

December 9

The Owls come up empty in their Atlantic-10 opener at State College, losing 61–59 to a very tough Penn State team. Temple has a chance to tie it up right before the final buzzer when Penn State misses the front end of a one-and-one with :05 remaining. The Owls get the rebound and Kilgore races upcourt with the ball. Hodge is ahead of him, wide open under the basket. By the time

Kilgore finally looks up, spots Hodge and heaves a long pass, a Penn State player has rotated over and gets a hand on the ball.

Although Chaney is upset with Kilgore for not looking up sooner, what has him really worried is his team's inability to handle the Nittany Lions' assortment of junk defenses designed to stop Macon, who winds up scoring ten points on four for sixteen shooting. "We're looking at the same things teams did to us all last year," Chaney explains, not wanting to go through another season like that. All this special attention on Macon should and does lead to open shots—especially open outside shots—for everyone else on the team. Tonight the Owls are unable to take advantage. "You can't assume that just because a player is wide open and loves to shoot he will score," Chaney says. "If you only have one player on the floor who is a good outside shooter [Macon], you'll have big problems with the box-and-one. But if you have two good outside shooters and a great player inside, you are moving more and more toward a well-balanced team, and these types of gimmicks can't work and they'll have to match up one-on-one or perhaps a straight zone."

In the game, Causwell scores fourteen, Hodge twelve, Kilgore eleven, Strickland seven, and Harden adds five. These are signs of balanced scoring, but Chaney knows he will need more, much more in the tough games ahead. Even though he doesn't tell his team, Chaney is pleased with his team's progress over the season's first four games—despite the 2–2 record. "I'm happy with them, but I don't want them to know," Chaney says. "Players who feel their coach is pleased with them settle in and don't aspire to higher levels. I want my players to keep working and trying to get better and the way you do that is to keep raising the ante. Every time they do something well, raise the expectation level with whatever motivation you have as a coach. And you must keep raising them up.

Every time you climb one fence, there is another. Every time you beat one team, there is another."

What doesn't please Chaney is the bus ride back to Temple after the game. In the back, several players become engaged in loud discussion of the top rap groups. Chaney, stewing over the loss in the front of the bus, walks back to tell his players to shut up and think about the game and what they did wrong. "He said we were treating it like a party when it was like a funeral to him," Kilgore said. "He wasn't that mad, but he just wanted to make sure we knew how he felt about losing."

"The fact of the matter is, when we lose a ball game, I expect my team to take on the same attitude as I do," Chaney explains. "When I lose a game, I look at it as if someone died. And I'm hoping it's not me. When I heard them talking, I went back to discuss my feelings. You only have to do that one time. That sets the tone for the whole year."

December 11

For the second straight day, Chaney concentrates on offense during practice, trying to get his players to recognize and attack the gimmick defenses other teams are running on Macon. "We're trying to get other players to recognize what's happening," Chaney explains after practice, "what the other team is attempting, so we can react and assert ourselves as a team. We're going to see it more and more, especially if the scouting reports keep saying it's effective."

While Chaney encourages other players to take more shots, he refuses to put the clamps on Macon. No matter how many players are on him, Macon has to keep shooting and scoring for the Owls to play well. This might sound like a contradiction, but it goes back to one of Chaney's basic beliefs that he would rather have his best player take a bad shot then a bad player take a good shot. "A great player like Mark has a built-in ego," Chaney explains. "When he sees obstacles, he challenges them. If you want to look at that as a negative, you destroy the fact he is a super player. If he gets into a situation where he's not scoring and helping his team, it's usually because his team isn't helping him. To help him they must begin to score."

After working on the different offensive sets, Chaney has the white team work on special situations, including the Jack-in-the-Box and other plays designed to free up a man—usually Macon—for a last-second shot. Chaney devised the Jack-in-the-Box while he was at Cheyney, and over the years it has almost never failed to get an open shot. Whether or not the player made the shot isn't what's important; the key is that the shot was there. The play begins with Temple inbounding the ball from under the opponent's basket with only a second or two remaining. The designated thrower heaves a long pass downcourt to the designated receiver, who is standing at his own foul line. Through a series of intricate screens and picks and fakes, all the other players, who start in a tight circle at the foul line, begin moving away from this spot, with the designated receiver suddenly popping free for the long pass. To be effective, the Jack-in-the-Box requires the timing of a Swiss watch, a perfect pass and a receiver who can catch the ball and shoot it in traffic.

In most situations the ref won't call anything. He just wants to get the game over with. Pretend like you're going for the ball and your man will follow you. Or walk him out of there.

140

By this, Chaney means that once the defensive player takes his position in front of the offensive player he is guarding, the offensive player should just try to walk through his man and push him where he wants him to go. Kilgore is the "pitcher" on the Jack-in-the-Box and his first throw sails over Macon's head. The next one is right on target and so is the one after that.

The success of a pattern in a last-second situation depends on whether you make a good pass.
Putting the ball in the basket is gravy.

Norman has been quietly watching practice for the past hour, but the coach in him comes out when he spots Causwell sitting at the edge of the court, icing his knee. "The man was playing you on your left shoulder all night," Norman lectures. "All you have to do is drop step and go around for an easy dunk. All night long that was there. I wanted to come out from behind that [microphone] and knock you out." As he always does, Causwell listens quietly and nods.

A few minutes later, Lovelace has to leave practice to prepare for a class presentation later that morning. "Maybe I'll come over and listen," Chaney threatens as Lovelace heads to the locker room. "Where's the class?" Lovelace just shrugs and keeps walking.

"I guess he doesn't want you watching," Demopoulos jokes.

Chaney just laughs, and adds, "I'll find out from Miss Davis." Fortunately for Lovelace, he's only kidding.

After practice, Maloney and Chaney work with Kilgore on his jump shot. "Try a stagger step," Maloney suggests, demonstrating how Kilgore should be set before he releases, with his right foot slightly ahead of his left. "That'll give you better balance." Kilgore hits three straight. "You could be a great shooter like that," Chaney says. Kilgore keeps shooting and hitting. "Coach," Demopoulos says to Maloney, "show Strick." He does and soon Strickland is hitting shot after shot, including six long jumpers in a row. "Guess what," Demopoulos tells Strickland as he keeps firing. "After a while, if you keep working on this, you'll be able to do it faster and faster, better and better and it will become automatic. You won't have to think about where your feet are, they'll just be in the right place."

December 12

In their home opener, Temple tops the St. Joe's Hawks 74–54. The win is Chaney's 400th as a college coach. "This win represents a lot of kids, a lot of teaching and working with kids. I don't know where I fit into the equation," Chaney tells the press after the game. "There's been a lot of good people involved, a lot of good kids."

Chaney is pleased with the play of Kilgore (fifteen points) and Harden (nine points, ten assists, three steals and no turnovers). They are starting to recognize that when other teams put the box-and-one on Macon they're going to get plenty of open shots. "We went to work the last couple days on recognition; recognizing what shots we could get against different defenses. I told Mik and Michael this is the shot I want you to take."

It's becoming apparent that the offense runs better when Harden is in the game and Kilgore is at the three position. "I didn't realize until today, but whenever I bring the ball up, I never got into the offense," Kilgore says. "Today I felt comfortable when Mike was on floor and I'm the three guard. We won't become a great team until I become a much better player."

142

The game also features a brief "One-Eyed Jack" stare from Chaney (his first of the season), midway through the second half, after Macon is whistled for an offensive foul. Chaney argues until he gets a technical and then stares at the offending referee for the next minute. This sounds harmless enough, but a Chaney stare is enough to melt the stripes off a referee's shirt.

Although Chaney has been staring at referees for years, it didn't receive national attention until the 1987–88 season, when Chaney twice treated a national television audience to full-blown "One-Eyed Jack" stares (which are not quite as powerful as his "Reckless Eyeball"). The first came in the big 83–66 win at North Carolina and the second was in the second round of the NCAA tournament during the Owls' 74–53 win over Georgetown.

The Georgetown "One-Eyed Jack" was a masterpiece. With 4:54 remaining in the first half and Temple up 24–18, Chaney was hit with a technical foul by John Clougherty after arguing a questionable traveling call on Evans. After Georgetown hit both shots, the game was stopped for a television time-out. For the entire two minutes, Chaney stood in front of his bench staring across the court at Clougherty, while Maloney instructed the team in its huddle. Clougherty couldn't help but feel the heat of Chaney's laser look. Instead of turning away he stared right back and the two locked eyeballs for what seemed like an eternity. The crowd began to notice and a murmur slowly built into a full-blown roar as the two remained locked in silent combat.

"What was he gonna do, give me a technical for what I was thinking?" Chaney asks. "He was lucky I only gave him my 'One-Eyed Jack' stare. I did not find it necessary to use my 'Reckless Eyeballs,' which is the kind of thing that could have gotten me killed in the South awhile back. The 'Reckless Eyeballs' is really heavy. The 'One-Eyed Jack' has a different purpose. [Clougherty] will remember

143

it. It will haunt him until he apologizes. One day he will sit down and write me a letter and apologize. Or maybe the phone will ring at two in the morning and it will be an anonymous apology. I don't know how or when, but it will still happen."

Tonight's version was not in the same league as the North Carolina or Georgetown "One-Eyed Jacks." The Owls were up by twenty at the time and Chaney's heart really wasn't in it.

After the game, in his office, Chaney has a chance to reflect on his 400th win. He is a little uncomfortable with the thought that many equate winning so many games with being a successful coach. "The most bothersome and misunderstood aspect of this business, as I see it, is that people who win are looked at as people who are good coaches. That disturbs me. I don't think you can measure a good coach based just on winning. A coach must be judged on some of the altruistic things that sports are all about: developing character, good sportsmanlike conduct, developing confidence, good will, good competitive spirit, the will to win and the knowledge to know and distinguish that winning has nothing to do with the score. A coach with a lesser record or from a less prestigious program could have a greater impact on the lives of people."

Chaney never set out to be a college basketball coach. After he graduated from Bethune-Cookman in May 1955, his main goal was to find a way to support his wife and son, preferably by playing basketball. The NBA was an option. Chaney was drafted in the fourth round by the Syracuse Nationals but didn't think his chances of making the team were very good. It had nothing to do with his assessment of his talent—Chaney was confident that he could play with any team—it was his understanding of the unofficial quota system for blacks in the NBA. In the 1950–51 season, Chuck Cooper became the first black to play in the NBA. By the 1955–56 season—which would have been Chaney's rookie season—the flow of blacks into the NBA was still only a trickle. In the eight-team league there was a total of ten black players. Three teams still had no black players.

Instead, Chaney accepted an offer to join the Harlem Globetrotters for $450 a month. "I was poor and needed to make money to support my family," Chaney explains. "All Syracuse was offering was a tryout and the odds of a black man making it in the NBA at that time weren't too good. So the Globetrotters looked pretty good to me."

On October 2, 1955, Chaney boarded United Airlines flight 31 from Philadelphia to Chicago—his first airplane ride—to join the Globetrotters, who were headquartered in the Windy City, despite their name. Chaney still has his ticket stub. It was paid for by Abe Saperstein Sports Enterprises and cost $34.10.

From the start, Chaney hated playing for the Globetrotters. "I didn't like the idea of having to be funny on command," says Chaney, who was being trained as the team's next great comic ball-handler. "I could trick dribble if I was reacting to something on the court, but to do it just to be clowning was something I couldn't adjust to."

Chaney wasn't a clown, he was a competitor. He detested being a part of games in which the outcome was decided before the start. Chaney lasted until December, when he decided to accept an invitation to come home and play for the Sunbury Mercuries of the Eastern Pro League and pursue a job as a phys ed teacher in the Philadelphia Public Schools.

With only eight teams in the NBA at the time and given the quota system for blacks, the Eastern Pro League—which was based in Pennsylvania cities like Easton, Williamsport, Reading, Scranton and Lancaster and had no quota system—offered big-time competition and attracted great players.

Games were played on weekends and most of the players held down regular jobs during the week. The pay was low and the competition fierce. "Back in the early days in the Eastern League, we got a two-hundred-dollar guarantee when we played away games," says Stan Novak, who coached Sunbury and is currently the director of scouting for the Detroit Pistons. "That was for the whole team and we didn't get any expenses. We only had eight players, and we would split the money evenly: twenty-five dollars a man. We'd pile into two cars, chip in a few bucks for gas and then drive all over the state for games. This was in the days before the Pennsylvania Turnpike, and we'd drive through the mountains and coal country in the dead of winter in the middle of snowstorms.

"At home games we got a percentage of the gate. Sometimes, if the stands were full, we'd get seventy-five or eighty dollars a game, sometimes more during the playoffs. But other times, when the stands were empty because of a blizzard or something, we didn't make much." Chaney remembers that players on the Lebanon team, which was owned by a meat-packing company, sometimes got paid in bologna.

The Eastern League had a reputation for being more physical than the NBA. Hard fouls and fights were common. The working-class crowds usually worked themselves up to a fever pitch. At Scranton, a balcony hung over the court and was directly over the visiting team's bench. "The fans would drop cigarette ashes and spit on you," Novak recalls. "Almost every game there was a fight. The referees just didn't have the control over the game they have now. If someone tried to hurt you, you had to hurt them back."

Chaney moved his family back into his parents' house

146

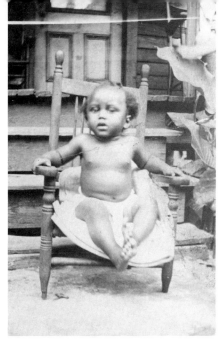

John Chaney as a baby.

The 1951 banquet where Chaney was embarrassed to accept his MVP Award (Chaney—top right).

ALL PHOTOS COURTESY OF JOHN CHANEY AND THE TEMPLE UNIVERSITY SPORTS INFORMATION OFFICE.

Chaney and his first
Temple team,
1982–83 (Terence
Stansbury at
bottom).

Chaney
congratulates Nate
Blackwell at his
last game at
McGonigle.

Chaney instructs
1988 #1 team.
From bottom,
seated: Evans,
Perry, Rivas,
Macon, and
Vreeswyk.

Chaney with Mike Vreeswyk.

Georgetown's John Thompson and Chaney after Temple wins in 1988 NCAA Tournament.

In 1988—accepting Coach of the Year Award.

Assistant Coach Jimmy
Maloney and Chaney.

Chaney and Mik Kilgore.

Rallying his troops from the huddle.

An animated Chaney signals the offense.

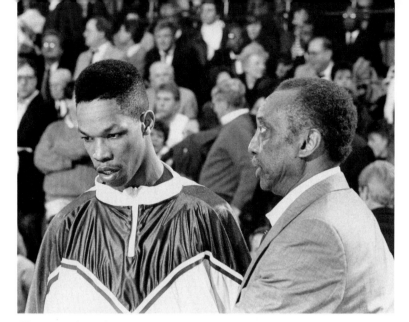

Chaney and Mark Macon.

The coaching staff, from left: Maloney, Chaney, Chris Demopoulos, Jay Norman.

Prowling the sidelines, Chaney unleashes his "One-eyed Jack" stare.

on Ellsworth Street for two years, before moving to Bartram Village, a project in West Philadelphia. He landed a job as a long-term substitute and taught at several different schools until he passed his teacher's examination and received a full-time position at Sayre Junior High.

As soon as he joined Sunbury, Chaney became the best player on the team, an immediate all-star and one of the top scorers in the league. Chaney was a crowd pleaser, a dribbler and scorer extraordinaire. He became the Eastern League's version of Bob Cousy. A Sunbury paper wrote: "In our opinion, no one in the Eastern League can compare with the overall dexterity of [Chaney]. His speed, dribbling artistry, baffling weave and shooting accuracy stamp him for our selection for the Most Valuable Player in the circuit. . . . Chaney can bewilder an entire opposing team with his devilment with the ball. Sometimes he will draw two and three players as he makes an effort to go up for a basket, but in the course of the leap he whips the sphere underhand to a [teammate] standing idly by, who then dunks the goal with ease."

"I would say I was like a Bob Cousy, only I could score more," says Chaney. "The modern player I would compare myself to is Michael Jordan. I wasn't as spectacular and couldn't jump as high, but in terms of being greedy and scoring, I was like him. People would make statements like 'John can dribble from here to Atlantic City and back without anyone taking the ball off him.' Once in fact, we were playing in a summer tournament and all our guys started fouling out. We were down to three guys and had the lead with five minutes to go. So I just dribbled for five minutes and we won."

In all, Chaney played ten seasons in the Eastern League, his last as a player-coach of Williamsport. He was a two-time league MVP, a seven-time all-star, and MVP in the 1959 and 1960 all-star games. His career came to an end on a snowy road in the mountains of central Pennsylvania late one night on the way home from a game. The car in which he was a passenger was hit head on by another, and Chaney suffered severe leg injuries that ended his playing days.

His first few years in the Eastern League, Chaney dreamed of being summoned by the NBA. As time went on, his dream began to fade. By this time he was a full-time teacher and coach at Sayre Junior High and had moved his family to the small row house in the Mt. Airy section of Philadelphia where he and Jeanne still live. His teacher's salary, Eastern League pay and the money he made working weekends for a caterer added up to about the same as an NBA salary. Chaney accepted his fate and began to get more and more into teaching and coaching. "You gravitate toward what is comfortable for you," Chaney says. "All my training at Bethune-Cookman was toward becoming a teacher and all my experience playing basketball helped me become a coach."

As a teacher and coach, Chaney was the same then as he is today: tough and caring. Chaney taught in the public schools from 1956 to 1972. "From the start, as a teacher and coach, I have been the same," Chaney says. "I would sit my students or players down the first day and lecture, telling them what we would be covering. I would establish the rules and roles. That's the way I've always done it and the way I feel comfortable."

After three years as the gymnastics coach, Chaney took over as the basketball coach at Sayre his last three years at the school. From 1966 to 1972 he was at Simon Gratz High in North Philadelphia, leading the basketball team to a 72–12 record. While at Gratz, Chaney and the other gym teachers started a breakfast program for the students. "When I got to Gratz, conditions were terrible," Chaney says. "There was such overcrowding, the school was running two shifts. Kids had classes at seven in the morning and were getting to school without any breakfast. So we

148

all got together and collected a few dollars and bought some boxes of grits and some bacon and cooked it up in the home economics room. We had so many kids in there eating that all the other teachers had to come down to see where all their kids went. That was a way to get them to come to school and make sure they had at least one meal a day."

Chaney's winning ways continued at Cheyney, where he was 225–59 in ten seasons starting in 1972. But his proudest moment came in 1978 when he was named one of the best teachers in the state. This was also the year the Wolves won the Division 2 national championship and Chaney was named Division 2 coach of the year.

Chaney would have never even thought of leaving Cheyney, where he had achieved such success as a teacher and coach and was so happy. But the school, which had promised to make him a full professor, kept dragging its heels. "It had nothing to do with money; there was no pay raise involved," Chaney says. "It was just the principle of the thing. Eventually I just got angry."

When Liacouris took office as president on July 1, 1982, the handwriting was already on the wall that he wanted a new basketball coach. At the time, Temple was in bad shape. Enrollment was down, tenured faculty were being laid off, and the university was losing money. "The place was close to bankruptcy," Liacouris says. "Plus we had a faculty revolt because of the layoffs. There was a white flight away from [the school's main center-city campus and toward Temple's Ambler campus in the suburbs] and an overall feeling that Temple was a second-rate institution. We have graduates who hate their own background and are embarrassed they went here."

Another negative is the school's location in the heart of North Philadelphia, a blighted neighborhood filled with drugs, crime, poverty and rows and rows of abandoned, burned-out buildings.

149

"One of the first questions I asked myself was, how can I get people to come to Temple?" Liacouris says about his first few months as president. "How could I turn around this negative attitude?"

One of the answers he came up with was sports. Liacouris envisioned McGonigle packed to the rafters with cheering students decked out in cherry and white, caught up in the atmosphere of an exciting basketball team. He wanted a team that played and beat the best of teams and he wanted national exposure. The only problem was he just didn't think Don Casey was the man to get him where he wanted to go. "I couldn't, in my own mind, move the university forward with him," Liacouris says. "We were moving into the Atlantic-Ten, which was a step up for us [from the East Coast Conference that included teams like Drexel, American, Lafayette, and Hofstra]. He wanted to play a soft schedule and said it would be hard to win in the new conference. This was the same problem the university had; they were afraid to succeed."

Another problem Liacouris had with Casey was the poor graduation rate of his players. "He claimed sixty percent, but it was really thirty," Liacouris says. "I still have all the records right here in my drawer."

Casey, by all accounts a good coach and a man respected throughout the basketball community, had compiled a 151–94 record in nine seasons and had two years left on his contract in the summer of 1982. "[Before I took office] we went to lunch one day, and I said, 'What are you going to do in the future, your long-term future?'" Liacouris says. "I said we could get him into administration. He interpreted this as me trying to get him out."

In July 1982, Casey accepted a position as assistant coach for the Chicago Bulls (he's currently the head coach of the Los Angeles Clippers but will be fired after the 1990 season). This cleared the path for Liacouris to hire a new coach. There was speculation in the press that Liacouris was set on hiring a black coach, with Chaney's name mentioned despite the fact that he had not been approached by Temple at this point. Liacouris denies this, saying he wanted the best possible coach, regardless of race.

Liacouris went to Sonny Hill, asking his advice on who to hire. Hill is one of the movers and shakers in Philadelphia basketball and the director of a huge summer league that bears his name. "I told him I wanted a national program, a clean program, a program that excited people," Liacouris says. "I thought he was going to recommend himself. But he said, 'John Chaney.' I said, 'Who's he?'"

Liacouris quickly found out. "I found a guy who was successful on every coaching level who graduates his kids." The two met for lunch and like most conversations with Chaney, the talk centered around life, not basketball. The two found they had similar backgrounds and philosophies and struck up a mutual admiration and friendship that has grown stronger over the years.

Liacouris decided Chaney was his man but met some opposition from a member of the school's board. "He said, 'You're not going to hire any niggers,'" Liacouris says. "I got mad and told him, 'I'm hiring John Chaney.'"

"To see John get this job is one of the outstanding things I've seen in Philadelphia in my lifetime," Hill said at a press conference on August 18, 1982, announcing Chaney's selection as Temple's coach. "What John will bring to Temple and the city involves a lot more than just basketball. He'll bring the alumni, students and community together. Regardless of what has happened at Temple in the past, I've always thought the school was a sleeping giant. Well, I believe the giant's gonna come alive now. John Chaney can be the rallying point, the stabilizing force, the perfect person to bridge the gap to the future."

One of the first things Chaney and Liacouris did was set

up a program to get some of the players who had left without degrees back into school. "That was very difficult, but we had some success," Chaney says, naming three or four players who have either gotten their degrees or are currently in school. One he spotted while driving down Broad Street; Chaney pulled over and talked him into going back. "Many of them had gone out and started a life, started a family and it was hard to convince them it was important to come back and get a degree. Having a family and having to support them and go to school all at the same time is a very difficult mix. But Peter and Pat [Swygert, Temple's executive vice president] made it a priority and provided funds and support."

What Liacouris had dreamed, Chaney began to make a reality. The Owls began winning and winning and suddenly McGonigle Hall was packed and alive and Temple students felt a sense of pride in their team and university. The number one team in 1988 brought Temple the national attention Liacouris had craved. The admissions office was swamped with requests for applications, the Owl Club (an alumni booster organization) reported donations were up substantially and sales of T-shirts and other novelty items relating to the team skyrocketed.

"I have made a lot of great hires since I've been at Temple," Liacouris says. "But he's easily the best appointment I've made as far as the impact it's had on the university and community. Temple is known as a place that must be pretty good if they have a guy like Chaney working for them."

6

Being Told You're Wrong Is the Best Way to Correct a Problem

December 13

Ready or not, the Owls start the most grueling stretch of their season. In the next month they will play five nationally ranked teams: Illinois (currently ranked fifth by the UPI) on December 16 at Illinois; LaSalle (6–0 and unranked, but ranked seventeenth by the time they play Temple) at home on January 3; North Carolina State (ranked fifteenth by UPI) in Atlantic City on January 6; University of Nevada, Las Vegas (the UPI's number twelve team) on January 13 at the Spectrum in Philadelphia; and Georgia Tech (sixteenth in the UPI poll) in Atlanta on January 16.

In the next few weeks, our season hangs in the balance in terms of postseason play. What this means is you can ill afford to go into any game

and not be ready to play. You're at a level now where the teams you are playing capitalize on mental mistakes. The teams you are playing are the top teams in the country. When you go to play with a lack of confidence or a lack of fire or vigor in you and a lack of concentration, you end up with a loss. Illinois was in the Final Four last year. Their talent says they are good. They are good in every spot. The guys that come from the bench are damn good. Don't fool yourself, you're not playing against anybody that is coming out of any other corral than the O.K. Corral. They are all O.K. They are all official players.

When Chaney arrived his plan was to develop Temple into a national program. He knew the only way to do it was to play a nonconference schedule that included games against the top teams—preferably on national television. Going up against these teams—even if Temple lost—gave Chaney and his fledgling program instant recognition and credibility. "You have to move with the times," Chaney explains. "And television is the best way to communicate what your program and school are all about."

Wanting to play the top teams and actually getting them on his schedule were two different things. Chaney sent out letters to what he considered to be the top fifty teams in the country, but favorable responses were few and far between. "We were not considered a high-profile team at the time. We had all kinds of problems getting the top teams to play us." Chaney had to agree to two-for-one deals in which he would agree to a three-year contract with another school, with two of the games at the opposing team's arena and only one at McGonigle. "Finally, in the last year or two, we've broken out of that mold and now we can talk to the top schools eye-to-eye."

Every year Chaney improved the strength of his non-conference schedule. In 1984–85, the first year he could have a major impact on scheduling, Temple played Bradley (a 57–56 loss), Wake Forest (a 71–61 win), and Wyoming (a 66–60 win in the finals of the Cowboy Shootout in Wyoming) during the regular season.

In 1985–86, they took on UCLA (a 79–59 loss), Wichita State (a 62–60 win in the Pizza Hut Classic at Wichita), and Wake Forest (a 64–59 overtime win).

The 1986–87 season was a big breakthrough for Chaney. The Owls were invited to play in the prestigious preseason NIT tournament, where they beat Virginia 79–75 and lost a heartbreaker to UNLV, 78–76, on a buzzer-beater. That season, Temple also played Memphis State (a 67–59 win), UCLA (a 76–65 win), Kansas (a 67–64 loss), and Alabama-Birmingham (a 67–60 win).

This year, Chaney has put together a nonleague schedule that ranks among the three or four toughest in the country. Three games will be on national television: Illinois, North Carolina State, and Vegas.

You can't go to Illinois hop, skipping and jumping. You can't get off the plane licking on a lollipop—an all-day sucker—because that's exactly what you're going to be when they're through with you. They come to play. If you don't believe me, go look at the tape of them playing Chicago State. Chicago State had ten people walking around the court with no heads because Illinois bit them off. Chewed their heads right off. All them Illinois players have scars on their arms. You can scar them up, they don't even stop. The referee blows the whistle and says, "You got fouled," and they say, "Oh, was I? I didn't notice."

December 16

The Owls arrived in Chicago two days ago. That night, looking forward to some prime Midwest beef, Chaney and Demopoulos order takeout ("I hate to go [out to] eat; someone might recognize me and want to talk") at a joint famous for its ribs.

"They were terrible," Chaney says. "They serve a lot of them, so they boil them first to cook 'em fast and then they put them on the grill for the last few minutes. They've been drenched and drowned in water and taste like jello. You're supposed to have to tear the meat off the bone with your teeth, but this meat just falls off like jello."

On road trips, food is perhaps the only distraction for the three coaches. Chaney usually does some shopping at the airport or at a local supermarket on the way back from practice the day before a game and stocks the refrigerator in the coach's suite with some smoked meats, cheeses and other favorites. The three always share a suite, with Chaney in one room, a room in the middle to watch films and hold team meetings, and a third room for Maloney and Demopoulos. The first thing they do upon entering—after staking their claim to one of the three bathrooms—is turn on the television to ESPN. If there's a basketball game on, they're in heaven. The next thing they do is order room service. Chaney and Demopoulos usually order the spicier, fancier items on the menu, while Maloney sticks to the basics. "That stuff they eat will kill you," says Maloney, as he orders a fruit salad or tuna sandwich.

"This was Syracuse revisited," Chaney says, after the Illinois game.

For a half and a little more, the Owls play like world beaters, giving the Illini all they can handle. At the half, Illinois leads 39–38, despite the fact that both Causwell and Hodge have to sit out much of the half after they each pick up a second foul. The Owls seem ready to make a move at the start of the second half. Twice, Strickland steals the ball and streaks downcourt on breakaways. He comes up empty both times. On the second attempt, Hodge gets whistled for his third foul while trying for an offensive rebound of Strickland's missed shot. Less than a minute later, he picks up his fourth, an offensive foul, as he fights for a position in the low post.

"Every game I've been thinking about getting a steal like that and being by myself," Strickland says. "The first one I think I got fouled, the second I just lost control of the ball."

These missed opportunities help ignite Illinois on a 19–4 run and the Illini take a 58–42 lead with 9:02 to play. Temple never gets within ten the rest of the way and loses 78–61.

Macon leads Temple with twenty-two points and plays a good part of the game at point guard. "With all the gimmick defenses the other teams are using, I thought the best thing would be to have Mark handle the ball and let everyone else develop their game." The strategy doesn't work, in large part because of the foul problems that keep Causwell and Hodge off the floor for almost half the game. With Temple's two big men out, Illinois controls the boards 42–27.

Several reserves get a chance to play with all the foul trouble. But just like in the Syracuse game, Temple's level of play drops significantly when Chaney goes to the bench. Later he tells a story from his school yard days to illustrate the panic that seizes some of his young players during the big games. "There was this one guy, Duke, I think his name was," Chaney says. "He would stumble out of the bar, drunk, onto the court, and play like a bitch. But guess what? The minute we had a real game, all he was was drunk. We'd say, 'Come on, Duke, we're playing the Apaches.' Duke would say, 'What? I can't play, I'm drunk." We'd say, 'Yesterday you were drunk in the school yard, but you played great.' Then he'd say, 'Yeah, but we weren't playing the Apaches yesterday.' "

December 20

Today Chaney works on getting his team ready for Saturday's game with Duquesne, a team Temple should be able to beat handily. "We should be able to steal the ball from them," Chaney says and then describes the Dukes' offensive patterns and how to cheat into the passing lanes for the steals. They work on this for half an hour, with the red team running the Duquesne offense. Then Chaney has the team scrimmage fullcourt for another half hour and ends practice with silent free throws. In this drill, no one can talk, while each player attempts to connect on five of six free throws. If a player misses two, everyone sprints fullcourt and back and the same player keeps shooting until he hits five of six. The Owls are not a good foul shooting team and this drill takes a while. Post is the worst free-throw shooter and he keeps missing and missing and missing. A few players start to grumble as they run. On his eighth sequence of shots, Post misses his first and makes three straight. When he misses his next, everyone should be running, but Causwell claims it's only his first miss. No one argues and Post hits his next two shots and is finally off the line.

In the huddle at the end of practice, Chaney talks about a bad attitude he sees starting to manifest itself in some of his players. It's just a tiny crack, something most coaches would never even notice, but Chaney isn't about to let it grow.

Every time someone says something to you [he points toward Hodge, but it could very easily have been directed toward two or three other players], you take a chip and put it on your shoulder. You can't do that. You get your ego involved. Your ego is not something you can deal with. It's a check you can't cash. You know where your ego should take place? When you are on that foul line. When you're up there by yourself and you have a couple of foul shots that are the difference between winning and losing. That expresses to me what your self-esteem is. Since the first day he has been here, [Post's] self-esteem has been built up. Because he's starting to make those foul shots. The first time we shot foul shots, he couldn't make one for ten days. He couldn't get past two. Now his self-esteem is going up as he's making more foul shots. Certainly he's not perfect—nobody is. But he's not afraid to go up there. He's not ashamed to fail. The foul shots all of you are missing in games, you have no business missing. You miss and your self-esteem goes down. Just like in the classroom. Then you get a chip on your shoulder every time someone says you're wrong. Being told you're wrong is the best way to correct a problem.

Demopoulos interrupts. "An error doesn't become a mistake unless you refuse to correct it. We all make errors. The mistake is not to correct it."

The biggest problem you [he points to Hodge again] have is every time someone says do this or do that, you take on a new personality and you put the blame on somebody else instead of yourself. And if you have a team full of players that put the blame on somebody else, you have a team full of losers. Born losers. In every game I ever lost when I played, I never blamed a teammate. I always blamed myself.

December 23

The Owls beat overmatched Duquesne 93–62, raising their record to 4–3 overall and 2–1 in the Atlantic-10. With the game tied at twenty-three midway through the first half, the Owls go on a 24–8 run to take a 47–31 halftime lead and the contest is never close the rest of the way.

The game is a chance for everyone to get their offense going. Hodge is eight of eleven for a career-high twenty-one and Causwell hits on seven of eleven for sixteen points. They both grab eleven rebounds. Macon is Macon, scoring a team-high twenty-three, plus eleven rebounds, three assists and three steals. Harden also comes off the bench to do a solid job. In thirty minutes he scores eleven, dishes off seven assists and does not turn the ball over.

With five minutes to go, Chaney clears the bench and Post scores his first basket of the season. But the highlight is the play of Joe Robinson, a freshman walk-on from Central High School in Philadelphia, who comes in with four minutes to play and connects on all four shots he takes.

Afterward, a reporter asks Chaney about Robinson. "I think Joe is putting some pressure on me," Chaney says tongue-in-cheek for the benefit of Macon, who is sitting next to him. "I mean, nobody we've ever had has shot like that. Joe has to be our best shooter. He's hitting those long shots, and it's gonna be your ass [he points to Macon] sitting on the bench next to me."

"I'll help you coach," Macon volunteers.

"See, Joe is putting pressure on me. The only bad thing I can say is he wasn't looking for anyone to pass to. The only thing that will keep him out of the lineup is he's pretty selfish."

"But he had one assist, Coach," a reporter says.

"He did? Okay, he's fighting for a starting job now."

Chaney isn't done teasing Macon. During the game he drove the lane and instead of pulling up for the jumper or going all the way to the hoop, Macon got fancy and dished off to a surprised Hodge, and the ball went out of bounds to the Dukes.

"Here you work hard to get in there and then throw the ball to Duane. That was ridiculous," Chaney says, suddenly forgetting all the great plays Macon made and remembering the one time he threw it away.

"I wasn't throwing it to Duane," Macon corrects.

"Shut up," Chaney shouts, laughing. "I saw what you did. You threw a two-foot pass."

"It was to Donald, Coach, and he was open."

Chaney gets up and grabs Macon's shoulder and tells him to never, ever make those two-foot passes.

December 25

It may be Christmas day, but the Owls are on the court for one of the longest practices of the season. It starts at ten in the morning and goes on and on until half past two in the afternoon. Their next game isn't until January 3, but it's a big one: the LaSalle Explorers at McGonigle. Speedy Morris's Explorers are led by Lionel Simmons, one of the top players in the country. Simmons is closing in

161

on 3,000 career points and is considered by most to be a lottery pick in the upcoming NBA draft. Surrounding Simmons is an excellent perimeter team. The Explorers' weakness is inside. Aside from Simmons, a small forward who rebounds like a power forward, the only other big people Morris can count on are six-foot-nine-inch sophomore center Milko Lieverst and backup Bron Holland, a six-foot-ten-inch sophomore who plays about ten minutes a game. The game will be a match between Temple's big people and Macon and LaSalle's little people and Simmons. Today, Chaney stresses the importance of Temple's inside game.

Our source of energy is right here in the paint. And it's also the secret to our success against LaSalle.

Next comes a story about his mother. It seems that another person from the nursing home was visiting her in her room and left their false teeth on the nightstand. Earley, nearly blind, thought they were hers and tried to put them in later. The point, which Chaney eventually gets around to explaining, is that inside players must begin to develop all their senses. They have to be able to see, feel and smell where the defense is. Chaney uses Kevin McHale of the Boston Celtics to demonstrate his point.

McHale has a thousand moves in the pivot and nobody can stop him when he gets the ball. You know why? Because he puts a body on the guy [defending him] and knows where he is at all times. He feels him.

Chaney positions Causwell in the pivot and takes an offensive position in front of him with the ball. He explains the educated foot and the educated ass and shows how to feel the man. "When you can't feel him, back up until you feel him. If you can get a foot around one of his, just roll strong to the basket. The only thing the man can do is foul you."

For the next three hours Chaney goes over everything in the Temple bag of tricks, especially offensive formations designed to get the ball down low to Causwell, Hodge and Strickland. Finally, after a huddle at midcourt, a short lecture and a "team together," practice appears to be over. But first Chaney has his weary and wary players line up at center court in four rows, one behind the other. He then hands out a big bag of chocolate-chip cookies to the person at the head of each line and tells them to pass them out. "Merry Christmas," he says and practice is over.

Later the team will get together at the Hershey for a Christmas feast. Chaney eats with the team and then heads home for another Christmas dinner with his family. "After dinner we sat around and watched some football and then around 11 o'clock I took my mother back to the nursing home. I got home around midnight and sat with my wife for a while. Then I took a bath and watched some tapes of the LaSalle–Southwest Missouri State game."

December 26

During practice today, Hodge, frustrated by his lack of scoring and constant foul trouble, takes out some of his anger on Post. Not very graceful, Post is a banger who never backs down from his more talented teammates. With Post scratching and clawing at him, Hodge misses a short shot. He grabs the rebound and dunks it, throwing a nasty elbow at Post's face as the ball goes through the net. Fortunately for Post's teeth, he misses. "Get the hell out of here," Chaney screams at Hodge. "Get off this court and get dressed." Without a word, Hodge leaves.

"You have to find a way to get your point across to players and show them you mean business," Chaney says later about the incident. "I've been watching him and I'm not happy with his attitude. And the only chance you have to change behavior is when you have something they want. I'll embarrass his ass and keep him from playing, which is what he wants, and if he does it again I'll throw him off the team. You have to be committed to change and growth, otherwise there's no point in being out here. I won't say anything to him, but I'll be watching him tomorrow."

In the huddle at the end of practice, Chaney talks about Hodge without mentioning his name.

A bad attitude translates into bad behavior out there on the floor. If you retaliate every time something happens, you're falling into the hands of the other team. I'm not here to stand around and call fouls in practice. When a guy is grabbing at your hands and pushing for position, that's one thing. It's not like he's throwing elbows, trying to hurt you. If a guy slaps at the ball and you lose it, instead of getting mad or trying to get even, what I would do is wonder why I'm losing the ball so much.

December 27

Hodge is back at practice and a model citizen. He works hard and plays clean.

At first he was mad at Chaney for throwing him out of

practice, thinking what he had done wasn't that bad. His justification was that Post had been pushing and shoving him around. But as he thought about it more and more, Hodge began to realize that his rationale was wrong. There is plenty of pushing and shoving in games and many times referees let the big guys in the paint get away with more physical contact than the rules allow for. Fighting back and throwing elbows is a quick way to pick up fouls and earn a spot on the bench next to Chaney. Hodge found Post and apologized. The next step was to prove something to Chaney. "I wanted to gain back Coach's respect," Hodge says later. "I can have something really good here and I don't want to ruin that."

Hodge represents a big part of Temple's future. A former star at Coolidge High School in Washington, D.C., and Chaney's second McDonald's All-American, he was one of the most highly recruited big men in the country during the summer before his senior year, in which he averaged twenty-three points, fourteen rebounds, and six blocks a game for a Coolidge team that went 27–3 and was ranked sixteenth in the country by *USA Today*. All the big guns were after him, but Chaney won out. "All along I had a feeling it was going to be Temple," Hodge says. "When I told all my friends that, they said I was crazy, that I should go to Georgetown or Syracuse."

It was expected that Hodge would step right into the starting lineup and make an immediate impact last season. However, Hodge didn't score the necessary 700 on his SATs and so he had to sit out the year. "When I knew I didn't have the seven hundred, I was scared to tell Coach," Hodge says. "It felt like I was telling a parent something I did wrong. I missed by twenty points and I felt like I had let him down. But he said not to worry about it, that we still love you and will stick with you."

Hodge has many natural athletic gifts. Despite hands that are small for someone so tall, he catches the ball well and hangs onto it. He has a natural feel for where the defense is and a wide assortment of power moves to the hoops. He can even handle the ball in the open court and has a nice ten- to twelve-foot jumper. The offensive skills it took Causwell two years to learn, Hodge already had when he came to Temple. Because of his height and talent, Hodge has never had to work that hard to be a star. But now, Chaney is challenging him to be great ("I've raised the ante"), and that requires a lot of hard work. Not just on the court and in the weight room, but in his classes as well. Hodge, who is one of the brighter kids on the team, is a bit rebellious and tends to take the easy way out of most situations, especially in the classroom. Chaney will spend the rest of this season and the next two trying to improve Hodge's attitude. Throwing him out of practice and denying him what he loves best—basketball—is one way.

At the end of practice today, as the team huddles, Chaney brings up yesterday's incident.

"Coach said I didn't have to apologize to him but to my teammates because I was hurting the team by not being there," Hodge says. "So I apologized and he said we could go on from there and he never wanted to see it happen again. So now I'll just come to practice and work hard."

"He said he was sorry and I accept that," Chaney says. "Now, what I do is observe his behavior and make sure that his promise manifests itself in his behavior on the court."

Most would agree that Chaney has a positive impact on his players. One of the few who disagree is Chaney.

"I'm conscious of what a thin line there is between a youngster who goes straight and a youngster who goes astray," Chaney says. "My problem is that when you say I'm responsible for my players [going straight], I can't give myself credit for that. I don't think anyone has the right to say that they've done that."

"But, Coach, none of your players have gotten into trouble," I insist. "A big part of that has to be your influence."

"You're saying that. What I'm saying is it's a coincidence," Chaney says, his voice rising.

"But it can't be a coincidence if it keeps happening. You have a big impact on your players."

"I don't want you or anybody to say that about me. I don't want to take credit. There are too many people involved with a youngster before I get to him. Mark Macon's behavior was in place before he ever got here. If his mother or Norwaine [Reed, his high school coach] wants to take credit, and they should, that's fine with me. Ernest's behavior was in place before he got here."

"I would become paranoid if I took the responsibility of turning every kid around. Sometimes I feel relieved when a youngster has gotten through this maze of problems unscathed. I know the challenges and problems a youngster must get through. I spend hours and hours trying to direct a kid, but not for one minute do I feel safe and confident in which way he's gonna turn out."

"You have to admit you've made some difference in their lives," I say.

"I would hope I have and I have had some players come up to me later and say it. But what happens tomorrow if I read in the paper they did something wrong? Do I think I failed if he's thirty years old and on his own and does something wrong? When do you stop feeling either responsible for or guilty [about] your players? Where do you begin and where do you stop?

"You must have a great understanding of what your limitations as a coach are in terms of working with youngsters and directing their lives. I've been at every level and worked with poor kids and rich kids and everyone in

167

between. And I've failed more times than I've been successful. I know the luck of the draw when you're working with kids. You can't put yourself in a position where you can predict how kids will turn out or wave a magic wand and change their lives. I don't have a litmus test like that. I just work until there is no more work to be done, and hope that when that youngster walks out of here, he will be something that is constructive and positive for himself, his family and society. But you can't become so smug that you take credit for every kid that turns out right."

December 31

Chaney is concerned about Strickland, who is still struggling to accept his role. In high school, Strickland was a dominating player and the star of his team. Now his role has changed. On offense he is not the first, second, or even third option. He is a role player whose job is to rebound and play defense. The other things will come with time as he proves himself. But Strickland is frustrated with his lack of production. When defensive players push and shove him and try to prevent him from getting into position, Strickland retaliates and quickly picks up needless offensive fouls and finds himself on the bench getting lectured by Chaney and Maloney.

Chaney starts off talking to the team about accepting their roles, but winds up singling out Strickland, comparing him to Dennis Rodman of the Detroit Pistons.

Rodman does not score baskets. Rodman is the best player in basketball who does nothing that is measured on the stat sheet. He took four or five charges in last night's game. He got rebounds. He got up and down the floor and played great

defense. He stopped players. He helped out. Guys were afraid to go to the basket because of him. The [Los Angeles] Clippers had twenty-seven or thirty turnovers and most of them were because of Rodman. They were just throwing the ball like Clint Eastwood—every which way and loose.

Let's say I use Rodman as an example, and I pointed out that you [he points to Strickland] could be a Rodman. I have a feeling in my heart that you could probably be a better Rodman because you can shoot a little bit better than him. If you could just be a baby Rodman [everyone laughs at this], that's all I ask from you. Forget about shooting. If you could play defense, real tough defense, I'd be able to say, "Okay, we're gonna put Strick on this boy, and we just shut him down because we have Strick on him. I can just cross him off the court." Just run and hustle. And if you could make good decisions, you could be a better Rodman.

The lecture ends and Chaney starts working on a new power formation for the offense, which should be effective against smaller teams like LaSalle.

You have to mean to score and be mean to score. When someone is playing up on you real close and you have possession of the ball inside, that's the most vulnerable position for a defensive player to be in. When he plays you tough, right up on you, he's vulnerable. He's in trouble, not you. You get up on [the 76ers Charles] Barkley's ass and you're in deep, deep trouble. He just rolls off of you and goes any way he wants. If I'm an inside player and the defensive man is up on me, all I want is the ball. Give me the ball. If his arms are all over

**me, I'm attacking those limbs. I'm attacking them
with the ferociousness of a killer. If I was a blade,
I'd just cut him to death. I would just cut his arms
off. I wouldn't be shooting any kind of shots
where I'm faking. All I'm doing is attacking.**

The new power formation has Hodge near the foul line
and Causwell and Strickland down low, with Macon and
Kilgore on the perimeter.

"What would you do when you get [the ball] and are
uncovered?" Chaney asks Hodge.

"Shoot it," Hodge answers.

"That's right. Now what would you do if a man was on
you? What kind of pass would be in order?"

"Pass it back to Mik."

"That's right. I guess you're not stupid."

Later Chaney switches Strickland to the foul line and
puts Hodge down low with Causwell and they run
through the pattern again. He keeps warning the big men
not to dribble, especially when they have the ball near the
foul line. "When a little man sees you dribble up there,
they just lick their chops. They just know they're gonna
steal it. When you get the ball down here [low], hold it
strong in both hands, make a little baby dribble and chase
the ball. The reason Duane has gotten better in traffic is
he's gotten stronger in his hands. He knows someone is
beating him on the hands and still he holds it and shoots
it. Last year he couldn't do that."

A minute later Macon spins one way, then the other out
of control and forces up a bad shot. Chaney calls him a
"liver-lipped blankety-blank" and everyone laughs, especially Harden and Kilgore. "You shut up," Chaney
shouts at Harden. "You and that roommate of yours [Kil-
gore] love to hear me talk bad about Mark. You love that.
'He got Mark. Yeah! He called Mark "liver lips." ' I bet
you'll be walking around campus calling him 'liver lips'

170

now. Come out from under there Mr. New Orleans and call him that."

Harden, who's from Baton Rouge, stays put along the wall under the basket laughing. "Strick, you love that too, don't you, when I get on Mark's ass? Shoun? You're his home boy and you love it too, don't you?"

By now everyone is laughing, including Macon, who enjoys it when Chaney yells at him. "Sometimes he'll tell me to yell at him more," Chaney says later. "He doesn't want to receive special treatment." The only problem is Macon seldom does anything wrong.

January 2

It's the last practice before the LaSalle game tomorrow night at McGonigle and Chaney continues his theme that "winning is within you."

I don't want you to be concerned about the other team and what they can do. If you move toward what the other team is about and worry about stopping what they do, you're moving toward their side of the court. The strength of a great team is they are effective in what they do and force the other team to surrender. You make the other team deal with who you are. You have to have self-esteem and the way you get it is try to understand the things that are important to you. If you're the kind of person who is always going to take a backwards step and be concerned about somebody else—overly concerned—you're going to lose some of your self-esteem.

Cheyney State head Coach Keith Johnson and his assistant Milt Colston—who both played for Chaney at Cheyney—attend practice and head into the office afterward with Chaney. Other than learning from watching Chaney coach, they have an ulterior motive for being here: They need some money for a new videocassette player. "You see these boys here, they're in here twisting my arm for money," Chaney says and breaks into a laugh. "That's the problem with being associated with so many different institutions. I have to give money to Bethune-Cookman, Cheyney and Temple. I've found as I get older I have more and more friends. But I have to start dissociating myself from them. They all want money. I can't afford so many friends."

Johnson and Colston know a soft touch. Chaney promises to send them a check. Meanwhile, the press is lining up outside to talk to Chaney about the LaSalle game—the hottest ticket in town. When Johnson and Colston get up to leave, the first television reporter enters the office. He starts with a little small talk, something all reporters try to do to lighten the mood. With Chaney it's not necessary and can often lead to lengthy discussions, which can be a big mistake if the reporter is on a tight deadline. The reporter brings up the subject of referees, and with Johnson and Colston still there, Chaney begins a lengthy and comical recollection about a game a few years back at Wichita State. It seems that the fans knew one of the refs, whom they had nicknamed Pee-Wee in honor of his diminutive stature. Chaney was not too pleased with the home crowd's seemingly intimate relationship with one of the referees. "Their fans always stand and clap until their team scores its first basket," Chaney explained. "But we went out to a ten–nothing lead and the fans were still up and clapping, but they were getting pretty angry. They started yelling, 'Hey, Pee-Wee, give us a break. Hey, Pee-Wee, we raised you from a pup.' I was starting to wonder who this Pee-Wee was and why the fans knew him so well. So I stood up and asked him. He hit me with a technical."

Chaney next offers the reporter a roasted peanut from the big bag on his desk. By this time the reporter wishes he had never started making small talk, but isn't sure if he should interrupt Chaney, who starts telling him where he got the peanuts—a little corner market a few blocks from Temple. "The first time I go there there's this long line out the door and I thought to myself they must have good peanuts. Then I get inside and see they're selling numbers. All I can picture is the cops coming in and raiding the place and they arrest me too, and I try to explain that all I'm doing is trying to buy peanuts."

Finally the reporter sees an opening and changes the subject quickly and asks Chaney to comment on the fact that Temple has beaten LaSalle five straight times. "I think Speedy [Morris, the LaSalle coach] has had some great teams and we've been very fortunate to win," Chaney says. "We should have lost every game. This year they've come together and are a great team and I'm hoping they won't be able to impose their will on us."

Chaney goes on for another five minutes, answering questions, saying nice things about Morris and Lionel Simmons and then the reporter thanks him and gets up to go. As he walks out of the office, the next television reporter walks in. Once again the reporter makes the mistake of trying to make small talk, while his cameraman sets up his equipment. He asks Chaney if he had a nice New Year's Eve. "We cooked some chitlins and black-eyed peas and at midnight got down on our knees and prayed," Chaney says. "We always celebrate that way. We're old-fashioned. We have to buy the right food. Have a lot of peas with some smoked meat in them for seasoning. That's good luck. I guess it's an old Southern custom. And we can't do certain things that night, like wash clothes."

173

Chaney goes on for a few more minutes, until finally the reporter sees an opening and makes his move and begins asking the same questions as the reporter who just left.

January 3

Down 61–52, with a little less than four minutes remaining, the Owls score nine straight points to tie the score at 61 with forty-one seconds to play. There is no question who LaSalle is going to get the ball to: Simmons. With eleven seconds left and point guard Doug Overton in possession of the ball just outside the three-point line, Simmons cuts from under the basket to the sideline. Macon is whistled for holding Simmons and Chaney jumps up from the bench to register his opposition to the call. "I don't want to comment on the call," Chaney says after the game. "But you just don't make a call like that. Let the game end with the kids."

Simmons sinks both free throws and the Explorers lead 63–61.

Once again there is no doubt who the ball is going to: Macon. As the clock approaches zero, Macon has the ball at the top of the key. He starts to make a move toward the basket and is fouled by LaSalle's Randy Woods. With one second remaining, Macon hits the first shot and the Owls are down by a point. "The first one felt good," Macon says. "But the second one felt kind of weak coming out." It misses. Causwell leaps over Simmons and grabs the rebound, putting it back up just as the final horn sounds. The ball rolls around the rim and out. LaSalle is victorious, 63–62.

While Simmons (twenty-three points, including four for four from three-point range, and fourteen rebounds)

174

and his teammates celebrate, Macon (twenty-one points and ten rebounds) heads slowly back to the Temple bench, where several of his teammates rush out to console him.

In the locker room, Chaney tells Macon he'll wind up missing a lot more last-second shots in his career. "That made me feel better," Macon says. "What he was telling me was that I'll be in a lot more pressure situations and sometimes I'll make it and sometimes I won't. But the important thing is to keep taking 'em."

Later, in the office, Chaney, Maloney and Demopoulos sit around mulling over the game and studying the stat sheet.

"These are winning stats," Demopoulos says, noting that Temple outshot (twenty-six of sixty-three as compared to twenty for sixty) and outrebounded (45–40) La-Salle.

Chaney studies one line in particular, the Owls' free-throwing shooting. "Seven for seventeen. Shit."

7

The Battles Are Getting Tougher and Tougher for the Poor

January 6

After this afternoon's game against North Carolina State, Chaney is so proud of his team he cries in the locker room. "I was ecstatic about the way we played," Chaney says later. "It's the first time all season I've had a chance to feel proud of them." The fact that the Owls had just lost 74–71 didn't matter to Chaney. The important thing was that his team showed signs of coming together and playing the way Chaney has been hoping they would all season.

State went into the game 10–2 and ranked eighteenth and were led by their guard tandem of Chris Corchiani and Rodney Monroe, considered by many to be the best backcourt in the country along with Bardo and Gill from Illinois. Chaney considers Corchiani one of the top point guards in the country. He's not flashy or fancy, but he always gets the ball to the right man at the right time and never turns it over. "Corchiani's a bitch," Chaney says in admiration. Monroe is a great shooter and averages twenty-two points a game.

The Wolfpack threaten to pull away several times in the first half, led by the long-range shooting of Monroe, who hits seven of nine shots in the first half—including an amazing five of six three-pointers—for twenty points. Hodge keeps Temple in the game with thirteen points and the Owls trail 43–37 at the half.

Down 51–45 in the second half, Temple goes on a 13–2 run to take a 58–53 lead with 8:50 remaining. State battles back to tie the score at 64 with 4:38 to play and the game remains tight the rest of the way, with the lead changing hands four times. With 1:39 remaining, Hodge hits one of two foul shots to cut State's lead to 72–70. With fifty-five seconds left, Temple forces a turnover and the Owls quickly call a time-out to set up the game-tying or -winning shot.

The ball goes to Macon, who drives the baseline and pulls up for a short jumper with two men in his face. The ball bounces off the rim to Causwell, who has perfect inside position. He grabs the ball and goes up quickly for a dunk, but the ball bounces off the rim. Causwell grabs the ball again and is fouled as he goes back up for a shot with thirty-two seconds remaining. His first shot misses short, the second is good and Temple trails 72–71.

State immediately gets the ball inbounds to Monroe. "We want the ball in Rodney's hands in that situation," State coach Jim Valvano said, sounding like Chaney talking about Macon. "We told him not to give it up." Up to this point, Monroe, who will score a game-high thirty-three, has been held without a field goal in the second half, but he has hit eleven of twelve free throws in the half, including State's last four points.

Macon plays Monroe tight, trying to draw a charge or

a steal but gets neither. With the clock running down, Macon is forced to foul Monroe. "We didn't want to foul Rodney, but it's just that he got the ball and kept it," Chaney says.

With twelve seconds to go, Monroe drills both free throws to give his team a 74–71 lead. Temple quickly gets the ball past midcourt and calls time-out. The play is once again designed to go to Macon, who gets the ball deep and to the right of the basket. With Corchiani on him, Macon dribbles to his right, pulls up and lets fly with a three-pointer that would have tied the game. It just misses, rimming out as the crowd gasps and the horn sounds.

"I think we did everything right, it just turned out wrong," Chaney told the press afterward. "I see this as a step forward, as a coming together process and I'm very proud of the way we played."

Chaney calls the game a "coming-out party" for Hodge (twenty points, nine rebounds) and Causwell (fifteen points, nine rebounds, five blocks) and also praises the play of Harden (six points, eight assists and two turnovers). "Michael played very well against one of the top guards in the country," Chaney said of his duel with Corchiani (two points, five assists and four turnovers).

Harden started for the first time and played thirty-nine minutes. His starting, the shift of Kilgore to three guard and Strickland to the bench, effectively ends Chaney's big man lineup for the time being. "This gives us a little more control of our philosophy of using a point guard to handle the ball and stepping Mark [Macon] off with less ball-handling responsibilities."

Strickland says he is relieved to be taken off the wing and put back under the basket where he is more comfortable. "It's home to me," he says of the four and five positions. But he's not happy about being a substitute.

"Being a [sophomore] and starting was a pretty good thing, so I was kind of upset at first."

The family and friends of many of the Temple players wait outside the locker room. Chaney makes his way through the crowd, chatting and joking with the families. He puts his arm around Mike Flicker's mom and tells her what a fine young man her son is. "She'll be talking about that for a month," Flicker, the team's student trainer, says. "She loves Coach."

Causwell has a group of about twenty relatives and friends waiting for him who came down from New York. It takes the big center at least five minutes to kiss and hug everyone, and then Chaney does the same. "All these people are here to see you?" Chaney asks Causwell mockingly. "If you mess up in school, all these people will get you."

These words turn out to be prophetic.

Causwell is a very shy person, unsure of his abilities on and off the court. He didn't start playing basketball until his junior year at Cardoza High School in Queens, where he sat on the bench the entire season. His senior year he began to show some of his vast potential, averaging 13.4 points, 13.1 rebounds, and 12.2 blocks and college recruiters took notice. His progress was a testament to his determination to become a good player and to the push he got from Cardoza coach Ron Naclerio. "He worked with me every day at practice, at night and on weekends," Causwell says. "At first I couldn't even go off the [correct] foot and make a lay-up. But then things started to come into place."

Demopoulos still remembers the first time he saw Causwell play, during a Cardoza practice. "I heard there was this good big man in New York and I went to watch him in practice," Demopoulos says. "During the practice

Duane was a nonentity on offense. He never got the ball. But I watched him chase down a guard from behind on defense. That kind of athletic ability really got my attention."

At Temple, Causwell has slowly developed into a dominating player under the constant tutelage of Chaney and Demopoulos. After sitting out his freshman season, he was a backup on the 1987–88 number one team, spelling Rivas and Perry. He played a little more than ten minutes a game, averaging 2.0 points and 2.6 rebounds. Last season Causwell came on strong, starting and averaging 11.3 points, 8.9 rebounds and 4.1 blocks to rank second in the nation. The pro scouts started to take notice. "Every time I see him he gets better," says Steve Rosenberry, a scout for the Seattle Supersonics, after a game earlier this season.

"At Temple we have a built-in success formula for big people," Chaney says. By this he means he teaches his inside players to do only a few things. But those few things they practice over and over until they are perfect. "Our offense is built around keeping a big guy in the low post and teaching him to play with his back to the basket." Although this is a skill not too many college—or even NBA—players can master, it is highly valued. "Chaney's centers never seem to stray too far from the basket," Rosenberry says. "He likes them down in the paint and that helps Causwell. There aren't too many players who can play the low post."

This season Causwell has continued to improve, especially on offense, where he is gaining confidence and a few new moves. But still he has been inconsistent, dominating one game and disappearing in the next. "Duane can be a very good player," Chaney says. "He's just starting to reach his potential. He just has to learn to run up and down and be hungry—like a seven-foot Barkley—on offense."

January 12

Practice this morning is at the Spectrum in South Philadelphia, where the Owls will meet Jerry Tarkanian's Running Rebels of UNLV in a nationally televised game tomorrow afternoon. It has been a long week for Chaney. On Tuesday, the Owls traveled to Washington and beat George Washington 60–57. Last night they edged West Virginia 73–69, despite shooting seventeen for thirty-three from the free-throw line. The two wins raised Temple's Atlantic-10 record to 4–1 (6–5 overall).

Chaney has also been closely following the events transpiring in Dallas at the NCAA convention, which started last Sunday and ran through Wednesday. One important item on the agenda was a discussion and vote on the future of Prop 42.

I'd like to go over some points from last night's game, and then I can go on to the next page.

Foul shooting is killing us. We shot seventeen for thirty-three. We only have two or three people who are making foul shots. Everyone else is just throwing them up without concentrating. It's almost traumatic. Seventeen for thirty-three is mind-boggling.

"We're shooting sixty-three percent as a team," Demopoulos says.

That's mind-boggling. We usually shoot close to eighty percent as a team. We're not a team with fifty All-Americans sitting on the bench, fellas. We can't win unless you do the little things. You have to make foul shots, especially at the end of the game when it's time to win.

181

I watched the tape from last night and your passing was terrible. What is it I'm teaching you that you don't understand? We have guys on this team who are senior citizens, who are still doing the same things wrong. We can't make turnovers [they had fourteen at George Washington and twelve against West Virginia) and win. I've tried everybody [at that point]. We just can't find the right key to open up the door. I don't have a problem with guys missing shots [the Owls shot twenty-two for fifty-one at George Washington and twenty-five of sixty-one against West Virginia]. I have a problem with guys throwing it away.

Now Chaney turns his attention to tomorrow's game with Vegas. The Owls have lost to the Running Rebels three straight years, by a combined total of five points. The common thread running through these three games, in addition to their closeness, was the Owls' refusal to let the Running Rebels run. Although Tarkanian's teams often score one hundred points and routinely average over ninety, they averaged only sixty-three in their three games with Temple.

Getting back on defense will be very, very important for us. If you take balanced shots on offense, you're halfway there. Then concentrate on getting back and covering players coming down the middle. You can't linger, you have to run down the court. If you're tired, tell us.

Chaney sets up a drill that forces the white team—Harden, Macon, Kilgore, Causwell and Hodge—to get back quickly on defense. In addition to the five men on the red team, Chaney stations another player at each of

182

the four corners of the court; two on each end, just outside the three-point line. These four players stay in that one spot and are part of the red team's offense. The red team remains on offense at both ends of the court, while the white team remains on defense. Once the red team scores, they just pick up the ball and head back to the other end, with the added advantage of two extra men already waiting in the corners for a long outlet pass.

There's seven guys on the court. I'm not worried so much about the two guys in the corners; I'm worried about the wings [Kilgore and Macon] not getting back to cover the man here [he points to a spot in the paint]. I don't want them getting here uncovered for an alley-oop.

After five minutes of racing up and down the court, the white team's jerseys are soaked with sweat and their legs are starting to feel like lead. Hodge is the first to crack. Lovelace replaces him and Demopoulos takes Lovelace's spot in one of the corners. In the next five minutes, other players start gasping for breath, and Chaney begins switching players back and forth to give them a breather. At this point Al McGuire, the former coach at Marquette and current college color commentator for NBC, walks in to watch practice. He and Chaney have known each other for several years. "He's a very special man," Chaney says later. "He's a man of the earth, someone who has identified himself with and helped so many disadvantaged youngsters."

The feelings are mutual. "John is a very special person," McGuire says. "I think he's the best coach in America."

Chaney spots McGuire. He comes over to say hello, while his team keeps scrimmaging. By this time he's called off the seven-on-five drill and has the white team working on offensive sets.

McGuire and Chaney exchange greetings (Chaney kisses McGuire on the forehead in lieu of a handshake) and start talking about basketball. Chaney steers the subject toward Prop 48, a subject very much on his mind these days, telling McGuire the networks should devote more time during the games to encourage kids in first and second grade to do better in school.

"You have to get to the kids when they're young," McGuire says.

"That's right," Chaney says. "If they can't read when they're in twelfth grade, then they couldn't read when they were in first grade."

McGuire changes the subject back to basketball. They start talking about foul shooting and how this game might come down to one at the end.

"What I'd do at the end of a game when it was close was run so fast they could never foul me," McGuire jokes. "When we were up by twenty, I'd just wait around for them to foul me."

"I was so nasty and mean, I didn't give a shit whether I made it or missed it," Chaney jokes back. "I just wanted to take it."

They continue talking and Chaney says that his team has been making poor decisions on the court. "Poor vision leads to poor decisions," he says.

"I like that. I'm going to steal that tomorrow," McGuire says.

A few minutes later, Chaney gets up to address his team as they huddle at center court.

Tomorrow there will be a tremendous amount of man-to-man pressure on our offense. The biggest test will be handling the ball against this pressure. Shooting is the easy part. If you can't protect it; we're in trouble. If somebody forces you into making mistakes when you have the ball, if you

cannot recognize time, situation and score, we're in big trouble as a team.

You have to concentrate every minute you're out there. You can't drift up and down the floor. You can't jog when you play against great teams. You can't run down the floor and be next to a guy and then let him get the ball for a lay-up. You have to position yourself so he doesn't get the ball. Just like I talk about positioning yourself in life. If you don't position yourself, you can't very well do anything for yourself.

All the keys tomorrow are what we do, not what they do. It's all up to us.

After practice and back in his office, Chaney has a chance finally to sit back and reflect on all that has happened in Dallas the past week.

Sunday, January 7. The convention opens, with Prop 42 as the major issue. Passed a year ago, Prop 42—which eliminates scholarships for those who do not attain a 2.0 and 700 on the SATs—is slated to go into effect starting in the fall of 1990.

Another issue that will be voted on is the restoration of a fourth year of eligibility to Prop 48 players who are within twenty-four credits of graduation after their first four years.

Monday, January 8. Prop 42 was overturned and replaced by Prop 26. This new proposition states that those who do not attain a 2.0 and a 700 on their SAT cannot receive athletic scholarships, but can receive institutional financial aid if they qualify and must still sit out their first year. The student can receive an athletic scholarship his second year if he is making satisfactory progress toward a degree.

Prop 26 passed by a vote of 258–66. Temple voted

185

against the new measure. Prop 27, which would have eliminated Prop 42 completely, was voted down 228–92.

"I don't see how this changes anything," Chaney says of Prop 26. "All it's done is change it from an athletic scholarship to institutional aid. But it is still the same foolhardy message being sent out by people in higher education to people in lower education that they must change and improve without them getting any kind of help or financial aid. All we see is cutbacks in education and the ones hit the hardest are the kids in the poor neighborhoods."

One of the most vocal supporters of Prop 26 at the convention was Penn State football coach Joe Paterno, who stated: "My experiences with blacks in forty years of coaching is in sports and in entertainment. [Blacks] have proven, whenever given an opportunity, that they can compete and be better. They've competed in a world where they have had to be better than whites. Not as good as whites, but better than whites, in order to be successful, and any time they've been given an opportunity, they've done it. Any time they've had a challenge, they've responded to it. . . . I think we owe it to them, to give them the opportunity to say, 'Okay, you've given us a challenge in an area where you're doubtful whether we can compete in that area. But give us a chance."

At this point, it sounds as if Paterno should be leading the fight against Prop 26. So far, he sounds just like Chaney. But suddenly he veers off in a new direction: "Just give them a chance. And that's what I think we'd be doing if we ratify [Prop] twenty-six. If you [approve] twenty-seven [and eliminate Prop 42], all you've done is send out another confusing message to the youngsters pounding that basketball in the streets of Brooklyn and other places. We'd confuse them again. We may sit up in this hall and talk about a lot of things, but the message that we'll get out to those youngsters is, 'You don't really have to study, because there's a back door. If you're good enough and you run fast enough and can catch a football . . . you're going to get in. And they're going to keep you eligible [once you're in college]. And you're going to get a couple of years in there, and you're going to be a pro athlete. If we rescind forty-two and pass twenty-seven, we take an enormous, great big step backward."

When Chaney heard Paterno's remarks, he was furious. "Here is a man who has been able to select and choose the elite blacks, the cream of the crop," Chaney says. "He gets the blacks with the best scores and the best chance to graduate. And then he has the nerve to say every time he's challenged them, they've met the challenge. Of course they did; they were handpicked. And suddenly he's an authority on all blacks and knows what's best for all blacks. That's nonsense."

In another important vote, Prop 38 was first passed and then an hour later voted down. Prop 38 provided that Prop 48 players would get back a fourth year of eligibility if they had completed 105 semester hours toward their degree by the start of their fifth year. Finally, something that made sense. Here was the NCAA providing athletes with an incentive to stay in school for a fifth year and earn their degree.

A half hour later, Prop 38 was brought back up for discussion and eventually another vote. It was defeated 199–125.

"I'm just appalled," Temple athletic director Charles Theokas said during the convention. "It's sickening what just went on. One minute, it's through, somebody says a few words, and how many—fifty or sixty people—change their votes. That's how much some of these people think about what they're voting on. That's the frustration we face here every year."

"The battles are getting tougher and tougher for the poor," Chaney says wearily. "I'm beaten, I'm really beaten. I've reached the stage where I'm spinning my

187

wheels. I don't have command of any lawyer that can overturn something like [Prop 48 and now Prop 26] when there's an immunity given to the NCAA against any legal action. Where do you go? Where do you start to fight this thing? I speak out when I can, but whether I'm talking to deaf ears or not I don't know. I just don't know."

"Why, Coach?" I ask. "Why is there such a negative perception of athletes in this country and why does it seem as though the NCAA is bound and determined to pass new propositions to deny kids a chance at college?"

"I think that what happens is a kind of hysteria came over [the NCAA and college presidents]. It was the kind of panic that comes over any leader when he is being criticized for any mishaps or unfortunate circumstances. But the fact of the matter is that all the publicity is being pointed at the athlete because he's highly visible and highly vulnerable. The two Vs. You can't get around the fact that if you see a youngster on television who's making a million dollars playing in the NBA, and he can't speak very well or maybe he can't read very good, there is a high degree of jealousy. And people use that athlete as an example and say all athletes are like that, when a statement like that is ridiculous."

"Do you think that a lot of this negative feeling is being directed at basketball because so many of the players are black?"

"A great deal of it comes from the fact that the evils in any society fall heaviest upon the poor and the needy. If blacks are in the poverty areas—and many are—everything negative is filtered down toward them. All the crime and drugs and evil in our society are put on their shoulders. It cannot be avoided. What happens when people start making a correlation between evil and blacks? Do they just identify all stealing with black? Do they identify ignorance with just black or Hispanics? Where do you stop with this?

"To the people who are looking down their noses at athletes and blacks, it's more digestible for them to read about so-and-so failing. They would rather read about someone flunking out than read about an uplifting story like Ernest's, about someone who has overcome so much."

"What if you were in a place where you could select the cream of the crop and couldn't recruit Prop 48 kids?"

"I think Temple is starting to move in that direction now. In the last two or three years they have raised their admission standards."

"Isn't this in conflict with what you believe?"

"Yes, in terms of my feelings about providing an opportunity for a wide range of kids to come to school. But [Temple is] still close enough to my way of thinking. They don't just look at SAT scores. They use other methods: they interview, look at the area he came from, look at his transcripts all through high school and see what other activities he's involved in.

"But if Temple ever moves in a direction where it becomes harder and harder or maybe impossible for me to get kids [like Pollard and Hodge and Strickland] admitted, I'll have to start thinking about quitting. I would feel that I am useless because I can't identify with that type of approach to higher education. I believe there is a growing need to bridge the gap between lower education and higher education, instead of higher education constantly setting rules to eliminate the poor and divorce themselves from their needs."

January 13

Once again, the Owls show their character, battling back time and time again—often without Macon—against the

189

team that will go on to win the national championship. But once again they lose, 82–76, to UNLV. "I could say a lot of good things about this team and how we've progressed [this season]," Chaney says, "but it means nothing until you win and establish a reference point as to how good you are."

Things start off bad and get worse for Macon as the game progresses. He shoots two for thirteen in the first half and picks up his third foul with 4:11 remaining and Temple up 33–28. Up to this point, the Owls have kept Vegas from running and Harden has been able to withstand the pressure of the Running Rebels' pressing defense. After Macon's third foul, Chaney replaces him with Conic and Vegas goes on a 12–4 run to close out the half and take a 40–37 lead.

Macon starts the second half by canning a three-point shot to knot the score at forty. But then Vegas hits three straight three-pointers to take a 49–40 lead. Temple pulls to 50–47, but then Vegas scores thirteen straight for a 63–47 lead with 10:02 remaining. By now, Macon has already picked up his fourth foul and is in the midst of a four for twenty-two night from the floor. Lovelace has already fouled out and Causwell and Harden each have four fouls. The only thing keeping Temple in the game is Hodge, who is showing a national television audience that he is a prime-time player. Hodge will wind up with thirty-one points and eleven rebounds.

With 8:41 to go and the score 68–53, a frustrated Macon fouls out and things look hopeless for the Owls. But they refuse to quit. Hodge hits four straight free throws, Causwell—playing with four fouls—hits a short bank shot, Hodge grabs an offensive rebound and dunks. With 6:04 to play, the Owls are back in the game 69–59.

With 4:36 to play, Causwell blocks a shot by Vegas' Larry Johnson, an All-American forward who will score twenty-six and grab twelve rebounds. It's a close call, with replays showing Causwell brushed Johnson slightly with his body on the way down after a clean block. Nevertheless, this is Causwell's fifth foul. Strickland takes his place.

With 3:47 to go, Harden fouls out with Vegas ahead 74–62. Amazingly, with Macon, Causwell, Harden, and Lovelace fouled out of the game, Temple battles back once more. Kilgore hits two free throws, Hodge hits a short jumper from the baseline and adds a free throw after he is fouled on the play, Randolph scores on an offensive rebound and it's 74–69 with two minutes to play. On Vegas' next possession, Hodge blocks Johnson under the basket, but Johnson grabs the loose ball and scores for a 76–69 lead. Conic answers back for Temple, hitting a three-pointer, Hodge adds two free throws on Temple's next possession and it's 76–74 with fifty-two seconds to play.

Then comes the game's most critical play. Temple presses, but the Running Rebels break it. Not content to run down the clock, Johnson takes the ball to the hoop. Kilgore jumps in to stop him and gets called for an intentional foul. Johnson makes the two free throws for a 78–74 lead and Vegas gets possession of the ball. Temple is forced to foul and Conic grabs Johnson with twenty-nine seconds to go. Again he makes both shots, for an 80–74 lead. Not known as a good foul-shooting team, Vegas makes thirty-one of forty-one in the game, including fourteen of nineteen in the last ten minutes.

Kilgore races the ball downcourt and drives to the basket. He misses but is fouled and cans both shots to trim the lead to 80–76 with twenty-two seconds left. The Owls are still alive, if Vegas would just miss a foul shot. Again Johnson gets fouled—by Kilgore this time—and once again he makes both shots for an 82–76 lead with nineteen seconds remaining to close out the scoring. A desperation shot by Kilgore just before the buzzer falls short.

"It was a strange game," Tarkanian says afterward. "There were so many times I thought we had it wrapped up, but then I'd look up at the scoreboard and they were right back in it."

Causwell's parents make the trip down from Queens for this game. While they're agonizing over the Owls' tough loss, a letter arrives at their home containing Duane's grades for the fall semester. Before the semester started, Causwell transferred into Temple's College of Health, Physical Education, Recreation, and Dance (HYPER-D). Temple is divided into twelve different schools, or colleges, and each controls its own admissions policy and sets its own academic standards. When Causwell transferred into HYPER-D, it was under the conditions that he would be placed on academic probation for a semester and would have to achieve at least a 2.25 in the fall semester to remain in the school. Causwell, who took seventeen credits in the fall (four more than the college recommends for students on probation), falls just short of the required 2.25, although he does make a 2.0. On Monday he will be dismissed from HYPER-D and the university.

By the time the Causwells get home and find the letter, their son and the Owls are already in Atlanta, preparing for Monday night's game against Georgia Tech.

January 14

While the Owls—including Causwell—are at practice, Mrs. Causwell reaches Theokas at home. The athletic director immediately calls the hotel in Atlanta and leaves a message for Chaney, who calls him back after practice.

192

"I was devastated," Chaney says.

Chaney calls Causwell into his room and explains the situation. Although NCAA rules would allow Causwell to play until the spring semester starts at Temple—which means he is still eligible for tomorrow night's game against Georgia Tech, Wednesday's game at Duquesne, and Friday's game against the University of Massachusetts—Chaney never even considers it. "It wouldn't be right," he says.

The two are in tears after a few minutes. "All I could do was tell him I still loved him and that there was nothing else I could do," Chaney says. But he is wrong. No matter how hopeless things look, Chaney still tries to move Causwell in a positive direction.

"He told me what I had to keep doing," Causwell says. "He told me I had to go back to school and keep working on getting my degree and to keep working hard for my shot at the NBA."

DiSangro drives Causwell to the airport for a flight back to Philadelphia. Liacouris is waiting at the airport and meets with Causwell and his parents, going over his options. By the end of the day, after his appeal for reinstatement has been denied, Causwell enrolls at Community College of Philadelphia. As they would do for any other senior with the possibility of playing professionally, Liacouris and Chaney set up a three-person committee of Temple administrators to help Causwell select an agent. "Everyone stayed with me and supported me," Causwell says.

After Causwell left Atlanta, his teammates quickly learned what had happened. "I think it hit everyone hard," Macon says. "We were very sad because we had lost a brother, a member of our family. But it taught me a lesson. It taught me that the closer you are to success, to the top of the mountain, the harder it is. Duane was close. Closer than close."

Hodge, who looked up to Causwell like an older brother, is devastated. "I couldn't believe it," he says. "I couldn't believe all of a sudden he was gone. Duane was always my inspiration. I always figured if he could do it, so could I."

In the evening, the team meets in the coaches' suite to talk about the situation. "We talked until about two in the morning," Chaney says. "We were all devastated and groped and grappled with how to handle it. I talked about how important education is and how we were all gonna stick with Duane."

Of all the players on the team, Strickland will be affected the most by Causwell's departure. Suddenly he is a starter again and has to fill the shoes of a player who could end up a first-round NBA draft pick in a few months. "I knew I would have to step it up," Strickland says. "The first few games I felt like my teammates didn't have confidence that I could do the job. Then Coach called me into his office and told me he didn't expect me to be Duane, that he just wanted me to go out and do what I could do. That made me feel better and I relaxed a little and started playing better, and I think my teammates got some confidence in me."

Causwell is not the only academic casualty. Joe Robinson has a bad first semester as well. Although the walk-on is eligible to keep playing, he and Chaney agree it would be in his best interests to leave the team and concentrate on his schoolwork. "I held out the carrot to him that if he did well he could try out again next year," Chaney says.

Lovelace also has a bad semester, although he too is eligible to remain on the team according to NCAA and Temple rules. However, Chaney decides that Lovelace can practice and play in home games, but cannot go on any road trips where there is the possibility he could miss a class. "I agreed," Lovelace says. "If I don't get my grades together, I could be out of school and lose everything."

January 15

At the end of practice this morning, the team gathers at center court of Georgia Tech's Alexander Memorial Coliseum. Since October 15, Causwell had been the one to shout, "Team!" but with him not there, there is a split second of uncertainty. Macon shouts, "Team!" and his teammates respond, "Together!" Two more times he shouts, "Team!" and twice more the Owls answer.

"I just did it automatically without anyone saying anything," Macon says. "I was sad about Duane, but I knew we had to move on."

For the rest of the season, the Owls will wear wristbands with Causwell's number thirty-two written on them. Several players will write his name on their game shoes.

January 16

If this had been Hollywood, Macon's last-second shot would have hit nothing but net and the Owls would have upset the eleventh-ranked Yellow Jackets of Georgia Tech—who wind up advancing to the Final Four before losing to eventual national champion UNLV. But this is

195

Atlanta, not Hollywood, and his three-point shot rolls around the rim and out and Temple loses 59–57.

"I thought it was in," Kilgore says later. "I was already thinking about how I was going to tell [the press] that this wasn't an upset."

With three seconds to go and Tech up 59–57, Dennis Scott misses the front end of a one-and-one. Harden grabs the long rebound and immediately signals for a time-out. Chaney sets up the Jack-in-the-Box, with Kilgore throwing long to Macon. Although everyone in the building knows the ball is going to Macon, he is still able to snare the long pass. As he comes down with the ball, Tech's Brian Oliver bumps Macon hard. The Yellow Jackets still have two fouls to give and it wouldn't have been a bad idea for them to foul Macon before he could shoot and force Temple to inbound the ball again. But the referee doesn't call anything.

Macon goes up for a shot and Oliver again makes contact, slashing him across the arm. Amazingly, the referee doesn't call a foul—despite the long scratch on Macon's arm—and Macon's shot misses.

"I was fouled, but I don't like to talk about the officiating," Macon says after the game, showing the scratch. "He got me good on the arm . . . after he bumped me."

The Owls play smart, aggressive basketball throughout, limiting Tech's "Lethal Weapon 3" attack of guards Kenny Anderson, Dennis Scott and Oliver (who average more than a combined seventy points a game) to forty-two points.

This marks the end of the Owls' grueling stretch of six games against Top 20 teams. Although they come within a few points of winning on four of the six occasions, the Owls lose all six, plus Causwell, and suddenly find themselves a disappointing 6–7.

"We had a chance to win," Chaney says after the game,

196

refusing to use the loss of Causwell as an excuse. "The only thing you can ask the kids to do is position you [to win]. I let them down. I didn't bring them through. . . . It was up to me as a coach to bring them through it, and I didn't do it. I just have to do a better job."

January 19

After the Georgia Tech game, the Owls flew straight to Pittsburgh for last night's game with Duquesne (a 67–43 win). This morning they take the first flight out of Pittsburgh and get back to Philadelphia early enough for a short practice before classes begin. This is the only chance they will have to get ready for Massachusetts tomorrow night at McGonigle in a very important Atlantic-10 game. Mass leads the league with a 6–1 record, followed by Temple at 5–1, and Rhode Island and Penn State at 4–2.

This morning, Chaney works on a new offensive set—the forty-one—which has Hodge down low and the other four players spread around the perimeter. After they're finished working on the new formation, Chaney calls the team together. He wants to talk about the events of the past week.

You should never lose by default. Too many people in this world lose by default. You know what that means? It means they don't show up. Not physically but mentally. I'm saying you have to put yourself in the game of life. There are thousands who are losing the game of life. There's no score sheet that tells you if you're winning or losing. The only person who knows is you.

I do the very best I can do by everybody here. Then somebody says, Well, you shouldn't have

recruited those guys, they don't belong in college. They say Duane didn't belong in college in the first place, that I knew he couldn't pass when I recruited him. There were hours and hours' worth of radio talk on your behalf this week. Those people said the school should have thrown him out long ago, but John Chaney kept his ass here to play basketball. Then the school does throw him out and shows integrity, because he didn't score what he was supposed to score and they say we used him.

The Causwell situation quickly became the hottest topic of discussion on WIP, an all-sports radio station, with many of the callers blasting Chaney. They say Chaney is a hypocrite, that he preaches education to the public but doesn't really care about his players and would bring anyone into his program if he could help win games, even if he isn't capable of doing college work. Causwell, they say, is a perfect example of someone who never should have been in college in the first place.

This goes on and on for a week, with all the people Chaney calls "closet racists" coming out of the woodwork to denounce Chaney and Temple. "I hear about all these people who go on the radio and say John Chaney is using people; he takes in kids he knows can't make it and on and on and on. When I hear this, I don't turn red. I turn *black!* Because all these issues—especially Prop forty-eight—are black issues. And the perception of people—although it's not true—is that Temple is a black school and a lot of people don't like that."

Chaney is particularly angry at one of WIP's hosts, whom he feels provided a platform for people to spew racist comments without challenging them or telling the real truth about what is going on at Temple. Two days ago Chaney was on WIP and called this person a "radio-racist" and threatened to punch him in the nose the next time he saw him.

"I'm not a racist," the host told me repeatedly when I saw him at a Temple game later in the season. This was one of only two Temple games he attended all season, and interestingly, he and Chaney have talked only twice in the eight seasons Chaney has been the Temple coach. "John just tries to intimidate people and I won't be intimidated."

It's impossible to say if this person is a racist. (Chaney doesn't want his name printed, saying he doesn't want to publicize and promote someone who uses controversy and racist remarks to boost ratings.) One thing is clear and that is this commentator loves controversy and is not above creating it to promote his show and himself. Not surprisingly, he hosts WIP's top-rated show. After Las Vegas—a team comprised almost entirely of inner-city black kids with a reputation as the bad boys of the college basketball—won the NCAA championship, he said, "I guess this proves you don't need any brains to win an NCAA championship." Is this a racist remark? Chaney thought it was. At the very least it's an incredibly insensitive thing to say.

"What he doesn't understand," Liacouris says of the announcer, "is that when you play with racial issues, you're playing with fire."

Because you're athletes, you're in a fishbowl. When you walk on a plane, are in the dorms, in a hotel, people know who you are. And people keep score and write down what you do. And people are going to carry that impression of what you are and who you are without ever having met you. It's like a fingerprint. It stays with you. You can't rub it off.

I don't like fighting windmills. I don't mind it

199

when I know I have a team of human beings that I like fighting for. You see, I brought every racist in this area out. Every bigot in this area—black and white—came out of the closet. Racism isn't just white. It exists in all races of people.

You've got to get in the race or you'll lose it by default. Every time someone calls your name, stand up. Never lose by default.

As Chaney finishes and the team meets at center court for a "team together," Causwell appears. This is the first time his former teammates have seen him since he left Atlanta. Everyone runs over to hug him. Hodge, in particular, is happy to see his buddy and calls an impromptu meeting for all the big men at the side of the court where they hug and talk and shoo away the guards every time they try to join in.

Later, in the office, Vreeswyk shows up. He's angry about all the things that have been said on the radio the past week. "I can't understand how [the radio host] could judge you without even knowing you," he says.

"The radio gives him the right to do that," Chaney answers.

"I'm gonna call him, I'm gonna straighten him out," Vreeswyk threatens.

"Don't worry about it, forget it," Chaney says. A minute later Vreeswyk weasels a tie from Chaney.

"I can't believe you gave him that tie, I wanted that one," Demopoulos says laughing. DiSangro comes in and pops on a tape of Massachusetts. Chaney, Demopoulos and Vreeswyk watch for a while, commenting from time to time on what they see.

It has been a week since the team left from the Vegas game for Atlanta and then Pittsburgh and everyone is anxious to get home. Maloney has already left and Demopoulos gets up to go while Chaney spends a few more minutes watching the tape. "I got to go home and play with Allie Wowie [his nickname for his daughter Alexandra]," Demopoulos says and a second later he's out the door.

Before he leaves, Chaney gets a call from Joe Robinson's mother, who thanks him for looking after her son and working with him to get his academic problems straightened out. After a week of listening to negative comments on the radio, Chaney is happy to hear from her. "This, getting a call from someone who really matters, makes up for all that other crap," Chaney says.

For the rest of the season, through the NBA draft and beyond, Causwell will be a frequent visitor in the basketball office. He's still part of the family even though he can't play. "I'm sure Coach was disappointed in me after he fought so hard against Prop forty-eight, but he's stood by me," Causwell says. "When I needed support and help, he was always there."

Although he is disappointed that he has let down Chaney and his teammates, Causwell says he is even more unhappy that he let himself down. "But I feel that I've learned something important," he says. "I learned that you have to take care of your own business. You can't wait around for things to just happen or for someone else to take care of you. It's up to you. I guess that's what coach was trying to tell us all along. I wish I learned it sooner."

After the college season ends, Causwell will solidify his position as a number one draft choice with outstanding performances in two NBA tryout camps and he is selected by Sacramento in the first round. In May, after passing his courses at Community College of Philadelphia, he'll apply for readmission to Temple and be accepted.

January 20

Temple and Massachusetts trade baskets for most of the first half. With 3:44 remaining and Temple up 32–30 and in possession of the ball, Kilgore picks up a technical for complaining to the referee. Massachusetts's Jim McCoy hits both free throws and then a ten-foot jumper from the left baseline for a 34–32 Massachusetts lead that reaches 37–32 at the half.

Chaney immediately takes Kilgore out of the game after the technical and just stares at him as he walks silently toward the bench. "If he would have said anything, any smart remark, I would have strangled him right there in front of all those people," Chaney says. "The police would have had to come and get me and take me away."

A highlight of the half are the antics of Massachusetts coach John Calipari, who does a great impression of a Mexican jumping bean. From the opening tap to the end of the half, Calipari is on his feet, often a foot or two onto the court, leaping up and down, exhorting and directing his team and working the officials.

Massachusetts scores the first six points of the second half for a 43–32 lead and Chaney decides to start pressing fullcourt. It works, and Temple starts scoring and cutting into the lead, finally going ahead 52–51 on a Kilgore lay-up. McCoy answers back for a 53–52 Massachusetts lead, but Hodge hits a short turnaround in the lane for a 54–53 Temple lead, and the Owls never trail the rest of the way. With thirty seconds to go and Temple up 80–69, Harper Williams goes over the top of Hodge and the referee calls a foul on the Massachusetts player. Hodge isn't satisfied with just getting the call and pushes Williams away. The referee correctly calls a technical on Hodge.

The Owls go on to win 86–69, taking over first place in

the conference with a 6–1 record (8–7 overall). Massachusetts falls to 6–2 (10–5). Macon leads Temple with twenty-five points, Hodge adds twenty-two and Kilgore eighteen plus a career-high thirteen rebounds. Harden also plays a solid game with a career-high fifteen points, seven assists and only one turnover.

But Chaney isn't happy with his team's play or the two technicals. With Kilgore sitting next to him, Chaney erupts while talking to the press. "I'm not too happy with my team. This is, perhaps, the worst team I've coached in my life. I can't coach a team that can't think. If you're brainless and spineless, I can't coach you. It's a terrible feeling to give instruction to youngsters who are not responding . . . for us to see that McCoy is an excellent shooter and not to go out and get him. I don't understand. Ask him [Kilgore] what's in his brain." With this said, Chaney walks out of the interview room, leaving Kilgore to fend for himself.

"Everything he says is correct. He's right," Kilgore says solemnly. "I got a technical that was really dumb on my part. But I'm learning. I'll get better and better as the year goes on."

It seems incredible that after last week's furor over Causwell's flunking out, Chaney would stand up in front of the press and call his players "brainless and spineless."

"Calling them brainless and spineless isn't dehumanizing, at least I don't think so, not in the athletic world," Chaney says. "My point is I've heard coaches say things worse than that. When you describe the behavior of an athlete, people outside athletics don't have a clue what you're talking about."

"But aren't you just giving all those radio racists out there more ammunition?" I ask.

"I can't sit here and separate those people out and figure

who's for me and who's against me and who's a racist or isn't a racist."

"And it's not embarrassing for them to be called brainless and spineless?"

"My team should never be embarrassed by anything I say. They know I'm talking about their behavior on the court, not their real personalities. What we as coaches often do is try to harness a youngster first, just like a scientist tries to harness energy. You have to harness energy before you can direct it. Sometimes the only way to do that is to strip a player of certain things, and one of the things you strip him of is having to be responsive to outsiders who really don't count. If you don't reach that stage, you can never direct a team. My players must look only to me and my coaches for what they think is right. They must recognize we are offering some kind of direction in terms of their play on the floor and in terms of their personalities."

January 21

When Chaney arrives at practice, he summons Kilgore and Hodge and the three go to his office for close to an hour, while Maloney runs practice. Chaney is disappointed in their attitude on the court and the technicals they picked up last night. He stresses that they are part of a team and are hurting their teammates with their antics. "You have a right to go off in the street by yourself and put your head down on the curb and let a car run over it, but on the basketball court you don't have the right to pick up a technical and ask your teammates to overcome that."

When the meeting is over, Chaney returns to practice and talks to the team about taking the right shots.

204

You can't win if you don't use this [he points to his head]. Teams that don't use their heads end up failures. If you say to yourself you're a failure, it becomes a noun. You become a failure. Shooting and missing the right shot isn't failing. But when you start to lose here, inside, I can't deal with that. I can't coach guys who don't think. Everything you did last night, all those points and rebounds, went for naught [he says to Kilgore].

We run into a box-and-one on Mark or a triangle-and-two every game. We should be able to feed off that. You other three [Kilgore, Strickland and Harden] should feed off that. You say there's Mark, there's Donald, everyone's on them, that leaves me free. Anywhere I went—Rhode Island, Massachusetts, Duquesne—I would walk right into the town and tell everyone where to find Mark and Donald. I'd say, "I know you're looking for them, let me help you find them." I would slip out from the hotel and go find the other coach and tell him what side Donald plays on and tell him what Mark does on the court. And if I couldn't find him, I'd send a note. Then I would feed off them.

When the point guard drives down the middle, he flattens out the entire offense. Who drove to the basket last night from the position of point guard and we wind up giving up an easy basket?

"Mark [Macon]," says Maloney. "And they got an easy basket."

They got an easy basket all because you destroyed floor balance. I put you back in [he says to Harden], and you did the right thing. You were like a windshield wiper [on offense]. You went

205

back and forth [around the perimeter] controlling
the ball. Every time they got the ball, you were
back. That's Temple basketball. That's the way
you play. With balance. Not too much milk. A
little of this, a little of that. A little sugar, a little
honey. A little dab will do ya.

What you did last was worth twelve points [he
says to Kilgore]. Then afterwards somebody says,
Why couldn't you say something nice about him
instead of calling him brainless and spineless? We
had the ball in our hands under their basket and
you're talking to the official and get a technical.
What did you say?

"I forget," Kilgore says.

You got to remember, or I'll think you're stupid.
Did you say something about his mother? I was
ready to choke you and kill you. One word from
your liver lips and I would have bludgeoned you
to death. Ernest, do you think that would have
been fair?

"No," Ernest says.

I know you're trying to protect these boys, Ernest.
But when they're wrong, they're wrong. What's
your sign, Kilgore, the Ram?

"No, Taurus. The Bull."

Same thing. They both got horns on their heads.
You know why the Lord put horns on their heads?
So they could ram into things. Any type of human
being that keeps ramming his head into walls all
the time, there has to be something wrong with

206

him. How about you [to Harden], what sign are
you?

"Taurus."

See, they both have hard heads. You're two
peas-in-the-pod. You [Harden] are slowly coming
out of it, but I still can't trust you.

January 24

With eight minutes to go in the first half of Temple's
game with Rhode Island, Causwell shows up and stands,
partially hidden, in the corridor to the side of the Temple
bench. Just before the start of the second half, the public-
address announcer says that Causwell is in attendance. He
receives a standing ovation.

Temple tops the Rams 81–70, despite an off night for
Macon. Still in the throes of a shooting slump, he hits just
five of twenty-five shots for twelve points. "What a hor-
rible night for Mark Macon," Chaney says afterward.
"But out of a bad situation comes something good." The
good was the play of Hodge, who has twenty-eight points
on twelve of seventeen shooting and nineteen rebounds,
ten offensive. Strickland also has a nice game, with ten
rebounds and nine points, and Kilgore adds sixteen.

The press wants to know what's the matter with
Macon; he is averaging 19.4 a game, but his shooting
percentage after tonight's game is down to .386 percent.
Chaney says there's nothing wrong and he's not worried.
"You start tampering with something that doesn't need
fixing and there's a strong possibility you'll get it com-
pletely out of whack and never get it back in shape again.
Because this [he points to his head] is what you're really

tampering with. We're concerned with his patience and him getting his feet underneath his shot. I've seen him go through stretches like this before. But he has a license to shoot a thousand shots a game. In fact, he should have shot more tonight. I'd much rather one of my better players shoot bad shots than have a lesser player shoot good shots. Because he'll keep putting pressure on that other team and sooner or later he'll get out of it."

True to his word, Chaney has not been tampering with Macon in practice. Maloney will work with him a little, telling Macon to slow down as he makes his move to the basket and to get his feet under him before he goes up. By getting his feet under him, Maloney means that Macon should be square to the basket, be balanced when he goes up for his shot and jump straight up.

As tough and focused as he is, Macon admits that he is getting a little frustrated. "I guess I got a little down on myself," he says later. "I wanted to do so good that I tried too hard and did bad. Coach hasn't said much. He doesn't try to get into my head because he knows what it can do to a person's confidence. He gives me confidence 'cause the only time he ever really says anything is when I stop shooting. He says I need to take twenty shots a game."

January 31

Two different Temple teams play at St. Joseph's tonight. The first stumbles and bumbles their way through the first half, shooting twelve for thirty-three, committing six turnovers and trails 38–30 at the half. A new team takes the court to start the second half and promptly uses a pressing, tenacious defense to go on an amazing 30–2 run in the first eight minutes of the half to take a 60–40 lead on their way to a 78–63 win.

Macon scores twenty-eight, Hodge and Kilgore each add seventeen.

"We knew it was coming," St. Joe's coach Jim Boyle, says of the Owls' press to start the second half. "Knowing it and doing something about it are two different things."

At the press conference after the game, reporters ask Macon about the big second-half run. "When you sow a good seed, you get corn," Macon says. He pauses for a second and then laughs. "I'm sorry. I know I sound just like Coach."

8

Heads You Win, Tails You Lose

February 1

We aren't going to go anyplace unless you start thinking. Heads you win, tails you lose. Anytime I've won, it's because I had players who were smart.

Chaney isn't happy with Harden's play, especially his decision-making ability. He uses one play from last night's game to illustrate. After Temple raced to a 60–40 lead, St. Joe's came back to cut the margin to 62–50. One of the key plays during this stretch was when Harden, fighting to bring the ball up against defensive pressure, tossed a pass to Kilgore and then proceeded to run into his teammate, causing a turnover.

That was one of the greatest plays I've ever seen. I want you [Harden] to practice that. I was waiting

for the official to do this [he crosses his arms as if calling an intentional foul]. A flagrant foul on Michael, Mik go to the line for two shots. If they would have blown their whistles and called a foul on you, then I would have seen everything in a basketball game. That would have meant I could make my exit, never, ever to return.

I could see one time when someone made a bad pass to you [he says to Harden]. You jumped up and tapped it over to someone else, which meant the difference between them intercepting. If you can see that, you have the ability to see more.

If we have to force-feed you as a team, if we have to open up your mouth, put the food in your mouth, and push your stomach in and out for you to digest it, we can't win. You just can't win if you don't play with your heads. Heads you win, tails you lose. If you play with your heads you win. If you play with your ass you lose.

February 6

Chaney thinks he's supposed to attend the Markward Club luncheon today, but Sonny Hill shows up at the office and tells him it's not until tomorrow. "Shit, you mean I got dressed up for nothing?" asks Chaney, who's in a suit.

Mike Missanelli, the *Philadelphia Inquirer*'s college basketball writer, is also in the office—waiting to meet with Causwell—and a discussion on basketball naturally breaks out. Hill (a former star at Northeast High School who played with and against Chaney in various summer leagues and in the Eastern Pro League) is a world-class talker who can keep up with Chaney when discussing the game.

Missanelli wants to know why Temple doesn't try to play a more up-tempo style of play. Not all the time, but sometimes. After all, he says, you have the talent, and he uses Strickland as an example of a player who can run.

"Look at the Illinois game," Chaney begins. "We could have busted the game wide open. Strick steals the ball twice in a row. He's out on a break. He took off a mile from the basket, loses the ball, picks up a foul. Knocked a guy down. Another time he did a crossover dribble in the middle and they took it off him. So now you say, 'Hey, why don't you run more?' You can't have it both ways. If you have the athletes and the subs to come in and replace them, maybe then you can take the reins off your team. Illinois has twelve Parade All-Americans on that team. Look at a Syrcause or a Las Vegas. They can do whatever they want. Fouls don't mean anything to them. I must manage my fouls. Another aspect of the game most people don't understand is floor balance. That prevents easy baskets on the other end."

"In a whole season, John's teams give up very few easy baskets," Hill says.

"So if you lose floor balance you destroy your chances of stopping easy baskets," Chaney continues. "The reasons I have for this are not popular reasons, not acceptable to a lot of people. A lot of people would like to see us do all kinds of monkeyshines. I'm not that kind of coach and I don't think I would be even if I had super talent on the floor. I would still like to have all the elements on the floor and I would want to control those elements."

"I agree with what you're saying," says Missanelli, who still clings to his belief that Temple should run more. "But I just think you should be able to get a few more easy buckets on transition."

"That could happen next year," Hill says. "When you have Macon, Harden and Kilgore with more experience, and you add in a Jonathan Haynes, John will have five mobile ball-handling players and he can begin to do more things because he can entrust the ball to the hands of more than one or two people. And that can create a break situation. We've talked about this before, and, every time we agree, those elements are not in place now."

"Pick any team that likes to run," Chaney continues. "The Lakers. They say we're gonna run every time, whether the other team makes it or misses it. But guess who they don't fast break on? The Boston Celtics. Not at all. Now you tell me why?"

"They can't outrebound them," Missanelli answers.

"That's not the reason," Hill says.

At this point I can't help jumping in. After four months with Chaney I know it cold. "Floor balance."

"That's right," Chaney says. "You take the game we played Las Vegas. Did anybody get any easy baskets? When you see us play them, how many games are in the sixties and seventies? How many easy baskets did they get?"

"Tell him where floor balance comes from," Hill says.

"It comes from the kind of offense you run. If you run an offense that's flat, you don't have floor balance. You know why Villanova beat Georgetown that year [for the 1985 national championship]? Floor balance."

"People get caught up in making things difficult, but's it's really simple," Hill says. "When I had John and Red [Auerbach] on my show [Hill hosts a weekly basketball show on WIP], what did Red say about the game? He said it's still the same fundamentals. You see a coach call time-out and four or five guys get together and discuss and computerize what they're going to tell their kids. John taught me, the way you form your team from October 15

213

is the way your team is gonna be. Because if you mess around and change it two or three times, then they don't know where you're coming from. The game itself is a simple game."

The conversation moves on to a discussion of Chaney.

"You know that most people in this city who cover [Temple] don't have a personal dialogue with John," Hill says to Missanelli. "But you know him. You come in and kibitz. You know what he's all about."

"A guy like Coach is open, easy to talk to," Missanelli says.

"You can't tell people that," Hill says laughing. "People think he's the boogeyman, the worst man in the world. They think he's crazy, volatile—which he is—but they don't understand that all that goes with the turf. Being someone who didn't get an equal opportunity, being someone who came late into coaching at this level, someone who never got the cream of the crop. If you don't deal with these kids here with discipline, if you don't get into their face, they're lost. Mik Kilgore, with that short fuse of his, if you don't stay on him constantly, it's a real problem. So you have to bring to these kids a certain demeanor. If you're dealing with blue-chip kids, you can sit back and cross your legs. They'll go to class every day and graduate. These kids here come from tough backgrounds. And for that radio racist to jump all over these kids and this school and John . . ."

Chaney's heard enough compliments for one day, so he turns the tables on Hill, telling Missanelli that Hill kept a whole generation of big men in this city from developing into great players. "He ruined their lives," Chaney says, laughing. "He never passed them the ball. He shot thirty-five times a game. Even when he gave it to them, he'd run right back and grab it from them and tell them to set screens."

"Everyone had a role in those days," Hill says, defending himself. "There was one shooter per team, sometimes two. Everyone else was a role player. I was good for thirty or forty a game."

"Shots or points?" I ask.

"Both," Hill answers and Chaney cracks up. "I could take ninety percent of the people off the dribble and get my shot off. John had the ability to play defense and he had a theory then that no one else had. He invented playing the shooting hand. It was something he learned innately. When you played against John, it was life and death. Even if I scored thirty points, I had to work so hard to score them. That's the kind of player he was. Guy Rodgers was one of the greatest ball-handlers of all times. That's a proven fact. And John was on a level with him. He just didn't get the opportunity [to play in the NBA]."

"Guy was lucky," Chaney adds. "He came out just when it was starting to open up. But nobody took the ball off of us. We were money in the bank. These kids today, they don't know how important the ball is."

"We didn't know why, but we knew someone on every team had to take care of the ball," Hill says. "His value was to run that ball club."

"Now they're trying to be a jack-of-all-trades," Chaney says. "But they're the master of none."

Causwell shows up at this point. He's late for his meeting with Missanelli, for which Chaney gives him hell. "Weren't you supposed to be here an hour ago?" Chaney asks. Causwell can only shrug. "I don't want none of your excuses; you apologize to him."

After Chaney finishes chastising Causwell, they talk about agents. "Before you make a final decision," Chaney says, "I want you to come and sit down and tell me why. Let me know what kind of instrument you're using to make your decision. I'm not going to tell you who to pick, I just want to know why you're picking them."

February 7

Today is the correct day for the Markward Club luncheon and Chaney makes it. He doesn't like to give speeches, but for the Markward Club he makes an exception. It has been around for as long as Chaney can remember and, in fact, was the organization that honored him back in 1951 as the MVP of the Public League. He still has the watch they awarded him and brings it with him today. After lunch, Chaney steps up to the podium.

I recently saw an article in the NCAA newsletter. The Secretary of Education made it very clear that we must take a strong look at educating minorities, at educating the people that need it the most, so that a youngster who participates in the game of life has an equal chance. If you don't give youngsters an equal chance, believe me, they won't have an equal future. The only chance we have is to constantly barrage people, focus in on our youth, and hopefully overcome what is a big problem in all of our lives today. While we sit in our own little comfort zone, whatever it might be—money or stature—we cannot divorce ourselves from those who need a chance.

Those of you that help people, the people in the Sonny Hill League that give throughout the year and never stop, are very special. And that's why it's very special for me to come here. Some of you here saw something special in me and gave me this watch. Basketball changed my life. It saved my life. And that's why I say education saves lives. Basketball gave me an education. You guys here [the high school players being honored] will keep playing, but one day you'll have to move on

and get a job and have a family. What you must pass on to that family is that we don't have to have money, we don't have to be rich to impart values. We have to be concerned about the total development of young people and make sure we can change the odds for young people.

February 11

The area of athletics is very closely related to war, according to Chaney.

A good example is today's game, an 83–82 triple-overtime win at Massachusetts. The contest is closer to a battle than a basketball game and features a near riot after Chaney and Massachusetts coach Calipari get into a brief shoving match.

The Curry Hicks Cage, completed in 1931, is one of the oldest arenas in the country and the 4,000 fans sit right on top of the court. Throughout the game the fans chanted, "Rage in the Cage!" and waved pom-poms, some just inches behind Chaney's head. The Minutemen's pep band was also right behind the Temple bench and took delight in drowning out Chaney as he tried to instruct his players during time-outs.

With just over four minutes remaining and the score tied at 64, Temple has possession of the ball. Calipari, on his feet and at the edge of the court as he has been throughout the game, urges the crowd on, and they respond, somehow increasing the decibel level another notch. As the 45-second clock winds down, Temple keeps looking for an open shot. Finally with the clock approaching zero, Macon takes a pass just outside the three-point line, turns, and fires up a desperate shot. Whether the shot beat the 45-second buzzer is anybody's guess; the noise from the crowd drowns out the horn. The shot is short of the basket, but Kilgore alertly grabs the air-ball and puts it in the basket for what appears to be a 66–64 Temple lead.

At this point Calipari goes berserk. First he runs over to the scorer's table, where he shouts something at the timekeeper, who in turn stops the clock and blows the horn. Calipari then runs onto the court and gets the attention of the officials, who didn't hear the horn, and they stop the game.

According to NCAA rules, all Macon had to do was get the shot off before the clock expired. If he did, the ball was alive and Kilgore had every right to grab it and score. This rule differs from the NBA, where the shot would have had to hit the rim for it to be in play.

The rules also state that Calipari cannot run over to the timekeeper to have him stop the clock or run onto the court to have the officials stop the game. What he could have done was have his team call an immediate time-out and then huddle with the referees to discuss the play and possibly rectify a correctable error, if it was determined that Macon's shot was released after the clock had expired.

Eventually the officals do meet with the timekeeper. After a few minutes they walk away from the scorer's table, confer with Calipari, then walk down to talk to Chaney. "When the ref came over, he said, 'Coach, you're not gonna like this,' " Chaney says. "They said the time keeper said the shot was no good. Now, first of all, I don't know what question they asked the timekeeper. If he went over and asked if the shot was good, that's an assumption that he knows the rule correctly. Maybe he didn't."

The official, with his arm around Chaney, continues to explain his decision. Calipari walks over from his bench into the huddle with Chaney and the official. Words are exchanged, and suddenly, Chaney pushes Calipari and attempts to go after him. Maloney and several Temple players jump between the two coaches and restrain Chaney.

"Here he has already handled the timekeeper and had his meeting with the officials, and now he wants to come down and handle my meeting with the officials," Chaney says. "I didn't see him until he was right on top of me, pointing his finger and saying something. I was outraged. I said, 'Get the hell out of my huddle,' and then I grabbed him across the throat or maybe the shoulder and pushed him."

"He was talking to the officials and I wanted to know what was going on," Calipari says after the game. "[Chaney] said, 'Get outta here,' and I said, 'No way.' I said, 'You're not talking to these guys unless I'm here.' He said something, and I said something back. He's competitive, I'm competitive. None of that stuff carries on. I have the utmost respect for him as a man, a coach and a person. It's over."

After Chaney pushes Calipari, the fans begin throwing things onto the floor and it looks like a riot is ready to break out. Calipari rushes over, grabs the microphone from the public-address announcer and starts screaming, "Stop! Stop! Stop! Cheer for us, not against them. If anyone throws anything, drag them out."

The uproar finally dies down and the game continues. With 1:45 remaining in regulation, Macon draws a foul as he drives to the basket. He makes both to give Temple a 69–66 lead. Macon is in the midst of a brilliant thirty-five point game, which includes several big baskets in the second half. However, he has four fouls. With a minute remaining, William Herndon hits one of two free throws to tie the game at 69. Neither team can score and the game heads into the first overtime.

Less than a minute into the first overtime, Macon commits his fifth foul and is out. About the same time, Rob Jones, the Owls' manager, tells one of the coaches that unless he takes Lovelace to the airport now, he'll miss the last flight back to Philadelphia, and that means he'll miss classes tomorrow. "Take him," Chaney tells Jones and they leave.

Each team can manage only two points in the first overtime, forcing a second five-minute period. With four seconds remaining in the second overtime, Kilgore drives and shoots, but misses. He grabs the rebound and shoots again. He misses, but the referee signals a foul on Harper Williams. The clock is on 0:00, but once again the noise of the crowd has made it impossible for the referees to hear it. After conferring with the timekeeper, the officials reverse their decision, saying the foul occurred after the shot. Television replays show that Williams fouled Kilgore with one second remaining. Chaney argues, but to no avail.

With just under two minutes left in the third overtime, Harden hits one of two free throws to draw Temple to 80–78. On Massachusetts's next possession, Strickland comes up with a steal and fires a long pass to Hodge, who fumbles the ball and misses an attempt at a backward dunk. Hodge comes up with the rebound and is fouled as he goes back up. He makes both and the game is knotted at 80 with 1:08 remaining. With :32 to go, Randolph fouls Rafer Giles, who hits both for an 82–80 Massachusetts lead. After a Temple miss, Kilgore strips Herndon of the ball and Harden hits a big three-pointer to give Temple an 83–82 lead.

"We were just about at the airport when [Harden] made that shot," Lovelace says. "I just about jumped out of the car I was so excited."

On their next possession, Massachusetts misses and Strickland grabs the rebound. He's fouled immediately but misses the front end of a one-and-one with five sec-

220

onds to go. Massachusetts gets the rebound and hustles downcourt, calling a time-out with one second remaining after they get the ball past midcourt. Tony Barbee misses a desperation shot at the buzzer and the game is finally over.

The win raises Temple's Atlantic-10 record to 11–2 (13–8 overall) and keeps the Owls ahead of Penn State (9–3).

"I thought it was extraordinary what they did after Mark left the game," Chaney says. "Michael Harden steps up and takes the big shot, and everybody else—Shoun and Strickland—stayed in their room and did what they had to."

A few days later, in the coaches' office after practice, the Massachusetts game is brought up for discussion.

"If I had known what you knew," Chaney says to Maloney, "I might have killed [Calipari]. I didn't know that he had run over and had the timekeeper stop the clock. I was only mad because he tried to get into my huddle."

"I think you're losing a step, Coach," Maloney says. "You used to be able to get the other coach in a headlock."

"You dirty dog," Chaney says laughing.

"What would have happened if they hadn't held you back?" I ask.

"I don't know, I may have punched him," Chaney says. "I'm a street fighter. I was outraged and upset, emotionally drained, frustrated, crazy. Think of any word you can think of, and that was me wrapped up in a bundle. So I'm capable of being anything. A gorilla. An asshole. A person who is afraid. I'm capable of every emotion at that point."

"But there could have been a riot," I continue. "How could you almost let that happen?" "Maybe I shouldn't be a coach," Chaney says. "How come presidents allow wars to go on? So, just like a president, I'm capable of

221

starting a war. When they hired me, they knew they might be hiring a loose cannon."

"You can't be defending your actions?"

"No, I'm not. I was wrong. I admit that. But I'm a human being and that means I'm prone to error. I'm prone to every emotion under the sun. I'm a person who can be out of control. It's only those who sit on the outside and think everyone else should be full of peace and love that don't understand. I'd like to have a match to put under their asses and see if they would sit there and burn up or get up and fight."

"But what kind of example is this sending to your players, especially when you tell them they have to control their emotions on the court?"

Demopoulos interrupts. "The test of a coach is how the kids act. They all acted very responsibly."

"I think they acted very well," Chaney says. "They restrained me. People were throwing cups of water and ice, and my players didn't go up into the stands after them. And I do not incite my fans here [at McGonigle]. I don't stand up and wave towels and try to create that kind of atmosphere. I do not put my band behind the other team. I do not put rowdy fans behind the other team. But, I can get out of control. Athletics are very closely related to war and when there is opposition, you try to overcome that opposition."

"Come on," I interrupted. "Basketball isn't war. It's a sport. It's a game."

"You can use any term you want, but athletics are combative. The whole concept of sports is contradictory. In football you ask someone to go out and hit someone as hard as they can and possibly knock them out of the game and then you're supposed to be a nice guy and help them up. What I'm saying is the concept of sports is contradictory and I have to operate within that. I'm not going to sit here and spit in your face and tell you that it's raining.

Other people will tell you no, that sports aren't like war. But then, when you're not looking, that same guy puts a banana peel under your foot or drops a hand grenade on you when you're sleeping. I play within the rules, I don't cheat and I don't want to see anyone get hurt."

February 13

The Owls beat Penn State at McGonigle 61–53 tonight to raise their Atlantic-10 record to 12–2, putting them in the driver's seat for the regular season championship. The second-place Nittany Lions drop to 9–4.

With nine minutes remaining in the game and Temple clinging to a 46–43 lead, Macon takes over. In the next minute he posts up and scores, hits a jumper, drives and scores and Temple's up 52–43 and on their way to a win.

Hodge leads all scorers with seventeen, Macon adds fifteen and Kilgore and Strickland twelve each. Strickland also grabs twelve rebounds and blocks four shots. However, he does pick up a technical foul in the first half for saying something to the referee after he got fouled going for an offensive rebound. But Chaney isn't that upset with Strickland. "It showed he has some fire inside," Chaney says. "He's a very shy person and he's just starting to feel his oats and assert himself. I can teach him to control himself easier than trying to build a fire inside him."

Macon and Chaney enter the interview room together, but Macon walks up to the podium first. "I'll be the coach tonight," Macon jokes. Someone asks about the Massachusetts game and the fact that the team was still able to win after he fouled out. Macon starts talking about the importance of each element on the team. "When you take the chicken out of the stew," he says, trying a Chaneylike

223

analogy, "you just have to throw in more carrots and garlic."

Chaney jumps up from his seat. "What the hell are you talking about?"

"That's my mom's recipe for chicken stew."

"It sounds more like possum stew to me. You don't know nothing about cooking. Now sit down." With that Chaney takes over the press conference.

Harden has had an off night, hitting only one of nine shots—all from three-point range—for a total of five points. Plus, Chaney isn't happy with the way he ran the team. In the office after the game, Chaney and Demopoulos argue about whether or not Harden took good shots. Demopoulos says he did, that they were in rhythm with the offense. Of course, Chaney disagrees. The argument centers around the last four minutes of the first half, when Conic came in to replace Macon, who had just picked up his second foul. Temple scored only one basket the rest of the half—by Hodge, inside—and Harden missed two three-pointers.

"I don't agree," Demopoulos says. "I don't think the shots he took were bad shots."

"You may not agree with me, but that's the way I coach basketball."

"I'll tell you what would happen," Demopoulos goes on. "If he doesn't take that shot, you'll say he has to take that shot."

"No I wouldn't," Chaney counters and he's starting to get loud. "It goes back to what I've been saying all along. I don't have players who have a feel for the game. If you have a feel for the game you don't take that shot."

Demopoulos holds his ground. "I can see coming down on a fast break and firing one up, or firing one up before we went through the pattern, but those shots tonight were good shots."

"For a point guard to put himself in a position where he's suddenly flailing up shots is no good," Chaney says. "He could be wide open, but he has to keep working the clock and the offense and get everyone else involved. What I'm saying is, if you look at basketball in terms of one guy having an asterisk next to his name saying he is the point guard, then he can't be throwing his hat in the ring along with Mark Macon and Mik Kilgore. Mark can afford to throw up bad shots. So can Mik. The point guard can never force up a bad shot. He must have a feel for the game. My point is, even if he hits the shot, we have a continuation of us running up and down the floor fast, when we want to slow the game down and use the clock because Mark isn't in there.

"Donald said to me after the game, he was never so tired as he was tonight. He apologized, he thought he gave a bad effort. My point is we can't have a guy like him running from foul line to foul line. The point guard has to stop, wait for Donald, and say, 'Donald, go in there.' Donald goes into the pivot, he throws it to him, the point guard's man drops to help out and Donald kicks it back out. Bap, that's a good shot. A structured shot. We might get a rebound out of it if he misses 'cause we have our big man working for us. That's what I mean by having a feel for the game."

February 14

Chaney is still upset with the way Harden orchestrated the game last night. Point-guard play is the topic of his lecture.

A basketball game has a kind of tempo to it and the only person who can regulate it is the point guard. If you don't understand that, we will never get there as a team. For instance, just before the half, when I took Mark out because he had two fouls, we were still going up and down the floor fast. We were lucky we didn't go off the floor down by ten. Because the pace was not ours. And the only person responsible for that is the maestro, the conductor, the point guard.

The point guard doesn't get in the race of seeing how many points he can score. I call it spitting in the wind when a guy doesn't have a feel for the game. You have to know who to get the ball to and when. If the wrong guy is going to shoot the wrong shot at the wrong time, we're going to lose. How many times do you think Donald will go up and down the floor, from foul line to foul line, and never see the ball, before he stops running? But guess what? You give a big man the ball and he's not tired anymore. Ever see a man on payday, when he gets his check? He could be sick all week, but Friday rolls around and he's there.

It's like Mark [Macon] said last night. If you have chicken stew, but no chicken in it, it's not chicken stew. I don't coach basketball, I coach elements. You can have great athletes on your team, but if the right elements aren't there, you're not going to win. So each player should take pride in what he is and not compete with each other.

Harden was a great high school player. He averaged twenty-five points, ten assists, five rebounds and five steals a game his senior season at Southern Lab High (Louisiana) and led his team to the state championship. "I was a totally different player than I am now," Harden says. "I was a slasher. We pressed a lot and ran a lot and I had a license to take control of the game."

Despite his style of play, Chaney thought he saw in Harden a player whom he could harness and control and develop into a great point guard. "Everyone told me I should go somewhere that played up-tempo. But I chose Temple because of Coach. I believed in him, that he could take me to a higher level. Everyone else was offering me things, telling me what they could do for me and my family. But I had a lot of friends that played college ball and I saw how these coaches used 'em and didn't care about them. Coach was different."

Harden was a Prop 48 casualty during the 1987–88 season. While Hodge, Strickland and Lovelace had one another for support in 1988–89, when all three had to sit out, Harden was alone and far from home. He is a very intelligent, sensitive young man who comes from a strong, loving family. "Once he came to one of our practices and sat in the stands and there were tears in his eyes," Chaney says.

As the Owls kept winning that year, Harden became more and more depressed. "I tried to work out on my own, but I lost all my incentive," he says. "I know my ball-handling skills deteriorated and my game still isn't back to where it used to be."

"I learned from watching and playing with Terence [Stansbury] for a year and Howie [Evans] learned by playing with me," Blackwell says. "What has made it hard for Michael is he had to come in fresh, after sitting out a year. He didn't have an idea what Coach wanted, or when to step off. Now it's to the point where he's trying to do everything exactly the way Coach tells him. He's becoming like a robot. He hasn't learned when and where to do things on his own or when to take chances and not worry about Coach yelling at him."

Harden will play well for a game or two and then have

an off night. Instead of just shrugging it off and coming back harder the next night, he gets discouraged and down on himself. And the more Chaney yells at him, the worse it seems to get. His statistics are solid—7.1 points, 5.1 assists and 1.6 turnovers a game—but he has yet to completely grasp what Chaney means when he talks about tempo and controlling the game. Harden still wants to run more and penetrate to the basket.

"I try not to let [Chaney's yelling] get to me, but it does," Harden says. "He's constantly coming at me. If I make a turnover, it's like 'oooh, he did a bad thing.' But basketball is a game of mistakes. If the point guard has the ball most of the time, he's going to make the most mistakes. I love Coach and try my hardest for him, but sometimes it gets hard. He says he's teaching us about life and how to be a man and I try to listen and develop into a man."

Harden is doing well in school, gets along well with his teammates and says he is starting to develop into a Temple point guard. Still, he is haunted by the question of whether or not Temple is the best school for him. "I'm glad I came here because I love my teammates and we have a great time together. But sometimes I question the system and I wonder how I would have done if I went somewhere else, somewhere that played more my style. But I'm not bitter. I trust in God and I pray for all the guys on the team and all the coaches."

February 20

Before Chaney arrives at practice, Maloney talks to the guards. "As soon as [the other team] went for Mark, I'd light 'em up." From just outside the three-point lines he fires up a shot. Swish. The ball rolls back to him and he

228

takes another. Swish. Maloney gives the players a little wink.

When Chaney calls his players together, he talks about Villanova, whom the Owls play tomorrow night at home. Both teams are badly in need of a win to cement their chances for an NCAA at-large bid if they don't win their respective conferences. Temple is currently 15–8, and the Wildcats are 15–11. After he spends a half hour telling his players about Villanova, the Owls begin scrimmaging. After a few times up and down the court, Chaney stops practice and addresses the team again.

There are two things you must have to be good in this business. In basketball or in any sport. Fear and anger. Fear says I will not leave any stone unturned. I will remember all of the things that I have to remember. Fear opens your eyes to what you must overcome. Anger says how I'm going to play the game: tough and mean. So fear and anger work together. You don't go out overconfident. Because overconfidence is close to being blind.

In the huddle after practice, Chaney discusses another important topic: cheating. At this moment, several schools are being accused of possible NCAA rules violations.

One of the things that is devastating a number of teams right now is cheating. Sooner or later, when someone cheats, it devastates an entire program. We played Illinois this year. It's a shame that those people there on that club took whatever [money] was given to them [the program is currently under investigation for paying players to attend Illinois]. They have devastated an entire program. All of the incoming recruits are hurt, the

students are hurt, the fans are hurt. They could be hurt for years. Just like Kentucky [which is currently on probation]. Because they accepted money and cars. How would you like to have your whole season wiped out because of something like that?

In the office after practice, the three coaches talk about some of the programs currently under investigation.

"The two conferences they always talk about as being so great are the ACC and Big Ten," Demopoulos says. "And those are the guys who are always getting caught breaking the rules."

"The truth is never brought out," Chaney says. "The system perpetuates itself. All these announcers on television say so-and-so is such a great coach and not one says he's a great coach because he has bought all these players. We continue to perpetuate this type of thinking, that a guy's a great coach because he has great players and wins. Recognition is never given to a coach who is honest and decent and works hard and gets the most out of his players."

"But they say nowadays the most important aspect of coaching is recruiting," Maloney says. "According to Vitale, recruiting comes first, then communicating with your kids, and third is Xs and Os."

"That shit irks me," Chaney says, "A guy who has fifteen All-Americans on his bench doesn't have to be a good coach to go out and win. It's like in horse racing. A great jockey doesn't ride a jackass. He goes out and gets Seattle Slew."

"That's why people who are bad coaches go out and cheat to get good players," Maloney says.

"But those announcers don't say that," Chaney says, his voice rising. "That's why I say [Princeton's] Pete Carril is a great coach. Then people turn around and say, 'I wonder what he would do if he had great players?' They always look for another angle, a way to tear him down."

"You know who they used to say that about?" Maloney asks. "Bobby Knight when he was at Army. They said when he got to Indiana he'd never be able to treat players like he did at Army."

"Bobby Knight can coach," Chaney says. "He showed that at Army when he took a bunch of nobodies and won a ton of games. He made a fire without a match."

"If you're a good recruiter," Maloney says, "you can be in this business a long time and nobody will ever know you were a bad coach."

Whereas Chaney and Maloney seem in agreement that a coach should be judged by how he molds and shapes the players he has, Demopoulos has a different idea.

"The definition of a good coach in college basketball today is being a good recruiter," Demopoulos says.

"That's not my definition," Chaney says.

"But you've always said the most important element was having good players," Demopoulos says.

"That's true, but that's not the measuring stick I use to judge whether or not someone is a good coach. It's the wrong measurement. I'm not saying I don't do that [recruiting] job. We have to do that job. I just don't think it's the right criterion for judging a coach. [Recruiting] is something I have to do, but that doesn't mean I have to like it."

In fact, Chaney hates recruiting. But in order for Temple to land the type of players Chaney needs to become a national power, he, Maloney and Demopoulos have to travel the country trying to persuade seventeen-year-old kids to come to Temple. According to Chaney, recruiting is done on two levels. The top programs in the country—schools like North Carolina, Duke, Syracuse or George-

231

town—don't recruit; they select the cream of the crop. This leaves the real job of recruiting to the coaches for teams that aren't considered the elite programs.

For example, on the plane ride back from a recruiting trip, Chaney and Demopoulos read an article that said one of the most highly recruited big men in the country just signed with an ACC school. "The reason he gave for picking that school was that they had sent something like fifteen or sixteen players to the pros in the last ten years," Chaney says. "Dean and I figured it out and came up with the fact that of those fifteen players, eleven had left school early without a degree. And this is a school with a good reputation. What if Temple had all these players leaving without degrees?"

Temple is a hard sell. The Owls aren't in a big-time conference that gets a lot of television exposure; they don't have a big arena; and the school is located in the middle of one of the worst sections of Philadelphia. "The only thing we have is Coach," Demopoulos says. Despite these handicaps, Chaney has been able to sign players like Macon, Hodge and Haynes. And he's done it the hard way—without cheating.

Chaney and Demopoulos continue their argument about what constitutes a good coach, while Maloney discreetly leaves the room. Once these two get going, he has learned that the best place to be is somewhere else.

"Who do you think is the best coach in the Big East?" Demopoulos asks.

"Rollie Massamino," Chaney answers, naming the Villanova coach.

"What's your definition of 'best coach,' because I don't know right now," Demopoulos says.

"His overall ability to—"

"Run a program," Demopoulos interrupts.

"No, his overall philosophy and strategy."

"But what if he had terrible players and never won a

232

game?" Demopoulos asks. "What if his players lost the ball every time and never got it past midcourt?"

"I would still be able to see his strategy."

"How can you see this if he has terrible players that can't do anything?" Demopoulos asks.

"I can tell by the direction they're going. Maybe his players don't have the ability, but I can see that he's trying to teach them. I can see if the point guard tries to protect the ball, if they try to get the ball to the right people, or play together on defense even if they get beat. John Wooden said very clearly that you can be a great coach and still lose. I've lectured on that. Some of the best coaches in the country are losing."

"So that's your definition of a great coach?"

"Yes," Chaney snaps. "And I've been saying that for an hour and very clearly your definition is different."

This should be the end of the argument, but it isn't. Chaney and Demopoulos go on for another half hour.

February 21

All the frustrations and problems of this difficult season are wrapped up in the final two minutes of the first half of tonight's game against Villanova. For most of the half, the Owls are all they can be. Macon is everywhere, creating havoc on defense and points on offense (fourteen points on seven for nine shooting). Harden runs the team to perfection, Kilgore positions himself for open shots. Hodge and Strickland are strong underneath at both ends of the court. All of this adds up to a 26–15 lead with 6:45 to play in the half.

Then the Owls start sputtering, missing open shots, and the Wildcats suddenly start hitting. The lead is down to 30–26 with 3:16 to play, but on Temple's next possession,

Macon hits a jumper in traffic to hike the lead back up to 32–26. Then disaster strikes. On Villanova's next possession, Macon reaches in and flicks the ball away from Greg Woodard as he heads toward the basket. It looks like Macon got all ball, but the official sees it differently and calls Macon for his second foul of the game. Chaney immediately replaces his star.

Woodard misses the front end of the one-and-one with 2:12 remaining and Temple rebounds. All the Owls' quintet of Harden, Kilgore, Randolph, Lovelace and Hodge have to do is hold on to the ball and play smart basketball for two minutes and preserve the lead so the Owls can regroup at halftime and come out smoking in the second half with Macon back in the lineup. Hodge has two fouls also, but with Macon and Strickland already out, Chaney gambles and leaves him in.

The Owls work the ball around and finally, with time running out, Harden takes a three. He misses, but Kilgore grabs the rebound. Instead of kicking the ball back out and taking another forty-five seconds off the clock, Kilgore fires up another shot with Maloney screaming at him to pass the ball back to Harden. He misses and Lovelace reaches over the back going for the rebound and is called for a foul. Lance Miller hits both to trim the lead to 32–28 with 1:32 to play. As Temple inbounds the ball after the second free throw, Massamino has his team switch to a fullcourt press. Randolph throws the ball away and Mark Dowdell hits a short jumper. The lead is down to 32–30.

Villanova keeps pressing and this time Kilgore throws it away. Lance Miller hits another short shot and the game is tied at 32. The Owls inbound to Harden. Villanova's David Miller makes a dive for the ball but fouls Harden. As Miller tries to untangle himself from around Harden's feet, the Temple point guard kicks at him and the referee whistles a technical foul on Harden. Woodard makes both free throws to give the Wildcats a 34–32 lead and possession of the ball. The Cats inbound the ball and work it around until Woodard makes a move to the basket. At the foul line he takes off, lands inside the lane and then takes another hop—a clear traveling violation—and passes the ball to center Tom Gries for an easy dunk and a 36–32 lead with fifty seconds to go. Chaney leaps up to scream about the obvious travel, but play continues.

In forty-two seconds, Villanova has just scored ten points and the Owls have not even been able to get the ball past midcourt. After hitting thirteen of their first nineteen shots, the Owls close out the half one for nine and do not score after Macon leaves the game. The half ends with Villanova up 36–32 and the packed house at McGonigle stunned by the turn of events.

In the second half, Villanova threatens to pull away several times, but the Owls keep scratching their way back into the game. With thirty-seven seconds remaining, Harden hits a big three-pointer to cut the lead to 67–64. The Owls have no choice but to foul and Harden quickly grabs David Miller, who misses. Temple gets the rebound and the Owls go to Macon, who misses an open three-point shot. The Owls foul again, as Macon gets Woodard. This is Macon's fifth and he leaves the game with nineteen seconds to play with twenty-nine points, eight rebounds, five assists and five steals.

Woodard hits both for a 69–64 lead, but Harden comes up big again, hitting another three with nine seconds left to cut the lead to 69–67. The Owls have to foul once again and hope Villanova will miss to give them a chance to tie or win the game. Conic fouls Chris Walker with seven seconds to play and he nails both for a 71–67 lead. There's only time left for Temple to inbound the ball to Strickland, who races in for an uncontested lay-up at the buzzer. Villanova wins 71–69.

The win drops Temple to 15–9 (13–2 in the Atlantic-10), with three regular season games remaining. It's starting to look more and more as if the Owls will have to win the Atlantic-10 tournament to make it into the NCAA tournament.

After talking to his team and the press, Chaney finally makes his way to his office. "What kind of defense can we play to keep Mark [Macon] in the game?" he asks Maloney and Demopoulos, not expecting an answer. There's no way to protect Macon, whose ferocity prevents him from ever backing off during a game. "When we lose him we lose everything."

"If we could have just put in someone who could score, it would have been all right," Maloney says.

"Score?" Chaney snorts. "We only needed someone to hold on to the ball. That's all and we would have escaped."

February 22

We lost the game right before the half. The ten points they scored, you gave them. That cost us the game. We don't have the kind of team where we can spot someone ten points and expect to come back.

"Up to that point they only had twenty-six points," Maloney says. "With a minute, thirty to go they only had twenty-six. Then they score ten."

You had a golden chance. You win last night, you set them back light years. We win, that puts us right in the driver's seat. But you take us out of that because you don't know how to win. It has

nothing to do with what's in your heart. You can want to win all you want, but you have to know how to win.

After practice, Hodge drops by the office. "You're doing pretty good," Chaney tells him. "But you have to encourage Strickland. I need to have more than Mark trying to bring this team together." Then he tells him a story about Tim Perry and how he told him to stop hanging around with this one particular guy, whom Chaney considered bad news. "Timmy says, 'You can't tell me who my friends are.' I said, 'Damn right I can.' The guy wound up stealing from Timmy's room, from Howie's room. See that hole in the wall, where the plaster is? He broke through the wall and stole a VCR."

There's a moral to this story. It's that as Hodge gets better and better, more and more people will suddenly want to be his friend and give him things. "Pick up some of Mark's habits," Chaney says. "Be careful in the friends you choose. A minute of fun can lead to a lifetime of pain."

February 25

After the Owls' 86–74 win over George Washington at McGonigle last night, they headed straight for the airport and a flight to Pittsburgh, where a bus was waiting to take them to Morgantown for Tuesday night's game against West Virginia. The plane was delayed for several hours and the team didn't arrive in Morgantown until close to three this morning. This doesn't prevent Chaney from holding an 8:00 A.M. practice, and, afterward, the weary Owls eat breakfast and go to sleep.

This evening, Chaney holds a team meeting in his room. Earlier in the day, the host Mountaineers topped

Penn State, which gave Temple the regular season Atlantic-10 championship. Chaney is worried that his team is headed for a letdown. "You have to know who the enemy is," Chaney says and begins a lengthy story about how during World War II the Japanese would do anything, up to and including flying their planes right into an enemy ship, to win. "That's what you're going to face Tuesday night. You better be prepared."

After the meeting, several players stick around to watch "The Simpsons." Afterward, DiSangro puts on a tape of Buster Douglas beating Mike Tyson. "When someone smothers your eyes with those jabs, it just befuddles your ass," Chaney says, as he watches Douglas take control of the fight.

"Would you have been a good boxer?" someone asks Chaney.

"I'd have been an octopus out there," he says, thankful for the straight line. "I would use my hands, my feet, my head, anything."

"But you can't strangle anyone with boxing gloves on," Rob Jones says.

"Shut up," Chaney answers and he breaks out laughing.

February 26

In the huddle at the end of practice this morning, Chaney again warns his players what it's like to play at West Virginia. "They'll be waiting with open [the pauses for effect] knives. When you walk in, you'll hear them say, 'lock and load.'"

This place is a test of character, spirit, a test of heart. If you don't have character, pretend you do.

You will always have high and low moments; this is a game of ebbs and flows. How well you hang on when you're in the valley, how well you hold on, shows your character. I want to tell you a little story and then we'll stop.

What follows is one of Chaney's stranger analogies of the season.

This is black history month, so let me tell you a story. Who was Uncle Tom? Donald?

"An in-house slave," Hodge answers.

You're pretty smart. So now we have to raise the ante. You have no business doing bad in class. Johnnie, who was Uncle Tom?

"Did he dress up in an Uncle Sam suit?" Conic answers. Everyone cracks up, with Macon leading the way and his high-pitched shrieks of laughter fill the big arena.
"I read the book," Post says next. "He was a black slave who lived in a little house."

All right, let me tell you who Uncle Tom was. He was a mythical expression of a black slave. During the days of slavery, he was considered someone who kowtowed to the white slave owners. He wasn't one person; he represented a lot of slaves. But I look at Uncle Tom a little differently than most. In those days nobody had a way of knowing how smart a slave was. Especially since he always took a humble attitude around whites. Every time he got slapped in the face, he turned the other cheek. He had a 'yes, sir' attitude. He took a low profile. But I ask myself, what would have happened if he had been stubborn? What would have happened if he was a ram head or macho? What would have happened to blacks?

"There wouldn't be many of us left today," Hodge says.

That's right. And who's the best example of that?

"The Indians," Macon says.

That's correct. The Indians have almost completely gone away. The one reason is they had so much pride. They refused to yield. Uncle Tom was one that yielded. In my book Uncle Tom was a hero. Without him there would be no me. If he did not take a back step, there would be no you. He stepped off so his family could survive.

I'll tell you this. When you're in a battle, in an arena where you are a gladiator, in front of a large audience that is testing you, challenging you, the greatest thing about an athlete is his ability to be on an even flow. Balanced. And that comes from control. Control the elements, control what's inside you. If you are swayed by outsiders, you will never, ever have balance. You will never, ever control what's inside you. You won't be able to control your destiny and your family's destiny. You know what Thor held in his hands? Lightning. That meant he had control of it, and lightning is the most lethal weapon of all. So you must be in control or you won't be able to direct your energy.

Later, there's a discussion on Chaney's Uncle Tom theory. Rob Jones disagrees. "He's no hero in my book," he says, adding that he wouldn't have backed off. Eventually

Chaney agrees, pointing out that he used the story to illustrate how sometimes—on the basketball court and in life—it's better to back off and control your emotions than to charge in like a ram. But still Jones has a tough time imagining Chaney backing off from anyone. "Coach will fight anyone if he thinks he's right," Jones says. "He'll never step off."

When the team gets back to the hotel, Chaney receives a call from West Virginia coach Gail Catlett. In articles in both the local paper and the West Virginia school paper, Catlett slams Chaney for arriving in Morgantown so early. "They [say they're] worried about education up there," says Catlett, who has been at odds with Chaney in the past over his views on Prop 48. "They come in here Saturday, Sunday, Monday, Tuesday, Wednesday—five days for one game." On the phone Catlett apologizes, saying he was misquoted, which is hard to believe since both papers misquote him identically. But Chaney, who hasn't seen either paper, is willing to accept the apology.

"Don't worry about it; I just appreciate you calling," Chaney says. "I understand what those newspaper guys do."

Chaney explains why he left so early. Ordinarily, Temple would have left Sunday night, practiced at West Virginia Monday, played Tuesday night and taken the first plane back on Wednesday morning, arriving home in time for classes. All he did this trip was leave Saturday night, a day—a weekend day—early. Eventually Chaney changes the subject to Prop 48 and the Mountaineers' Chris Brooks, a Prop 48 casualty now playing and averaging thirteen points and 5.7 rebounds. "We tried to recruit him too," Chaney says. "I know what kind of kid he is, what kind of background he came from. Education is the only thing that will save his life. He needs a chance."

241

February 27

While the two teams warm up before tonight's game, Chaney watches from high up in the stands at the West Virginia Coliseum. He does this before most games, home or away. Several Mountaineer fans spot Chaney and a few come over to say hello, wish him luck or ask for an autograph. Although Chaney is concentrating and focused on the game, he is polite and friendly, as are the West Virginia fans.

As the game clock winds down to twelve minutes, DiSangro waves up to Chaney from down on the court, signaling him that it's time to head to the locker room to talk to the team. Chaney rises and begins walking slowly down the bleachers toward the floor and the entrance to the Owls' locker room. As he makes his way, the fans along his route rise as if they are doing the wave and begin booing and hissing Chaney, some even throwing empty cups at him. Chaney continues, expressionless, and even stops briefly to shake someone's hand while a hail of insults and paper cups fly past his head.

Once the game begins, the Owls play like a team that has already clinched the regular-season conference title. They shoot sixteen for fifty (32 percent), commit seventeen turnovers and are outrebounded 36–32. This adds up to a 55–51 loss.

After the game, a crowd of reporters waits outside the Temple locker room, listening to Chaney rant and rave inside. It goes on for more than five minutes, with no one brave enough to go in. Theokas says, "Go on in," but no one moves. Finally Chaney emerges.

"I'm very frustrated," he begins, his voice reduced to a hoarse whisper. "We made too many mistakes. In the past our teams have just not done that. A couple players on the floor panicked and just didn't know how to win. We got nothing inside (Hodge had nine points and Strickland zero), and after a while we were reluctant to throw it in."

Macon also struggled, scoring twenty, but hitting only five of twenty shots. "He's trying too hard," Chaney says when asked about Macon. "He can't do it alone, but he's not getting any help. The ball is not given to him in a timely manner. He was wide open, but [the point guard] waited until he was covered to get it to him. It's almost like in the days when people were shaving points. They would wait until the big scorer was covered and then give it to him when he couldn't do anything with it."

The questions continued for another half hour, with Chaney patiently answering the same ones in separate interviews for two television crews and three radio guys. Finally he's done and heads toward the team bus. "This was a big setback for us," he says wearily.

March 1

The Owls (16–10, 14–3) close out the regular season tonight at McGonigle against Rutgers (15–14, 11–6). It's a night to say good-bye to seniors Ernest Pollard and Rob Jones. It could also be the night Macon becomes Temple's all-time leading scorer. Going into the game, Macon has a career total of 1,794 points in ninety games (a 19.9 average), leaving him just seventeen behind Terence Stansbury's school mark of 1,811. Macon has been hot the last six games, averaging 27.0 points a contest, and twice equaling his career high of thirty-five. His average per game is up to 21.0.

"It's been in the back of my mind; it's hard not to think about it," Macon says. "But I just wanted to keep focused and help us win the game."

The first summer Macon was at Temple, he would often

play one-on-one against Stansbury. At the time, Stansbury was playing for the Indiana Pacers. He's currently playing in Europe. "He killed me," Macon says. "I'm not saying I didn't score, but he did a lot of damage to me. And he taught me something, how when I spin off a man to spin far off him so I have an open shot. He didn't tell me that; I watched him and picked it up."

With 10:47 remaining in the second half, Macon gets the ball to the left of the basket at the three-point line. He fakes a shot and gets the defender off his feet, drives to the baseline and pulls up and hits a twelve-foot jumper in traffic to give him a new school record of 1,812 points. The fans immediately begin yelling "Macon! Macon!" and shower the court with confetti. The referees stop the game (calling a technical on the Temple fans for throwing things onto the court) and award the ball to Macon, who is then engulfed by his teammates. After they untangle, Macon heads toward the Temple bench with the game ball. First he and Chaney hug and then Macon presents the ball to a stunned Pollard. "It was something I thought about doing a couple of days ago," Macon says after the game. "Ernest is my pride and joy. He's the lone senior on the team and I get emotional thinking about him leaving. But he's prepared and Ernest is going to make something of himself. I wanted to cry when I gave it to him, but I had to keep playing."

"It was very emotional for me," Pollard says. "I hope he heard me in all the noise. I told him I look up to him so much as a person on and off the court. You know, I don't show my emotions much, but I was pretty choked up."

This would have been a nice way to end the game. The Owls had just completed a 21–9 run to start the second half, taking a 52–44 lead. But they still have more than ten minutes to play and the Scarlet Knights are intent on spoiling Macon and Pollard's big night. After Macon's historic basket, Rutgers goes on a 13–2 tear to take a 57–56 lead with 5:56 remaining.

The game is close the rest of the way, but Temple moves out to a 64–57 lead with 3:53 to go. Again Rutgers battles back, tying the score at 64 with twelve seconds remaining after they press and steal the ball from Macon. After a time-out, Temple works the ball around, trying to free Macon. But two men are on him and Kilgore has to shoot. He misses at the buzzer and the game goes into overtime.

Temple has a chance to win at the end of the first overtime, but Macon misses a spinning, leaning shot from the foul line. In the second overtime, Macon decides enough is enough. After Hodge scores on an inside move, Macon hits a jumper, after spinning his way away from two defenders, for a 71–67 Temple lead. After Rutgers scores, the Owls get the ball back to Macon. Again there are two men on him and again he spins and stutter-steps his way toward an open space, rises up, and hits a jumper to give Temple a 73–70 lead. Two foul shots by Macon in the last minute seal the 75–70 win.

Macon finishes with thirty-one points, Hodge adds fifteen and Kilgore thirteen.

9

This Basketball Game
Meant Nothing

March 4

At 8:14 this evening, while Penn State is beating George Washington 83–72 in the third Atlantic-10 quarterfinal matchup of the night (Rutgers has already beaten Rhode Island 80–79 and Massachusetts topped West Virginia 78–55) and the Temple players in their locker room are preparing for their upcoming game with Duquesne, Hank Gathers collapses on a basketball court 3,000 miles away.

At 9:55, during the first half of the Owls' 61–50 win over the Dukes, the former graduate of Philadelphia's Murrell Dobbins Tech High School and current star for Loyola Marymount is pronounced dead of an apparent heart attack. The word of Gathers's collapse and subsequent death sweeps through the Palestra and finally reaches Chaney as he heads off the court after the win.

Chaney, who knew Gathers very well from his playing days at Dobbins and the Sonny Hill and Baker Leagues, is immediately overcome with emotion. His eyes redden

246

and fill with tears as he gathers his team around him in the cramped locker room. "All the winning and losing is put in perspective," he begins softly. "I was just told that a young man died. Hank Gathers collapsed and died during a game." No one moves or says a word for what seems like several minutes, with disbelief slowly giving way to sorrow.

Chaney emerges from the locker room several minutes later and makes the long walk across the court and down several corridors to the interview room. Chaney makes his way to the podium and sits between Macon and Harden. "Any questions?" he asks softly.

"I guess by now you heard about Hank," a reporter says. The room is absolutely quiet, and Chaney stares straight down for several seconds trying to compose himself. "I was told about it before we got to the dressing room. It's amazing that we fight and fuss about athletes all around the country . . . and yet when everything is said and done Hank Gathers just epitomizes so much of what life is all about. This basketball game meant nothing. This is a kid who is a soldier for a lot of kids, he champions a lot of causes. To hear this just devastates me." At this point Chaney, who has been speaking very slowly, pausing after every few words to try and collect himself, stops. He is overcome with grief and the tears well up in his eyes. Macon and Harden sit next to him helplessly, wishing there was something they could do to ease their coach's grief. Harden rubs Chaney's shoulder. Throughout the press room there is complete silence and even a few tears.

"How unfair this is. I knew three kids, Robert Liburd, who died from [Marfan's syndrome], Hank Gathers and Timmy Claxton [a former Temple star who dropped dead from a heart attack in 1980]. There are some good stories in life and these three guys represent all of them. They all come out of the same mold, young athletes who are just working their tails off. Somewhere I know Hank perhaps has a smile, because [playing basketball] is where he really wanted to be. But the game we participated in tonight is all lost when you think about kids like these."

With this Chaney stops, unable to say any more. Someone asks Macon if he knew Gathers.

"Yes I did, not as well as Coach and some of the other guys," he begins. "I'm saddened by it, but it makes me put my life in perspective. So many times people, as well as myself and maybe some of you all, take life for granted, thinking it's okay, and we're going to wake up tomorrow. But some people, they don't wake up."

That's it, the conference is over. Nobody has the heart to ask about the game, which has suddenly lost all its importance. "Are you okay, Coach?" Demopoulos asks. Chaney nods and slowly begins the long walk to his car.

In September 1985, doctors discovered Liburd had Marfan's syndrome, a connective tissue disorder that seems to affect tall, thin people and damages the heart valves and blood vessels. Liburd was advised that any physical exertion such as playing basketball could kill him and his promising career was over before it started. Liburd still wanted to play and went so far as to have a lawyer draw up papers that would relieve Temple of all responsibilities and liabilities if anything happened to him. "But I just couldn't let him play, even though I knew it was breaking his heart," Chaney said. "To have been an athlete all his life and then suddenly not be able to play was devastating. I made him come to practices and stop by the office and go to tutoring sessions and study hall. We wanted him to know he was still a member of the family."

On November 22, 1984, Robert Liburd, about to start his senior season at DeWitt Clinton High School in the Bronx, signed a national letter of intent with Temple.

Chaney said, "He's only been playing organized basketball a couple of years, but you can't teach tall. At AFBE [Athletes For Better Understanding basketball camp], he was blocking shots accidently and incidently just by standing in the low post near the bucket." Chaney couldn't wait to teach Liburd—seven feet, two inches and the biggest recruit in Temple history—how to block shots purposefully and mean to score and be mean to score. But Liburd never put on a Temple uniform.

Liburd remained at Temple and pursued his degree in communications. "He was really coming along and doing very well in school," Chaney said. "The adjustment seemed to be there and he seemed to have a good feeling about himself. He came in the office one day all excited because he had a summer job with a newspaper in New York."

The very next day—May 26, 1987—Liburd's roommate, Darrin Pearsall, a member of the basketball team, found him slumped over in a chair, dead of a heart attack. "It was a shocking thing for me and all our players," Chaney says.

And now, with Gathers gone from a heart attack, Chaney has to come to grips with the loss of another young basketball player.

March 7

It's down to Temple (19–10) and Massachusetts (17–12) tomorrow night at McGonigle (Temple's reward for winning the league's regular-season championship) for the Atlantic-10 championship and an automatic bid to the NCAA tournament. The Owls topped Rutgers two nights ago by a 65–57 score in one semifinal. Macon continued his string of great performances, scoring twenty-eight and pulling down a tournament record fifteen rebounds. Hodge was a tower of strength underneath with nineteen points and twelve rebounds, and Strickland finally played like Dennis Rodman, with six points, ten rebounds and five blocks. In the other semi, the surprising Minutemen beat Penn State 64–59.

Mass gives people a lot of trouble.

This is how Chaney begins his lecture this morning. He's confident, but still concerned. Calipari has his team playing inspired basketball.

They are smart enough to utilize their best players [McCoy and forwards Tony Barbee and William Herndon]. The ball goes to their best players. The point guard [Cary Herer, who averages 3.8 points and 7.9 assists] gets them the ball. Herer can't shoot, fellas. From anywhere. He's fifty percent from the foul line [56 percent], thirty percent from the field [41 percent, 35 percent from three-point range], yet he has gotten his team to the championship. I've been saying that since October fifteenth. The importance of point guard is getting the ball to the right people. Penn State is a better team, but they had twenty turnovers in that game [23].

[Massachusetts] has nothing to lose. They weren't supposed to be here and now they're playing for the championship. You must raise your game to a higher level. Play with your skill and will. If you don't and you let them come out and play freewheeling basketball and run and press you and push you around, you won't walk away with the prize. You'll walk away with a surprise. You must come mean and tough. If you don't have

enough heart, enough spirit inside you, think of what I have inside of me. That's all you have to do. Anytime you don't think you have enough heart inside you, play with what's inside of me.

March 8

Nothing has come easy for Temple this season, so why should tonight be any different? The Owls seem on the verge of an easy win as they race to a 25–15 lead and a 34–23 halftime advantage on thirteen for twenty-six shooting. The second half is a different story. Nothing will go down for the Owls, who can connect on only six of twenty-one shots. Massachusetts chips away at the lead, until finally, with fifteen seconds to play, Rafer Giles hits two free throws and Temple's lead is 51–49.

Already, Temple has been involved in eleven games this season that have been decided by five or less points, winning five. Two of the losses—to UNLV and Georgia Tech—were to teams that will advance to the Final Four. Although the Owls have yet to develop the cohesion and intelligence on the court that Chaney has been trying to hammer into them all season, they have never backed down or given up.

With eleven seconds remaining, Massachusetts's William Harper fouls Kilgore. He makes both to push the lead up to 53–49. McCoy races downcourt and fires up a three-pointer that misses. Kilgore comes up with the rebound and is immediately fouled with five seconds to go. He misses. Herer gets the outlet pass, dribbles up the floor and scores with a second left. It's too little, too late and the Owls win 53–49.

When it is finally over, the Owls explode, releasing all the frustrations of a tough season. They hug and jump up and down. While Chaney is hustled off to be interviewed on television [the game was on ESPN] and radio, his players begin to cut down the net.

Strickland, a huge smile on his face, waves to the crowd as he climbs the ladder and cuts down a strand of the net. He's struggled all season to find his niche, but he finally seems to be coming on as a consistent force. In three games in the tournament, Strickland scored twenty-nine points on fourteen for twenty-four shooting, had twenty rebounds and ten blocked shots and is named to the All-Tournament team.

Hodge, who had two men all over him in the game and was held to just three points, is reluctant to take his turn cutting down the net. Despite the win, he's upset with the way he played (three points on zero for five shooting from the floor) and immediately afterward, he sat on the bench with a towel draped over his head. His low output was to be expected, Chaney says later. There were two and sometimes three men collapsing on Hodge whenever he got the ball. He did the right thing by kicking it back out and working hard on the boards (nine rebounds) and on defense (three blocks). "We are starting to see teams do that more and more," Chaney tells the press afterward. "That's why it has been so important that Strick has given us something and for Mik and Michael Harden to step up and take the timely shot." The thing that has Chaney a little upset is Hodge's attitude afterward. He should be happy his team won, instead of upset because he thought he played poorly. "That's something I'll talk to him about," Chaney says later.

Kilgore takes his turn. He may have led the team in stupid plays and tongue-lashings from Chaney, but he never backed off from anyone. As he told Chaney earlier this season, "Coach, I may not make good decisions, but I'm a warrior." Tonight he came up big when he was needed the most, hitting four of eight shots for eleven

points, plus eight rebounds. Twice in the closing minutes
he came down with crucial offensive rebounds. "On the
first, I thought about making a move back to the basket,
but I decided to bring it back out," he tells the press
afterward.

"You almost did what?" Chaney says, jumping up from
his seat to the left of Kilgore and slapping his shoulder.

Macon, the tournament's MVP, takes his turn and the
crowd goes crazy. Once again he's come through in an
important game, scoring twenty points, including four of
Temple's last seven. It's been a long and difficult, sometimes frustrating season for Macon. But he's handled everything that opposing teams, the press and the fans have
thrown at him and emerged a stronger person and better
player. "I never had any doubts about us [winning]," he
tells the press. There was no way Macon was going to let
his team lose tonight. Early in the game he shouted,
"Come on!" at McCoy as he guarded him closely on defense, daring McCoy to make a move. With Mass control-
ing the boards early in the game, Macon began shouting
at his teammates, trying to pump them up. "I got mad. I
knew we had to rebound better."

"Does tonight make up for a long year?" a reporter asks
him.

"I don't worry about those things," Macon says, slip-
ping back behind his mask. "I don't look at yesterday's
news. I look at today, and tomorrow is a new day."

The last to climb the ladder is Pollard. He didn't play
tonight or at all during the tournament and only played
seventy-one minutes all season. But he never got frustrated or upset and remained a leader and an inspiration
to his teammates.

As Pollard cuts the final cord and the net falls into his
hands, he tries to pass it down to a teammate. But they
won't let him, insisting that he put it around his neck. He
shrugs, puts it on and turns to the crowd behind the

Temple bench and waves to his mom. The crowd cheers.

By this time Chaney is finally done with his interviews and heads back over to join his team. His eyes are red, his voice just about gone, his shirt soaked through and his tie loosened so the knot is halfway down his chest. Chaney and DiSangro come together in front of the bench in a bear hug that lasts thirty seconds. When they separate, both are in tears. Chaney hugs Demopoulos next. "We're back, we're back," Demopoulos says over and over. His first four years, the Owls were in the NCAA tournament, and he had begun to take it for granted. "But Coach Maloney told me you can never take it for granted. Last year, when we didn't make it, was the longest, worst year of my life. I think I finally understood what Coach Maloney was trying to tell me."

The Temple players get their first-place awards and head for the locker room. Liacouris ("My good-luck Jonah," Chaney will call him) and Robert Liburd's father join the team. Later, Chaney will give Mr. Liburd his tournament watch. "I have a hundred watches, what do I need another one for?" Chaney asks, trying to downplay his gift.

Fellas, I said to you success has a narrow door. Everybody's dealt the same number of cards: five. Everyone has a hand. Some guys might have aces, some guys might have deuces. But you have to play the cards you're dealt. You're in the NCAAs. I can criticize you for things, but being in the NCAAs spells success.

October fifteenth, when I said our goal was to be in the air in March, that was my promise to you that if we worked hard we'd be successful. Now we have to work even harder. Sixty-four teams are hoping to be the one. Now we have to find a way to go through that narrow door. Believe

me, it can happen. It can happen for you. I've
never seen anyone hit a home run from outside
the ballpark. We're in the ballpark. We're up to
bat. Here comes the pitch.

We have to work hard this next week; come
ready to play, and when that door opens up, be
ready to step through it. From now on, if you win
one, you buy one.

IO

We Win Ugly Games

March 10

This is the first practice since the big win over Massachusetts and Chaney is ready to prepare his team for whom-
ever they will meet in the opening round of the NCAA
tournament.

> Teams that win and go on are teams that are in as
> a family. And they win in tough situations
> because their energies are all pulled together. They
> are all in the same pot. You can call that pot
> anything you want to, possum stew, chicken stew,
> with carrots, peas and everything else in that pot.
> But what comes out is a fine stew. They are
> clearly focused. When they come to the basketball
> court, they are identified as a force you have to
> reckon with, have to deal with and they are ready
> to meet any odds.

After the win over Massachusetts, a reporter asked Chaney what he thought his team's chances were in the tournament, despite the up-and-down season and the loss of Causwell. "Coach, are you happy just to be back in the tournament?"

"I've been here before," Chaney answered calmly. "And I'm never happy until I've exhausted all efforts to get to the top. There have been teams in the Final Four before that were not expected to get there. If you have the right chemistry it can happen. I know that. But how do I get that across to them? In the next few days we will spend a lot of time trying to convince them they are more than what they think they are. Hopefully they will take on that kind of image. If they don't, they can play in my image. If they don't have a strong image about themselves, then damnit, they can go out and play in my image."

Chaney is worried how his young team will react to the pressures of the tournament. Only Macon and Pollard have been there before. "We never lost confidence this season," Macon says. "Our goal all season was to make it here and we've accomplished that. Now the door's open a crack and we want to go in. If we have to knock it down, we'll do that." Kilgore adds that everyone on the team is looking toward Macon as they prepare for the tournament. "We'll take our cue from Mark," he says. "He's been here before and he knows what it's like. I guess he'll tell us about it and we'll just watch how he works and prepares and do the same."

Chaney's teams have always been prepared in March. In five previous tournament appearances, Chaney's Owls have won their first-round game every time and put together an overall mark of 7–5. In 1984, Stansbury's miraculous shot topped St. John's and gave Temple its first tournament win since the 1958 team reached the Final

Four. It was a huge win that put Temple back on the basketball map. "One of the things every team needs to do in terms of spelling out success and establishing some kind of strong feeling about winning is for kids to understand and get a strong feeling for the NCAA tournament," Chaney said in explaining the significance of the win. "Something like that spells success for the coach, the players, the university and the alumni." In their second-round game in 1984, Temple played North Carolina and Michael Jordan—the number one seed in the East—and were close the whole way before finally losing 77–66 in a game played in Charlotte, North Carolina.

In 1985, Temple topped Virginia Tech 60–57 in their first-round tournament game, which meant they had the unenviable task of going up against Patrick Ewing and the mighty Georgetown Hoyas—ranked number one in the country at the time. This was the Georgetown team that would eventually be beaten by Villanova in the championship game, one of the biggest upsets in Final Four history. Again Temple stayed close for more than a half, but eventually Georgetown's superior talent and depth and the dominance of Ewing over the smaller Temple players allowed the Hoyas to pull away to a 63–46. "It feels good knowing we can play with those caliber players," Blackwell said after the game. "We lost the game and you're never happy about that, but I felt good that it wasn't a total blowout. And I think we might have gained more from this experience than they did. I mean, they won, but Temple, as a university, might have gained from the exposure."

In 1986, Temple beat Jacksonville in their tournament opener, before losing to Danny Manning and the Kansas Jayhawks 65–43. In 1987, Temple beat up on Southern 75–56 in their opener, then dropped a 72–62 heartbreaker to LSU in the second round. This was the first tournament game Temple lost that it should have won. It also marked the final game of Blackwell's brilliant career. Temple shot only 36.5 percent (twenty-three for sixty-three) in the game and only 31 percent (nine for twenty-nine) from three-point territory. "This isn't the way it was supposed to be," said Blackwell after the game, who, like his teammates, thought Temple had a shot at making the Final Four that year.

"We honestly thought this was a great team and that we could make it," Vreeswyk added. "Now . . . now that it's all over, it's hard to take. It just stops so suddenly. There's no tomorrow."

While there would be no tomorrow for Blackwell, teammates Vreeswyk, Evans, Perry and Rivas got another chance the next year, along with freshman sensation Macon. The Owls were the top seed in the East and beat Lehigh 87–73 in their opener. Next came Georgetown and a chance for revenge. All the elements were on target in this game and Temple romped to a 74–53 win. Next came a 69–47 win over Richmond to set up a showdown with Danny Ferry and the Duke Blue Devils for a trip to the Final Four. Once again poor shooting did in Chaney's team; they hit on only 28 percent (eighteen for sixty-three) of their shots and only 22 percent (four for eighteen) on three-point attempts. Now Chaney prepares his team for the Owls' sixth trip to the NCAA tournament in the last seven years.

So today, as we go back to the beginning, remember how we started. Because how you start is how you finish. The only thing we have to do now is turn the volume up and be a little tougher, a little stronger in what we're doing. The very same things that got you into the NCAAs are the very same things that will take you further. And if we're lucky, you just might meet one of the teams that you lost to, a team that beat us by two or

three points in the last second. If you're lucky, you just might get another chance. And what you didn't do that time, we must do now. And your attitude is what leads you to doing it.

If you approach the game with apprehension or some degree of fear to take this step because you're afraid you might lose, if you're afraid to take a class because you might fail, if you're afraid to take a test because you might fail—then surely you will fail. Surely you will fail. Because fear provides a degree of darkness and darkness ultimately destroys vision and puts you in a position to make bad decisions.

Suddenly Chaney stops and glares over at Kilgore and Hodge, who are engaged in a game of footsies.

Kilgore, here I am talking about rude and crude—about you—and here you are demonstrating your shit.

"But Donald's kicking me, Coach."

I know he is, but Donald loves this. He loves to get you. Think of it like being in a barrel with a hole in it. And every time you turn around and your ass meets that hole, you're gonna get screwed. That's because you're rude and crude. That's how your personality is developing. Now leave Donald alone.

"Coach, is being rude and crude better than brainless and spineless?" Kilgore asks and everyone laughs.

Let's say it doesn't make any difference because you're all of them. How about that.

After Chaney's lecture, the Owls get down to work. What follows is the hardest practice of the season, starting with sprints up and down the court. Hodge manages to cut his left index finger during a drill for the big man, but continues playing and just wipes the dripping blood onto his white practice jersey. Soon Strickland's jersey is also covered with Hodge's blood because the big center continually reaches back with his hands to find out where Strickland is while he fights for position in the low post.

After the drills, the team scrimmages, running up and down the court for more than an hour, with Chaney stopping play every few minutes to correct an error. Finally, at half past noon, three-and-a-half hours after practice started, Chaney stops the scrimmage and has everyone shoot silent free throws.

"This was great," Harden says. "I wish we scrimmaged like this more."

"I'm gonna work you until your legs drop off tomorrow," Chaney tells his team in the huddle before the end of practice. "Tomorrow we're gonna work on man-to-man, zone coverages and keep looking at the same problems of guys dozing off or waiting for someone to tell them what to do. All of the excuse boys, the breakdown boys, had better be ready tomorrow."

March 11

As promised, this morning's practice session is long and grueling. The first half is devoted to running offensive patterns. "Each pattern has a reason," Chaney explains, after stopping play. "The purpose is to set up a player or players for a certain type of shot. In the thirteen we want to get Donald down here [in the paint]. Every player must

261

be on the same page and understand what we are trying to do."

After practice, Chaney and Demopoulos hit the road recruiting. Although not by design, this evening, when the NCAA Tournament pairings are announced on CBS, they will be watching television in the living room of a player they want very badly. The team, Maloney, Liacouris and a few assorted Temple administrators gather in a private room next to the President's office and sit down at a long wooden table ("This table's bigger than my house," Hodge says) for an old-fashioned southern meal of ribs and chicken and black-eyed peas and greens and plenty of ice tea and cheesecake. "This is my kind of food," says Harden, as he tucks his napkin into his shirt collar and digs in to the first of several platefuls.

After dinner, the team troops over to a large reception area where two televisions are set up and the press awaits to film the reactions of the players to their seed. At 6:30 the sets are tuned to CBS and a few minutes later Tim Brandt starts going through the pairings, starting with the Eastern Regional. The Owls don't have to wait long to hear their name called. It will be St. John's—the region's number five seed, against Temple, the number eleven seed, in Atlanta on Friday, March 16. The winner will take on either Duke or Richmond on Sunday. "All right," Harden says and gets up to walk around the room and shake everyone's hand. Everyone else is calm and accepts the news matter-of-factly.

"I can't complain," Kilgore says. "It sounds good to me."

Strickland, who's from Atlanta, just shrugs and says, "I'm going home."

The television crews and reporters surround Macon for a comment, but he's not in a talkative mood. "I don't have much to say. I'm ready to play."

DiSangro, who had a premonition Temple would be

playing St. John's, quickly finds a phone and starts making travel and practice arrangements. "He said last night it would be St. John's and we'd be in the East," Mike Flicker says. "He was right."

Lou Carnesecca's Redmen are a beatable team, especially since they lost Jayson Williams, their six-foot-ten-inch starting power forward and third-leading scorer (14.6) and second-leading rebounder (7.8), a month ago to a foot injury. St. John's finished the season 23–9, but the Johnnies are currently struggling to regain their earlier form. Although they finished fourth in the Big East with a 10–6 record, the Redmen lost their regular season finale to Seton Hall and lost to Villanova in the quarterfinals of the Big East tournament.

St. John's is led by senior point guard Boo Harvey, who averages 16.5 points and 6 assists per game and has a knack for hitting big shots at the buzzer. Harvey is lightning quick and knows how to control and run the offense. Senior Jason Buchanan, who struggled offensively this season, starts as the other guard. He averages just 6.1 a game and shot only 33 percent from the field. Inside, despite the loss of Williams, St. John's is still big and strong and talented. Robert Werden, a six-foot-eleven-inch sophomore center, is a solid low-post player, who averages 9.6 points and 7.8 rebounds. Billy Singleton, a six-foot-seven-inch junior, moved into Williams's starting spot at power forward and has done a very good job, averaging 10.1 points and 6.9 rebounds. Malik Sealy, a six-foot-eight-inch junior, is the Redmen's most gifted player. He can hit the open jump shot or take the ball to the hoop. He averages 18.1 points on 52 percent shooting and 7.0 rebounds.

"St. John's creates balance very much like us," Chaney will tell his team later in the week. "They have a great point guard. They control the tempo of the game. And the guys inside do what they are supposed to. They have a

structure for success. They go where they can be successful and a team like that always has a chance to win. If the
salt and pepper is supposed to be on the shelf, that's
where it is. You don't go in the bathroom and find the salt
and pepper. It's on the shelf in the kitchen."

March 13

Since it is spring break week at Temple, practice is scheduled for 9:00 this morning. Still, several players wander in
late. Demopoulos is the only coach here—as always,
Chaney won't be in for a while and Maloney has called
in to say he's having car problems and will be a little late.
Demopoulos just stands at the edge of the court silently
until about 9:20 when all the players are finally dressed
and out on the court. "Practice was supposed to start at
nine, not nine-fifteen, not nine-thirty," Demopoulos begins. With each word he grows more angry. "None of you
should be late, especially now. Weren't you listening [to
Coach] when he talked about your attitude? That's what
wins games. Now isn't the time to be late. I could understand, maybe, if it was five-thirty practice, but not nine
o'clock. It's NCAA time."

Chaney arrives a few minutes later and calls his team
together. This is the first time he has talked to the team
since it was announced they would play St. John's.

**We win ugly games. We win ugly games. I'm
serious. We win ugly games. There's not another
team in the country that wins ugly games like us.
Ugly games. How do you win a game when you
play bad? How do you win shooting thirty-seven
percent? How do you win twenty games like that?**

Let's go back to October 15. I said that if you average ten or less turnovers a game, you stand a chance to win some basketball games. We possessed the ball more than any other team in the country. If we shoot only thirty percent, that means we may have to have the ball twice as many times as the other team. We win by not turning the ball over.

This means if we play smart, we might not even have to score a basket to win. Scoring baskets is not our value system. Our value system is in taking more shots than the other team and taking the right shots. Shit, look at this boy right here [he points to Strickland]. This boy is shooting thirty percent from the foul line. Nobody in the history of basketball shot thirty percent at foul line. But you see, we're good at missing. We're good at being bad. How about a point guard who three minutes out of the dressing room already has three turnovers? Unforced errors. But we still win. How did we win? I don't have a clue. How about this boy [Kilgore]? He gives a team eight points just for being liver-lipped. But we win ugly games and we're going into this tournament as the ugliest team in America.

"We played the ugliest game in tournament history," Demopoulos interrupts, bringing up Temple's 61–50 overtime win over Jacksonville in 1986. "Timmy [Perry] shot an air-ball from the foul line."

That just shows we've been an ugly team for a long time, so don't worry about being ugly. Now if you're crude and rude, that's bad. You can't win that way. But we can win ugly, no question.

After his lecture, Chaney puts the ugliest team in America through its paces. He starts off by working on pivot play, hoping to set up situations for Hodge to get the ball down low or at least force St. John's to exert so much pressure guarding him it will free things up for other players. "You are a very efficient player," Chaney tells Hodge, who is still a little upset about his low offensive output in the Massachusetts game. "If someone is looking for an NBA-type player, someone who can position himself to get the ball and roll inside for the shot and the foul, they might just find you. You don't have to score any points to be effective. Certainly it's great, but if three people have to play your ass and you make good decisions and your teammates score, I don't care what the newspaper people say, you played a great game."

The remainder of practice is spent working on the offense and Chaney methodically goes over each formation, the pattern each player must run and the shots they can expect to get. Things don't go well, and as they have all season, the white team struggles to set up good shots. This seems as good a time as any to pull out a metaphor.

Johnny Appleseed [Chaney begins, combining and confusing this story with "Jack and the Beanstalk"] reached a stage of frustration trying to make things grow. He used fertilizer, watered them every day, but nothing came up. Finally he just said shit, forget it and threw the seeds out the window. Two days later shit starts springing up everywhere. That's what a coach will do from the bench. He'll say, "I tried everything; I give up."

"I never heard you say that," Randolph interrupts.

I'm not talking about me. I'm talking about coaches. I'm not a coach; I am Brutus. I'm brutal.

266

Coaches are nice people. They say nice things about their players.

Conic, who's having trouble with his contact lenses, interrupts and asks if he can go get some eye drops.

Just sit down. You don't need to see anything, just listen. Now, see? That's brutal.

Chaney laughs and Ryan Kling brings over the bottle of eye drops for Conic. Later, in the huddle after practice, Chaney is still frustrated that after all these months of hard work and practice his players still aren't running the offense the way it should be run.

There's not a forward in this country who has more potential than you [Strickland]. But as long as you dwell on making excuses, your ability will never rise. And you [Kilgore] have the opportunity at six–eight to play guard. Who else in this country, six–eight, can handle the ball like you? But if you keep up this stupidity I swear you will never reach your full potential. There's a lot of former basketball stars walking around this city like bums. They live for yesterday and they're going nowhere fast. I don't want any bad attitudes with me when I go to Atlanta. I want to go to Atlanta with a lollipop in my mouth.

"Why a lollipop, Coach? Why not some raw meat?" asks Randolph, always the wise guy.

You shut up. I'm still looking forward to you playing one good game of basketball.

"Coach, are we gonna practice tomorrow?" Kilgore asks.

Yes. Do you think you can make it?

Kilgore smiles and nods.

Thank you.

March 14

At a little past 4:00 P.M., the Owls are in the air and on their way to Atlanta and the NCAA Tournament. When they arrive at their hotel around 8:00 P.M., the players head to their rooms and the coaches to their suite. The first thing the coaches do is turn all three televisions to ESPN, which is showing several first-round NIT games. Less than a minute later, they watch a replay of Stansbury's game-winner against St. John's six years ago in the NCAA tournament.

"They're still playing that shot," Chaney says.

"Think that's a good omen?" I ask.

"Let's hope so," Chaney says.

With that, Chaney flops down in bed and begins munching from the jar of Hot Crisp Pickled Okra he picked up at the airport. He tries to get Demopoulos to try one, but there's no way. "My mother used to make me eat okra and I hated it," Demopoulos says. Chaney just laughs and keeps eating.

March 15

This morning's eight o'clock practice is the final preparation for tomorrow's game. The team will practice again in the afternoon, from three to four, but this is an open practice at the Omni in front of the press and assorted visitors—including opposing coaches—and no team is dumb enough to do anything but loosen up and shoot around and get a feel for the arena.

The Owls work hard for more than two hours this morning at Georgia Tech's arena. Chaney starts with the white team on defense and has them work on stopping the red team's transition game.

"When a guy gets the ball in front of you in the low post, turns around and scores, you're saying, 'the hell with you, Coach,'" Chaney says after Lovelace gets the ball down low with his man behind him and scores an easy basket. "Or you're saying you just don't give a damn about winning. If that's true, then you come to my room. Room 747. And you say, 'Coach, I'm not ready to play.' And I'll put your ass back on a plane. I don't want any excuses. There are no excuses for not winning. I didn't get this far to have you bullshitting up and down the floor."

Two more trips up and down the floor and Chaney stops play again, still unhappy with the white team's defense. "If you want to win you have to do more. How do you do more? You do more on defense. You move your feet. You make your presence felt. The other team must know you're out there. It's like Muhammad Ali. One boy he was fighting kept calling him Cassius Clay. Wouldn't call him Ali. So he gives him a whipping. Every time he hits him he says, 'What's my name? What's my name?' What he was really saying is, 'I want you to always remember who this is whipping your ass.'"

A few more trips up and down the court and Chaney switches the white team into the standard 3–2 defense. He warns that St. John's will attack this with a 1–4 offensive set, with Harvey up top and everyone else spread out in a straight line parallel to the foul line. "They'll try to flatten you out and sneak behind," Chaney warns.

"Hey, Strickland, that's a foul!" Chaney yells, stopping

practice after Strickland fights to get defensive position in front of Lovelace. "How many minutes you gonna play tomorrow? Two?" Next time down the floor Strickland does the same thing. "That's your second foul, Strickland. What are you gonna do tomorrow, just keep reaching and pulling?"

"This is disgusting," Demopoulos says. "This is the worst practice we've had all year."

Practice continues like this for another hour, with Chaney continually stopping play to make corrections. It's obvious everyone is on edge. There's a lot more cursing and head shaking than normal. No one seems in the mood to be yelled at, but Chaney, always relentless in his quest for perfection, doesn't let up for a minute. It's his way of saying, play in my image, play strong and don't relax for a second. Finally he ends practice and calls the team to the center of the court for their huddle.

The effort you gave today is the effort you will give tomorrow. You can't turn your game on like a water faucet and say, "Now it's time to play."

Chaney, Macon and Harden head over to the Omni before the rest of the team for the mandatory press conference at 2:30. It's a chance for the large gathering of reporters to get a few quotes. Carnesecca comes up with the day's best line when asked about Temple's patient offense. "They try to give you a little bit of anesthesia, lull you to sleep," he says with an impish grin. "We just have to keep our concentration and sustain our defense for up to thirty-five seconds."

Carnesecca says he's worried about Macon ("He'll make a helluva pro") and the Temple zone and adds that

270

the two teams are alike in many ways. "They have a great player in Macon and we have one in Boo. They have several other good people, and so do we. We play similar and like to work for good shots. I make it a pick 'em." Finally he's asked about the 1984 game and Stansbury's shot. "I'd much rather remember the seventy-nine game" (a 75–70 St. John's win in the opening round of the tournament).

Chaney is just as quotable. He talks about how Temple is an "ugly team." Someone asks him to elaborate. "A number of people consider our style slow and methodical, uncharacteristic of black players. I guess we don't do a lot of Barnum and Bailey stuff, people think we should. Our games are not pretty games. In fact, I haven't enjoyed a lot of them myself."

After comparing the current team to the 1988 version, commenting on the big win over the Redmen in 1984 and complimenting Carnesecca and Harvey and Sealy and all the other St. John's players on the fine job they do, someone asks Chaney if he thinks Prop 48 is working. While several NCAA tournament officials sit there cringing, Chaney attacks this question.

If you guys were to really look at and print the truth you would see that it has failed. We have more students failing in high schools than ever before. People who supported this thing refused to recognize that no athletic body can impose an educational piece of legislation on a disadvantaged group of youngsters and force the entire educational setting in this country to change. You can't do it. We have more failures today than ever before. An article in *USA Today* about a month ago showed six point two percent more athletes are failing [to achieve a 700 on their SATs]. Prop

forty-eight has failed and has not accomplished anything.

"Why?" a reporter asks.

Because we're grabbing the ass of the horse instead of the head. The problem is simply like I've stated from the start; poverty. The solution is to start at the beginning, to direct all your energies and resources at the first-grade level. If you're gonna change things and change it for people, that's where it should be changed.

After the formal press conference, a group of six or seven reporters surrounds Chaney as he tries to head back to the court for his team's practice. He'd rather be out with his team, but he'll never pass up a chance to attack Prop 48. "Educators today are divorcing themselves from what an educator is all about. I wish Dewey [who came up with the Dewey Decimel System and is the man Chaney calls the father of the American educational system] could wake up for one minute. He'd probably stab himself with a knife if he looked at educators today.

"Let me give you two statistics and then I have to leave. In 1940 to 1945, in eighty percent of all black families and disadvantaged families—poor families—there were two parents in a household. Only twenty percent didn't have two. Today, in eighty percent of all those poor families, there is only one parent in the family. Only twenty percent have two.

"Here's another one. We have more black youngsters in jail today than we have in college. That's a tragedy. So if you want to print the truth, print those things. If we can level a country like Japan and they can bounce back and educate ninety-nine percent of their entire country, why are we still bullshitting around? Think about that."

272

March 16

The day doesn't get off to a good start. Two players are late for the Owls' 10:30 A.M. pregame meal. Although Chaney isn't there, he hears about it. "Something like that can cost us the game," he says later.

The bus for the Omni leaves at 1:30 and everyone is on time. After they arrive, Maloney leads the team to their locker room, while Chaney and Demopoulos find vacant seats along press row and watch the first game of the day: Duke versus Richmond. A few minutes after the Blue Devils finish their 81–46 demolition of Richmond, the Temple players head out onto the floor. Chaney keeps watching from press row, occasionally signing an auto-graph or acknowledging the greetings of a well-wisher. Finally, with the clock reading 16:00 until game time, Chaney heads to the locker room, and a minute later the team follows.

"There's not much to say," Chaney tells his team. "You're in a tournament that says you have a chance to be national champions."

The Owls head back onto the court for their final warmups, while Chaney, Maloney and Demopoulos wait in the hallway outside the locker room. As the buzzer sounds to signal the start of player introductions, Chaney and his assistant walk onto the floor and over to the Temple bench.

As always, the Temple players walk out onto the floor slowly and without emotion as their names are called. Macon is last and with a raised fist he joins the other starters, with the rest of the team right behind him.

St. John's wins the opening tip-off, and Temple quickly gets back in their 3–2 defense. The Redmen work the ball around and Harvey hits an open Singleton in the paint. Just as Chaney said he would, the burly junior goes strong to the basket. Strickland blocks the shot, but also gets Singleton with his body and picks up his first foul only seventeen seconds into the game. It's exactly what Chaney told Strickland would happen if he and Hodge didn't get good defensive position in front of their men.

Singleton misses both free throws and Strickland grabs the rebound. St. John's opens in a man-to-man defense, with Buchanan on Macon. Harden quickly organizes the offense and gets the ball inside to Hodge, who is able to front up Werden. He misses, but Strickland is there for the tip-in and Temple leads 2–0.

The two teams continue to trade baskets for the next several minutes. Hodge cans one of two free throws at 10:24 to knot the game at 12. Buchanan then nails a three-pointer for the Johnnies at 10:03 for a 15–12 lead. Hodge forces up a shot with Werden all over him and St. John's grabs the rebound. Harvey spins into the middle and hits a jumper for a 17–12 lead.

On their next possession, Harden makes a pretty inside pass to Hodge, but he misses an easy shot. The Redmen rebound, but Werden throws the ball right back to Temple. Harden misses an open three-point attempt, but Hodge and Strickland are there for the rebound. They both grab it and wrestle for possession and the referee calls a travel.

St. John's gains possession and Harvey swings the ball to Sealy, who in turn feeds a wide-open Werden under the basket for a dunk and a 19–12 lead with 8:02 left in the half. The two teams take turns missing, with Macon coming up empty on a three-point attempt at 6:40—his first shot of the game. After a Singleton miss and a Hodge rebound, Macon finally gets on track, draining a fourteen-foot pull-up jumper to push Temple to 19–14 at 5:46. This is the first score for Temple in four-and-a-half minutes.

Macon realizes it's time for him to take control and he starts firing away. "What I tried to do was stay calm,"

Macon said. "I didn't think about there being any pressure. I just wanted to take over the game and take the shot or make the pass."

After Macon's basket, Buchanan answers with a jumper. Macon, as promised, begins to take over, but not with the results he had hoped for. On Temple's next possession he drives to the hoop, but the ball rolls around the rim and out and St. John's gains possession. Harden quickly steals a lazy pass and feeds Macon, who then misses a pull-up jumper. Harvey hits a jumper, Kilgore misses a three and Harvey nails another jumper and suddenly St. John's is up 25–14 with 4:08 to go.

Temple keeps missing and the Johnnies keep hitting, until Macon finally ends a five-minute Temple drought with a three-pointer to cut the lead to 32–17 with :52 remaining. A Harvey three-pointer with :07 to play gives the Redmen a 35–17 halftime lead.

In the last ten minutes of the half, Temple is outscored 20–5, illustrating what Chaney meant when he said this was an ugly team. In all, Temple shot 28 percent (seven for twenty-five) and 22.2 percent (two for nine) from three-point territory. Macon is two for nine and Kilgore zero for six. St. John's is an incredible 71.4 percent (fifteen for twenty-one).

Things seem to get worse at the beginning of the second half. Werden scores off an offensive rebound and is fouled by Hodge, his third of the game. He misses the free throw, but St. John's' lead is up to 37–17.

Suddenly the Owls catch fire. Strickland hits a short turnaround jumper and then comes up with a steal. Macon scores on an offensive rebound, strips the ball from Buchanan and hits Harden for a wide-open three-point shot. He connects and suddenly the lead is down to 37–24 with 18:44 to play.

The Owls finally get the lead down to ten points: 44–34 with 15:15 to play on a Kilgore three-pointer. After a dreadful first half, Macon comes alive. He scores twenty-seven points in the second half (thirty-two in the game) on nine for fifteen shooting.

But St. John's slowly builds the lead back up and takes a 60–45 advantage. The Owls fight back again and cut the deficit to 60–49 with 4:58 to play and it's free-throw shooting time for St. John's. The Redmen are up to the task, hitting seventeen straight before Sealy finally misses the back end of a one-and-one with :33 to go and the Johnnies comfortably ahead 79–62. Macon hits a three-pointer with :21 remaining and David Cain scores at the buzzer for the Johnnies for a final score of 81–65.

The Owls quickly head for the locker room, where they sit quietly and wait for Chaney to start talking. He stands silently at the front of the room for several minutes and then begins speaking softly.

If you were to look back at our season, you would see it was one of peaks and valleys. Throughout, it has been a struggle. But as you look back, look inward. Look inside yourself. That's what we do as coaches. Not to second-guess, but to look inside and see if we did everything we could to put you on that floor ready to win. Don't look outside to anyone else: Look inside yourself.

Getting here was quite an accomplishment. Now ask yourself: Was it enough just to get here? Was there a growth process from the beginning to this point, or are you the same person and player now as you were then?

Is St. John's that much better as a team than you? Look inward. Is Boo Harvey that much better than you? Should I attribute your mistakes to youth? Look inward, fellas. The train we are on is hopefully a train that is moving on. You'll be playing again next year. If we can improve a little bit, will it be enough to beat the odds? Reflect. Look at how we want to be in the future. Every situation you face in life, you should grow from. Always take another step forward. If you're satisfied with what just happened, what you just accomplished, you're not growing. What more could each of you as an individual have done? Did we work hard enough as a team? Did you work hard enough as an individual? We're a young team, but I guess we're a little bit older after this game. And we should be a little bit better. There are a lot more things we can do as a team, and how well we do them will determine if we become a better team. I don't have any criticisms of any individuals. We're past that. Now is the time to think of the direction we're going and to heal up our wounds. I'll heal. I'll be all right. You must be too. Let's get together.

For the final time this season, the team huddles and Macon leads the cheer. "Team!" he screams, and the room reverberates as everyone answers, "Together!" Two more times, and that's it. Chaney, Macon and Harden head over to the interview room and DiSangro starts making arrangements for a flight back to Philadelphia this evening. On the way, Chaney runs into Singleton, a player he once recruited. The two shake hands and Singleton asks for an autograph for his mother. Chaney doesn't have anything to write with or on, but promises to drop one off in the St. John's locker room before he leaves.

"I think St. John's played an excellent game," Chaney tells the press. "They had a very good game plan and just ABC'd us to death. The leadership of Harvey was excellent." While the last few players get their gear together, Chaney quickly finds a program and pen and writes a note for Singleton's mom. He starts walking over to the St.

John's locker and runs into Carnesecca. "You just ABC'd us to death," Chaney says, complimenting him on the fine job his team did. "All those people saying they want to see teams run up and down the court and score don't know what they're talking about. You just keep ABCing them to death and you can go a long way." He hands Carnesecca the program to give to Singleton, they shake hands again and Chaney heads for the team bus.

DiSangro is able to get the team reservations on an 8:30 P.M. flight back to Philadelphia, and everyone has to hustle to pack and get ready for the ride to the airport. Demopoulos is staying overnight and will head to Florida in the morning for more recruiting. He asks Chaney if he wants to stay over and go with him, but he says no. "What kind of signal would that be for the team?" Chaney says. "It would be like I was abandoning them. It's important I show them I still love them."

Naturally the plane is late—two hours late—and finally arrives in Philadelphia a little past midnight. The Owls are back on the ground and out of the big show.

II

College Is the
Fountain of Life

March 24

Today is the last time the Owls will meet as a team until October 15, 1990. The meeting starts at 9:00 A.M. in a small classroom in McGonigle. For the first half hour, the strength coach goes over the off-season lifting program. At 9:40, Chaney enters and begins talking.

I hope you're prepared to have an open mind and endure a long session with me.

This proves to be the understatement of the season. Chaney will talk for more than four hours. It's only in the last hour, when the players realize that the cafeteria is closing and they'll miss out on lunch, and that they're about to miss the 1:00 P.M. tip-off of the first quarterfinal game of the NCAA play-offs, that they begin to show signs of impatience and start fidgeting in their seats. For close to four hours, they have been listening intently as

279

Chaney sums up the season and everything he has tried to teach in the last five months.

You can say we were successful in winning twenty games, but to me that is mediocrity because there was a little bit more in this team than twenty wins. What I'm saying to you is I thought you had a little bit more in you. You could have gone further up the road.

You [he points to the two who were late to breakfast the morning of the St. John's game] made us lose that game because you weren't in the ring. And there is no other reason except that you didn't give a damn. I want that to stay in your minds for the rest of your lives because sooner or later you're going to have to wake up and realize you can't be late for life. There's only one thing you won't be late for and that's your funeral. I'm serious. That's one thing you don't manage; the Lord manages that for you. But you have a chance to manage your life. But you say I'd rather be late, and guess what, that's a life-style that stays with you.

We're charged as a coaching staff to teach you something; that you're in college to learn about life. If we can't convince you of that, you have no reason to be here. You're being paid to be here. This school is giving you something like eleven, twelve thousand dollars a year to be here. That's what it costs. You're being paid to work for yourself. Ask yourself where would you be and what would you be doing if you didn't have this? Find out what Duane Causwell is doing right now. He's sweating bullets because he's not in school. Why? Because he might not be drafted in the first round. What happens if he breaks a leg practicing, if he doesn't get drafted? What does he have? He came in the office yesterday, trying to be readmitted to this institution. How long has it taken him to realize he has to get a degree? Now, whether he's fooling me with that shit, I don't know. But I know I got mine. I got my degree. You can fool me, trick me all you want into believing you, but I still got mine.

The biggest contribution I can make is to go right out and put up a big sign that says I'm a fortune-teller for youth. I could make a lot of money because every one of my predictions comes true. I can predict right in this room the lives of every one of you 'cause I've seen you all before. You're not new to me. Your names are different, but I've seen you before. There is nothing new under the sun.

Fellas, you have a responsibility to recognize that you have something here. You have to look at the fact that this is a four-year investment in yourself that will last a lifetime. College is the fountain of life. You have to drink from it. Some of you come here behind. High school doesn't prepare your ass for college. You can't sit around for a whole semester and hope something will happen. You have to work at it. If I don't tell you that, then I am shirking my responsibility. But you don't have to follow what I say. You can choose to do what you want to do. But I have warned you, taught you as best as I could.

If something or someone will drag your ass down, stay away from it. It's a hard decision, but a man, a *good* man, makes the right decision for himself, even if it's not always the easy decision. You have elevated yourself from the guys you used to hang with. The same jokes aren't funny anymore, the same shit they talk about isn't any good anymore. You have been in college, you have elevated yourself. Your friends that didn't go to college stood still and they're standing there in quicksand and going down. You have developed for yourself a whole new set of life circumstances. You've elevated yourself, you've moved on. If you want to drift back to that, there's something wrong with you. If you want to remain in the same spot the rest of your life, there's something wrong with you. You have to want something better for yourself.

College is something that moves people in a positive direction. It cultivates and develops, and if you allow it to, it will nurture your development. Having a good attitude, a responsible attitude, is the only way that you can be successful. I'm serious. Every year I spend this time at the beginning of the year and the end of the year telling you this. We can't meet anymore as a team, it's against NCAA rules. If you choose not to take my recommendations, that's up to you. But we as a coaching staff will not stand still. We have to have a team of good people with good attitudes; people who want to study and go to class. We can't be there to check on you every day. That's not our job. College is for responsible people. If you're looking for a shortcut, an excuse to lose, you'll always be able to find one.

Next Chaney pulls out index cards. On each he has listed a player's name and their strengths and weaknesses. He goes over each card and tells each player what he accomplished during the past season, what he should work on during the summer and what his role will be next season. Finally, at 2:20, the meeting is over. The 1989–90 season has come to an end.

"You think that was long enough?" Chaney asks as he, Demopoulos and DiSangro walk down the hall toward the basketball office.

They answer yes.

"I think I wore 'em down," Chaney says and the three start laughing.

March 26

Funeral services for Earley Chaney are being held today. She passed away five days ago.

More than 200 people crowd into the Emmanuel Johnson Funeral Home. Many knew Earley, but most are there to show their support and love for her son and his family. There are former and current players, friends that go all the way back to the school yards of South Philadelphia, friends from Gratz and Cheyney and Temple; people Chaney has known for fifty years and people he met less than a year ago. There are blacks and whites, old people and children. As Chaney hugs and kisses and draws strength from his friends, he alternates between tears of sorrow and nervous laughter as he tries to joke around to ease the tension of a very difficult day. In a sense, Chaney is alone now, the only one still living from his immediate family. Since he has been at Temple, he has buried his stepbrother, stepsister, stepfather, and, now, his mother. "As you get older it seems all you see is death," he says sadly.

A woman kisses Chaney on the cheek and says she'll miss Earley, now that she's gone. "She's not gone," Chaney says, holding his hand over his heart. "There will always be a little piece of her right here inside me."

All of his players take a little piece of Chaney with them when they leave Temple and head out into the real world. They'll remember the 5:30 A.M. practices, the thousands of lectures, the yelling, the laughing, the hugs, the wins and the losses. Most of all, they'll always remember that winning is indeed an attitude. And maybe, just maybe the little piece of Chaney they carry inside will help them flip the record over when things are bad.

"As I get older, more and more of what Coach says makes sense," Blackwell says. "Everything he's ever said to me about life has come right back to me as right. I always remember he said that you can only take out of the bank what you put in. This means you have to pay your dues and work hard or you won't reap any rewards. Maybe if I had listened better and worked harder when I was in school, I wouldn't be working full-time now and taking courses to get my degree."

Pollard says he's already starting to repeat some of Chaney's catch phrases when he talks to his family and friends. "The things he says can't help but rub off on you," Pollard says. "It makes me feel good that I got a chance to play for him and maybe pass on what he taught me to other kids."

"He's the best person there is to teach me about life," Macon says. "He's taught me so much already, but I know there's so much more to learn and I'm going to make sure I get it all."

Postscript

It's been a long, difficult season for Chaney. The wind-mills seem to be gaining and he is growing weary of the constant battles. "People do not have a clear understanding of what the real problems are: the problems of poverty and the problems of people who will never, ever get a chance in life," Chaney said earlier this season and the words have cruelly come back to haunt him. "We have to start opening our minds and our hearts to these people before it's too late."

In mid-April Chaney is still feeling the effects of the long and trying season. "Another year, one more year for Mark [Macon]," Chaney says. "The struggle is just getting too tough. I don't feel like I'm making a dent."

It's hard to tell if Chaney would really carry out his threat to retire once Macon graduates after the 1990–91 season, and ride off into the sunset, or if these are just the words of a man feeling the cumulative and lingering effects of a long season. Fortunately we'll never know. A few days after Chaney says these words, someone comes along to remind him of the importance of what he has always fought for and that the small victories—the Ernest Pollards and Mark Macons—are just as important as the big victories that are beyond his control. As he told his team earlier this season, "The key is to control the little things. No human being is capable of overcoming all the big things in life." Not even a man as strong as Chaney.

The "someone" who reminds Chaney of this is Aaron McKie, an all-public player from Simon Gratz High School (the same school Chaney once coached) who in late April signed a letter of intent to play basketball for Temple.

"Aaron lives in perhaps the darkest, bleakest community in this entire country," Chaney explains. "His father died when he was in ninth grade and he doesn't even know where his mother is. He lives with his aunt, who is very old."

When McKie signed with Temple, he hadn't scored 700 on his SATs, although he did have the required 2.0 grade average. "If you only looked at his SATs, here you would have a kid who many would condemn and cast out and never, ever give an opportunity. But this is a kid who has overcome so much and here he is about to graduate high school. And he wants desperately to become something, to make something of himself and go to college and graduate.

"The only thing that should count in judging Aaron is what you can really count on in a man: character, integrity and attitude. Is he honest? Will he work hard? That's all that matters. If that's how you measure a man, you'll never go wrong."

McKie represents everything and everyone Chaney has been fighting for for the past thirty years. "I, being poor, have only my dreams," Chaney says, quoting William Butler Yeats. "I have spread my dreams under your feet. Tread softly, because you tread on my dreams," Chaney was once McKie, spending hour after hour in the school yards of Philadelphia, dreaming of a better life, a life other than the poverty and despair he saw all around him. Chaney had his opportunity and he made the most of it. Now he's not about to let anybody take away McKie's chance. "If you don't give youngsters an equal chance, believe me, they won't have an equal future," Chaney told the audience at the Markward Club luncheon.

A few days after McKie signs with Temple, he and Haynes are on the radio together. McKie and Haynes have played together on summer league teams and have developed a deep friendship. The Haynes family is a loving and supportive group and have all but adopted McKie as one of their own. On the radio the two talk about their lives, their dreams and goals and about how happy they are to be going to Temple together to play for Chaney and get the opportunity to make the most of their lives on and off the court.

The next day a man Chaney doesn't know approaches him and tells him he heard the program and was impressed, even inspired, by McKie and Haynes. "This man told me he was a Villanova graduate and a Villanova and LaSalle fan," Chaney says. "But after he heard Aaron and Jonathan, he was inspired and enlightened and said from now on he'll be rooting for them and Temple.

"I was all set to quit after Mark left, but now I'll stay. I think I want to fight a little longer."